Charles Francis Adams
1835-1915
An Autobiography

Charles Francis Adams

Charles Francis Adams
1835-1915

An Autobiography

With a *MEMORIAL ADDRESS*
delivered November 17, 1915, by
HENRY CABOT LODGE

NEW YORK / RUSSELL & RUSSELL

Note

In 1913 Mr. Adams sent to the Massachusetts Historical Society a sealed package, containing, as he expressed it, "an autobiographical sketch," to serve as material for a memoir to be prepared for publication in the *Proceedings* of the Society, when the occasion should arise. Full authority was given to the Editor of the Society to make such use of this "sketch" as seemed to him proper. Of the contemporaries of Mr. Adams no one remained qualified, by knowledge or sympathy, to prepare a memoir, and the autobiographical sketch, on examination, made a search for a biographer unnecessary. It is full and characteristic of the writer.

The Memorial Address by Mr. Lodge was delivered in the First Church in Boston, on the afternoon of Wednesday, November 17, 1915, at a public meeting of the Society in commemoration of Mr. Adams. The proceedings were marked by great simplicity and deep feeling. The invocation was made by the Rev. George Angier Gordon, and the benediction given by the Rev. Charles Edwards Park.

W. C. F.

Contents

Memorial Address

No man who reflects, certainly no one who gives rein to his imagination, can approach even the slightest attempt to tell the story of a man's life upon earth, whether it be his own or another's, without feeling that he is doing so in obedience to one of the overruling impulses, one of the deep-seated instincts of humanity. He cannot escape the vision of the successive generations of men as they pass by in long procession recounting, each in its turn, the lives and deeds of those who have gone before.

> The form remains; the function never dies.

We fain would learn where the function and the form began and when they issued from the darkness. There comes no answer to our questioning. We cannot know, we can only guess.

In those dim, mysterious regions of the past, about which conjecture alone is possible, we may nevertheless be sure that, as soon as men secured command of language, the first use to which they put it, after passing beyond the base needs of daily communication, was to talk of themselves and of each other. When Browning's Eurydice cries to Orpheus:

> No Past is mine, no Future; Look at me!

we listen to the passionate voice of an old, sophisticated and complex civilization. Primitive man was the very reverse of this. He clung to the past and grasped blindly at the future. A little speck in the vast spaces of time and eternity, his overwhelming spiritual need, the craving hunger of his soul was to bind himself to those who had gone before and strive to clutch that which was still to come, so that he might in his ignorance rescue himself from the loneliness in which he wandered, helpless and unaided. Memory and imagination were his sole resources; so he turned to the singers, the reciters, the ballad-makers, the minstrels, and the rhapsodists to tell him of his past, of the heaven-born heroes from whom he liked to think that he was descended, of the wars, the deeds of arms, the conflict with forces of nature, of light and darkness, of the vague traditions and legends which were to him unchanging and unquestioned truths. This to him was history, and he sought the future in the prophecies and predictions of his sibyls and priests and soothsayers, in the signs of the heavens, in the flight of birds, and among the entrails of animals.

When some great genius, when more than one, perhaps, like him to whom the Greeks gave the name of Cadmus, discovered a method of expressing language by certain arbitrary signs, men began to carve those signs on stones, paint them on walls, bake them on bricks, and finally to write them on papyrus, on skins, on bark, and on parchment. Thus they recorded events which seemed to them memorable, facts began to rear their hard, unfeeling heads, and imagination slowly withdrew from a world in which it had once reigned supreme. One form of these records was the epitaph, the attempt to tell upon the tombstone something of the life of the dead who lay beneath, of the ancestor to whom primitive man had always clung in the wide wastes of the universe, which he could not understand, and to whom he had given his worship. Thus biography began, and, as Carlyle says, "History is the essence of innumerable biographies." Compared to the untold myriads of human beings who have lived and died, the number of biographies, of epitaphs, of bare mention even, in lists or catalogues, is trifling, and yet each one of the countless and unnoted millions had his trials and sorrows and joys, his virtues and his crimes, his soul history, deeply interesting if truly narrated and rightly considered. But we can only deal with what we have, and from what we possess must infer the rest, for that alone is permitted to us. The inference thus drawn is history, which is not a science, for it can never be exact, which is at best an approximation to truth. From it we can learn greatly, but it is as barren as a table of statistics unless informed by imagination and presented with the finest skill of which literature is capable. Moreover, the biographies, the recorded lives of men, whether brief or copious, whether resting on a few allusions or filling volumes of minute detail, are not only the material of history, but are each and all the picture of a human being, of a human soul, in its short and troublous pilgrimage from the cradle to the grave. If we look upon them with considerate eyes, there is nothing of equal interest and importance in the whole range of the great literature of knowledge. I have no intention of embarking upon this vast ocean of inquiry or of attempting to examine the development of the written lives of men and women. I would merely note here one fact: that not only from the time when men scrawled the names of their fellow-men on stones, but from the much earlier day of the history preserved in the trained memory of those who recited poetry and ballads, we almost always find an effort at least to tell the names, if nothing more, of the father and mother, perhaps of the more remote ancestors, of the hero whose deeds the minstrel chanted, or even of the unsung dead lying in perpetual calm beneath the carved stone. The impulse which gave rise to this habit was wholly natural. The desire to define the man or woman who had gone, for the benefit of the generations yet unborn, would be quite sufficient to account for it. Yet one cannot help feeling that there was a vague idea working in the minds of these remote people, dim shadows as they are, in the dawn of recorded history, that ancestry not only defined but explained. At all events, certain it is that the primeval habit continued, and also expanded and developed as civilization advanced, so that by its influence and pressure a great literature came into being. In all the historical writings of Greece and Rome, wherever an account is given of any man something almost always is said of his parents, often of his ancestors. This was the custom from the days of Herodotus to those of Plutarch, whose biographies, so sweepingly condemned by Macaulay, have none the less delighted succeeding generations of readers, who cared naught for the writer's political principles, but rejoiced in the stories which he told. Thus has the practice passed on through the centuries until it has reached the days of the evolutionists, of Darwin and Mendel and the modern biologists. Now parentage and ancestry are no longer in biography merely a means of definition, the creators of the atmosphere and the influences amid which the hero or heroine of the tale grew to maturity and achievement. They have become scientific necessities, preliminaries absolutely essential to any just comprehension of the human being whose life and work arrest our attention and invoke our consideration. In simpler phrase heredity is now not only an inseparable but an indispensable part of the task of the biographer, whether he tells his own story or that of some other man, whether the life so written fills volumes or is but the merest outline and suggestion. We no longer smile at Dr. Holmes's remark that a man's education should begin one hundred and fifty years before his birth, for the saying involves a great scientific truth which Dr. Holmes foresaw, as he did much else for which he did not receive due credit, in the wide regions of thought and speculation.

In Charles Francis Adams, second of the name, whose life and character, whose manifold activities and public services we seek fittingly to commemorate to-day, the hereditary element of biography is marked and conspicuous in an unequalled degree. I say "unequalled," which is a perilous word, for a universal affirmative, if not as impossible as a universal negative, is almost as dangerous. Yet I think the word is justified. It would be difficult to find in history another case of four successive generations of intellectual distinction and the highest public service equal to that shown by the Adams family during the past century and a half. In some of the long royal dynasties instances of great ability are no doubt found, but they are as a rule isolated and the high position itself is inherited, not won. Among the Plantagenets even, the dynasty more productive of remarkable men than any other of modern times at least, the highest ability came at intervals and the union of ability and character only at very protracted intervals. The house of Orange-Nassau in William the Silent, his two sons and later his great-grandson, William III, presents a very famous case of inherited ability; but there again the great opportunity and the high position were a birthright.

There have also been many instances of long descent where the same family has held through centuries the same titles and estates, but this means little because the titles and estates usually sustain their possessors instead of the possessors upholding and adding glory to the honors and property won by the hard-handed, hard-headed founder of the line. No doubt from these distinguished families, both in England and on the Continent, have sprung some great men as well as many men of strong abilities; but the men of mark have been sporadic and not in close succession during four generations. Frequently there has been only too much justification for Pope's oft quoted lines:

> What can ennoble sots or slaves or cowards?
> Alas! not all the blood of all the Howards.

Very rarely does one find a case like that of the family of La Trémoille in France, where a strain of vigorous ability combined with energy, force, and character runs in varying degrees through several generations; but the Trémoilles never touched the summit in either political or military life and the favoring opportunity was a birthright. We have, of course, the famous instance of the elder and the younger Pitt who both reached the zenith of power, but then came the end, as it did in the less conspicuous case of Lord Burleigh and the Earl of Salisbury, after whom the line waited two hundred and fifty years before it again shone forth in the high places.

But in our American family, with no adventitious aid of titles or estates, without the lucky chance which Lord Thurlow described as "the accident of an accident," the first two of the line by their own ability, their own energy and force, their own strong, fine characters, rose to the highest pinnacle of public service and public distinction. Each, in the words of the son, fulfilled his aspiration that he might be permitted, "By the people's unbought grace to rule his native land."

To the third, to the grandson, was given the opportunity in the darkest hour of his country's trial to perform the greatest service rendered by any civilian except Lincoln himself, with whom none other can be compared. He took the "Master of human destinies" by the hand and gave the great service in full measure. To follow even in the most meagre outline the careers or to endeavor to describe in the most superficial way the characters and achievements of John Adams, John Quincy Adams, and Charles Francis Adams, would be to review the civil and diplomatic history of the Thirteen Colonies and of the United States during more than a hundred years. I shall not attempt to do this, for time and space forbid, and my sole purpose is to speak of one of the fourth generation who were born heirs to this family history.

It was a great inheritance, and unless we realize something of what it meant in all its aspects, we cannot justly appreciate him in whose honor we gather here to-day. It was an inheritance of which the possessors, unless false to all that is best in human nature, could not fail to be proud, one which any man might justly envy and desire; so pervading in its influences that a biographer of any one of the fourth generation might well make his theme a study in heredity. Yet at the same time it must not be forgotten that this remarkable heritage brought to those who received it burdens as well as honor. The famous ancestor, still more immediate ancestors of the highest distinction in successive generations bring to their descendants with an unrelenting insistence, from which the average man is free, Carlyle's question, "What then have you done?" The effort, not unfamiliar, by which a man of independent spirit strives to show that he has merits of his own, stands on his own feet and refuses to be simply "the son of his father," is a severe one. How much more severe the ordeal when a man is forced to demonstrate that he is not only something more and other than the "son of his father," but also more and other than the "grandson of his grandfather," and the "great-grandson of his great-grandfather." If the possessor of such a heritage is a man of strong nature and vigorous mind, the determination to assert himself, to do work which the world will recognize as his own, to prove that he is an independent, individual entity and not simply a descendant, becomes a dominant factor in his whole growth and development. Moreover, the fact of such continued success and celebrity in one family for over a century implies necessarily a stock of unusual robustness, physical, mental, and moral, as well as strong qualities of mind and character which become more emphasized by each transmission and which pass into and govern, almost like the hand of fate, those who inherit them. In the *Education of Henry Adams* weight is given to the introduction of another strain from beyond the New England borders by the marriage of John Quincy Adams. But, to the dispassionate observer, the Southern blood thus brought in seems to have had a sentimental rather than a real effect. The Mendelian law of the dominant and recessive qualities would appear to apply. The dominant qualities reassert themselves; the recessive, although still existent and with the possibility of reappearance, fade away, especially after only a single crossing, to a dimness which in human beings is a practical effacement. This one infusion from without could not overcome or even affect materially the qualities and tendencies of a strong Puritan stock carried in three generations to the highest power by unusual abilities and exceptional force of character. The heirs of the qualities thus fostered and developed could not escape them, they were life companions and controlling influences. They brought their own exceeding great reward, but by the doctrine of compensation they also brought their penalties. As an example the independence of thought in John Adams developed in John Quincy Adams both mental solitude and minute introspection which passed on to his descendants with no waning force. The peril involved in excessive introspection is obvious, for,

> Thus the native hue of resolution
> Is sicklied o'er with the pale cast of thought;
> And enterprises of great pith and moment,
> With this regard their currents turn awry,
> And lose the name of action.

That the third and fourth generations not only avoided this danger, but conquered the tendency which so strongly gripped them, is abundant witness of their mental and moral strength as well as of their vigorous intellectual honesty.

To such an inheritance Charles Francis Adams, second of the name, son of Charles Francis and Abigail Brooks Adams, was born on May 27, 1835, in a house on Hancock Avenue, then and now, although upon the brink of change, a narrow lane for foot passengers only which runs by the State House grounds from Beacon to Mount Vernon Street. In Boston and Quincy his boyhood was passed, and he had as a birthright all that was best in the community into which he was born. An unprejudiced outsider would justly have said that in home, parentage, and associations he was exceptionally fortunate, and this judgment, broadly speaking, would be true. But human nature both in boy and man is so constituted that the good things of life are taken as a matter of course, while the spots on the sun or the flies in the ointment loom large. With some temperaments the things disliked are pushed aside and the pleasant aspects prevail both at the time and in memory. With other temperaments the exact reverse occurs. In the case of Charles Francis Adams, as with many other boys similarly situated between the years 1835 and 1865, Boston was inextricably associated with winter, short days, cold, snow, and schools, while the summer home, in his case Quincy, meant the long days, warmth, sunlight, out-of-door life, and a pleasing absence of lessons. Boston, therefore, he earnestly disliked and Quincy he regarded with distinct although not exaggerated approval. Upon him, again as with other boys of like condition, the lingering forms of Puritanism, the serious Sundays, burdened with much church-going and ample Biblical instruction, weighed heavily. Most boys took this ancestral bequest as the work of a malignant fate, tried with a strict economy of truth to evade it so far as possible, and bore what they could not escape with the odd philosophy characteristic of boys when they meet the inevitable. Charles Francis Adams, however, was not an average boy, and he not only hated the Boston winters and the solemn dreary Sundays, but actively resented them, and found no philosophy, odd or otherwise, which would save him from kicking against the pricks. The spirit of the reformer was strong within him even in those earliest days although he was no doubt unconscious of its influence. In the brief autobiography which he bequeathed to the Historical Society, he not only vents his feelings in regard to these conditions of boyhood, which were common to the time, but he also dwells upon two additional grievances, one of which was, I think, exceptional, while the other was largely shared by his contemporaries, who for the most part did not regard it as a misfortune or indeed with any hostile feeling. The first of these grievances concerned outdoor sports and exercises. He learned to swim, but this he says was the only athletic accomplishment he had opportunity to acquire. He unquestionably learned to skate, although he puts it down as one of the things he missed, together with boxing, fencing, and riding, in which boys ten or fifteen years younger were certainly instructed and which they all enjoyed. Nor did he have apparently in the usual ample measure the games and sports common to boys of that time or a little later. His brother, in the *Education of Henry Adams*, says that there were no trout streams on the Cape. This shows that the youth of the family did not wander far afield as sportsmen, for there are trout streams in that region even now, some carefully preserved; and in the "forties" of the nineteenth century they were more numerous and full of fish. I printed not long ago a letter from Webster to my grandfather, who was also an expert in the gentle art, describing a day's trout fishing in Plymouth County and giving the weight of his spoils which he sent to his correspondent. There was no lack, then, of trout streams, nor of deep-sea fishing, and there was an abundance of shooting along the coast, for the shore birds, now departed, were in those days plentiful. The boys of my time had all the shooting and fishing they could reasonably desire, but it is clear that the atmosphere in which Charles Adams found himself was not favorable to sports and outdoor life, a situation no doubt to be regretted in the case of any vigorous boy. Charles Adams felt it as a grave misfortune and in his autobiography attributes this mischance to his father. There were many boys of those days who managed to get their fill of sports and exercise without any especial paternal sympathy, so that the failure in this phase of boy life cannot in this case be charged wholly to the shortcomings of the head of the house. At the same time it is clear that the elder Charles Francis was not one who would stimulate or actively encourage in his sons the athletic side of life or the love of outdoor sports. His own childhood had been passed in Europe during his father's long diplomatic service. He had never suffered from or enjoyed in the usual measure the education or habits of the ordinary boy. His education, varied as it had been, was undoubtedly better than that of most American boys, but by the very circumstances of his life abroad he lost much in the way of boyish associations, sports, and mischief. He was not likely, therefore, to appreciate the value of these things to his sons. Charles Adams in his autobiography quotes from his father's diary where the writer speaks of a morning, passed with his boys fishing for smelts, as a day wasted, and the son makes the very reasonable comment that no time was less wasted than that. But Charles Adams made too little allowance for the difference of temperament. In his father the Puritan strain was very strong, the New England conscience which insists that unattractiveness is a powerful evidence of duty was extremely vigorous. The traditions of race and family were with him commanding. To the country, to public affairs, to the care of his family and estate, to work of all sorts, with pen and voice, but always to work, he felt that all his energy and all his time should be devoted. As independent in thought, as determined and fearless in warfare against a public wrong like slavery as any who ever bore the name, in the lesser matters, in literature, in science, in manners and modes of life and standards of conduct, the elder Charles Francis Adams was conservative. He was not wholly free from the influences and thought of the eighteenth century which were still potent during the first thirty years of the nineteenth. That particular frame of mind seems a hundred years later not without charm, but the charm does not appear to have been felt by Mr. Adams's son who came into the world just as the eighteenth century really passed away with the coming of the railroad and the departure of the stage-coach.

The son Charles says of himself as a boy that he was not original, but that he was individual. He was by no means destitute of originality, but he was certainly individual, and his normal, instinctive attitude was one of questioning and even of revolt against anything existent, established, and accepted. Here he differed from his father, as I have just said, in temperament, and because of this difference he did not make sufficient allowance.

In the *Education of Henry Adams* the writer thus describes and estimates his father:

Charles Francis Adams was singular for mental poise, — absence of self-assertion or self-consciousness, — the faculty of standing apart without seeming aware that he was alone, — a balance of mind and temper that neither challenged nor avoided notice, nor admitted question of superiority or inferiority, of jealousy, of personal motives, from any source, even under great pressure. This unusual poise of judgment and temper, ripened by age, became the more striking to his son Henry as he learned to measure the mental faculties themselves, which were in no way exceptional either for depth or range. Charles Francis Adams's memory was hardly above the average; his mind was not bold like his grandfather's or restless like his father's, or imaginative or oratorical, — still less mathematical; but it worked with singular perfection, admirable self-restraint, and instinctive mastery of form. Within its range it was a model.

Upon one young man who had the privilege of knowing Mr. Adams after his return from Europe, and to whom he was very kind and considerate, he made precisely the impression so admirably given in the sentences just quoted. That impression was deepened by all the young man learned, as he grew older, from the letters and history of the time. On only one point would he now disagree. It is his opinion that Mr. Adams's mental faculties were unusual in depth and range when applied to any subject with which it was his duty to deal as a public man and he thinks that this is abundantly proved by his work as Minister to England and on the Geneva Tribunal. But such qualities and such a temperament, however much he loved and admired his father, did not appeal to Charles Francis the younger so strongly as they did to others. There was too much calmness and reserve, too much acceptance of the existent and the traditional, too little "divine discontent," too little of the spirit of general revolt, to be wholly sympathetic. Hence the criticism, not without foundation, of the lack of sports, games, and outdoor life in his boyhood, and also upon another point with much less reason. This last dissatisfaction was with the failure of his father to send him to a boarding-school. He felt, quite rightly, that association and attrition with other boys were the best part of education and, not so rightly by any means, that he could not and did not get them at the Public Latin School of Boston whither he was sent with his elder brother and the rest of his contemporaries. It is not quite easy to understand why he felt so strongly upon this point. The boarding-schools of that day were by no means what they have since become, and, judging from my own experience and that of my contemporaries, there was an ample association and attrition with other boys both in the public and private Latin schools of Boston, if one chose to avail one's self of them, as most boys did. If a boy did not find in these schools the valuable education to be gained by contact with his fellows, the difficulty, so far as my observation went, was in the boy, not in the opportunity which seemed to be in all ways sufficient to those who took advantage of it.

Charles Adams was in like manner dissatisfied with the instruction given in the Boston Latin School. At that period we had the old-fashioned classical curriculum, Latin, Greek, mathematics, a little classical history and geography, and exercises in declamation. The methods of teaching were largely mechanical: learning by rote the Latin and Greek grammars, which were reviewed every year, writing Latin exercises, memorizing the Greek and Latin prosodies in order to read and to recite Latin and Greek verse, and in those days to make a false quantity in Latin was little short of a crime. It was not the best method of learning languages, which should be acquired as we acquire our own tongue by practice and ear and then syntax and prosody can follow. But there was nevertheless a real mental discipline in it and boys came out of school with a considerable knowledge of Greek and Latin. Since then the field of studies has been greatly extended and the methods of teaching in some directions no doubt improved, but the net result seems to be that boys now know less about more subjects than they did in the middle of the nineteenth century and it is not apparent that they are any better fitted to use, control, and apply their minds, which is after all the real purpose of education. But the narrow range of studies and the faulty methods of instruction were a sore trial to Charles Adams and made him in later years an effective and most valuable educational reformer. At the moment they filled him with disgust and drove him to revolt, so that at the end of three years in the Public Latin School he persuaded his father to let him study with a tutor and thus prepared he entered the class of 1856 at Harvard in the sophomore year. To have thus omitted the freshman year seemed to Charles Adams long afterwards to have been a serious mistake, as it undoubtedly was. Yet his career in college was a success and his college life a happy one in contrast to that of his much disliked and contemned schooldays, although the methods of teaching then in vogue at Cambridge were not ideal, and were certainly not suited to Charles Adams. He was well on the way to being a good Greek scholar, to the possession of the language, so that through life it would always have been a pleasure and resource. Like others in similar cases, discouraged by the mode of instruction, he let it go and again like others never ceased to regret his loss. But there was large compensation in other directions. He made friends and his friends were the best men of a time when there were in Harvard many good men destined to future effectiveness and success. Thus at last he came into contact with his kind in the way he had always desired, and he felt, rightly no doubt, that it did him a world of good. He became a member of the college societies and took therein an active part, for his literary capacity was even then easily recognized by his fellows. He did not seek rank in scholarship and failed to rise above the middle of the class list. This, however, was of no great consequence, for he read much and widely, his mind expanded and intellectual growth and development began. There is no greater satisfaction than this sensation of growth and advance in mental power and Charles Adams realized and appreciated it. Most important of all, what he modestly calls his "aptitude," what others would term a natural gift and marked talent, now found an opening and showed itself forthwith. He began to write. It was an inherited gift. He himself says that his chief boyish recollection of his grandfather was that he was always writing. So the inborn tendency to think and then to seek expression for the thoughts broke forth at Harvard and found easy opportunity in the societies, in the college magazines, and presently in the newspapers. This it was, more than anything else, which made his college career a success and caused him to look back upon it with less severity of criticism than that awarded to the preceding years. There was much, no doubt, that was wrong in existing conditions, in modes of instruction and the like; there were, as he thought, many mistakes and lost opportunities, due entirely to himself, the statistics of which he kept with great care, and yet the general effect of the Harvard years was not only satisfactory but happy. To the onlooker it seems as if there were every reason why it should have been so. When a man at the age of twenty has found something worth doing, which he likes to do and can do well, as was the case with Charles Adams's writing, he may be deemed to be fortunate in no common degree. I believe Charles Adams realized the satisfaction and happiness he had found in writing, but I do not think that he regarded himself as particularly fortunate therein. The proverb is something musty, but one cannot but recall the familiar Latin line, "O fortunatos nimium, sua si bona norint."

Graduating in 1856, Charles Adams, deciding to be a lawyer, as the obvious thing to do, did not go to the Law School, which later he thought was a mistake, but entered as a student the office of Dana & Parker, which was certainly a very wise choice. That he learned much law there is not apparent, but he was brought into close and daily contact with two very unusual men, which was in itself an education. Richard H. Dana, Jr., whose biography Charles Adams wrote many years later, was a man of the finest character and an idealist as well. His *Two Years Before the Mast*, so aptly called by Mr. Adams "The Odyssey of the Pacific Coast," gave Mr. Dana a permanent place in our literature. He was also one of the leaders of the bar, distinguished alike in the law of admiralty and as an international lawyer. Above all, he had devoted himself to the anti-slavery cause and to the defense of the fugitive slave, with a courage and disinterested zeal which did him the utmost honor. His partner, Mr. Francis E. Parker, did not take the position either in literature or public life which would give him a place in history, but he was none the less a remarkable man. An eminent lawyer, he was also in the best way both cultivated and accomplished, a lover of art and of literature, with a keen and penetrating wit, delightful as a friend and companion, familiar with men and cities and a wise judge of both. Charles Adams fully appreciated and valued the two partners, and only a few days before his death I talked with him about Mr. Parker and his opinion of him fully coincided with that which I have just expressed. From close association with such men he no doubt profited largely, but if we may trust his own account he did not learn much of the law and he gave a good deal of time to the pleasures of society, all very natural to his age and opportunities. "Take thy fair hour, Laertes; time be thine." Who would have age and experience speak otherwise to generous youth? One would be a churl, indeed, to refuse to give the kindly permission. None the less, within two years our Laertes managed to pass the formal, easy examinations of those days and was admitted to the bar by Chief Justice Bigelow.

Thus duly certified professionally he took an office, first with his brother John and then by himself, and sat him down to wait for clients. This is a dreary, trying business at best and was peculiarly so to Charles Adams, not merely from temperament but because neither then nor later did he have any real liking for the law. To become a lawyer was an obvious thing to do, but the obvious was in this case wholly unsuitable. If clients did not come, however, events did. The storm of civil war was gathering, as we can see now, the political atmosphere was heavily charged and dark clouds were beginning to drift across the sky. Mr. Charles Francis Adams the elder was elected to Congress, the Boston home was closed, and Charles Adams the younger found his way to Washington to see his family. Politics and public questions were to him with his inheritances a second nature. Here there was no innate repulsion as with the law. They attracted him and absorbed his thoughts, and the extracts from his diary describing men and events in Washington are deeply interesting. No one realized what was coming, no one gauged the future correctly. It is all so natural and yet so tragic to see through the eyes of the young diarist the men of that day stumbling forward in the darkness to conclusions of which they had no conception.

Then came 1860 and the fateful election of that year. Charles Adams had the good fortune to accompany his father and Mr. Seward in the latter's wide-reaching campaign tour in behalf of the Republican candidates. He saw the West for the first time, a very different West from that of to-day, which he also lived to see and which he helped to develop and build up. The scenes of that journey, the travels by land and water, the popular meetings and the public men he met, all pass vividly before us in the pages of his diary. Then it was that he saw Lincoln, who came to greet Seward, for the first time. Here again was education, not to be found in law books or offices, most valuable to the keen and eager mind of the young observer. The teachings of those days remained with him through life. In the Boston intervals the dull waiting for clients went on, relieved only by the "aptitude" which reasserted itself, found public expression in the newspapers, and finally in an *Atlantic* article upon "King Cotton" which had a marked success. The lurid campaign of 1860 ended. The Republicans won. The Union began to drop to pieces. The winter of 1860-61 dragged slowly by. Charles Adams watched closely the rapid march of events, striving hard to judge them as they passed and to guess the future which no one could fathom, which indeed men recoiled from anticipating. Seward and his father, utterly declining to believe in war, in which it is now easy to see that they were wrong, were laboring by every means of delay, by the consideration of impossible compromises and hopeless arrangements, to hold the Government together until the 4th of March, and in this effort they were absolutely right, no matter what their view of the future might have been. At last the day so longed for came, and Charles Adams saw Lincoln peacefully inaugurated. He, like all Republicans and Union men, breathed a sigh of relief. They thought, or tried to think, that the worst was over. The worst, of course, was yet to come, but the first great danger had none the less been passed. The Government at last was in loyal hands. In the hands, too, of the greatest man of his time, although this fact the men of that day did not and could not know. Mr. Adams and his family returned to Boston. Every one was hoping for the best, now that the change of administration had been safely accomplished. There came a few weeks of anxiety, of hope, of fear, and then the storm broke. Sumter fell and the war began.

The immediate impulse of Charles Adams was to throw everything aside and go at once to the defense of the country. Amid the universal unreadiness for war, in which the mass of Americans could not believe until it was actually upon them, Charles Adams was better prepared than most of those about him. He was a member of the Fourth Battalion of the Massachusetts Militia. On the 24th of April (1861) his battalion was ordered to garrison duty at Fort Independence. There he had five weeks of real service and learned much, more perhaps than he realized. But he could not on the completion of this duty make up his mind simply and directly, as so many of his friends did, to do that which above all things he desired and which in reality he was certain to do in the end. The strong inheritance of introspection asserted itself and for five months he struggled with himself. It was all so needless and yet for him so inevitable. His patriotism, his courage, his high spirit, all drove him forward irresistibly.

The cold fits, the arguments in which he never believed, would come, would recur again and again, although each time more weakly. But the glow of the right and natural impulse burned ever stronger as the weeks passed, and at last one clear October afternoon as he was riding the decision came. "Why should I not go?" he said to himself. The negative vanished in the brilliant lights and gleaming colors of that autumn evening. He applied for a captaincy in the First Massachusetts Cavalry. On the 19th of December his name went in for a commission as First Lieutenant and on December 28, 1861, he left Boston with his regiment.

So far as the men who made up that regiment were concerned, no better ever went to war. But to Charles Adams it was an unlucky choice. He was unfortunate in his superior officers, not merely in the two in chief command, but especially in the one to whom he was immediately subordinate. No man ever went to the front with a clearer determination to do his full duty to the best of his ability than Charles Adams and no man ever kept better to his purpose. Yet he was treated at the outset in a way which would have driven many a man of good quality to desperation, to insubordination, to resignation, perhaps to ruin. The wrong and injustice of it all were very bitter, very hard to bear. There were recurring hours then and later when it seemed to him that he had lacked manliness in submitting to what he bore and in not breaking through everything, even leaving the service, that he might preserve his self-respect. But he overcame the temptation which was at once so natural and so strong, and there is in his whole career no more convincing proof to be found of the fineness and strength of his character and of the really noble conception of duty which throughout his life underlay all his acts and thoughts.

The regiment went first to South Carolina and then to Virginia. In the autumn of 1862 he was promoted to Captain; he was rid of the worst torment from his immediate superior and light began to break. He saw constant service and was in many actions, always and simply brave, cool, and efficient. He was at Antietam and Chief of Squadron in the Gettysburg campaign, then separated from his regiment on special duty at headquarters, and during the subsequent advance upon Richmond. In the autumn of 1864 he was transferred to the Fifth Massachusetts Cavalry, a colored regiment, as Lieutenant-Colonel, joining his new command at Point Lookout, Maryland. For some time he had been suffering from illness caused by hardship and malaria and now became so much worse that in November he was ordered home. He grew better, rejoined his regiment once more, grew much worse, and was again ordered back to Boston. As the winter drew to a close Colonel Russell resigned and the command of the regiment was given to Adams. At the same time came the offer of a place on General Humphreys' staff as Inspector-General. He esteemed Humphreys very highly and an important staff appointment was what he had longed for above all else. Nevertheless he refused the staff appointment from a sense of duty and obligation and took command of the regiment. He always felt that this was a grave mistake and bitterly regretted it. His decision certainly deprived him of being present at the close of the war in the happiest manner and in the way which above all others he desired. Yet as one calmly considers his action fifty years later, while the mistake from his point of view may be admitted, the thought of the self-sacrifice to the sense of duty rouses an admiration which overshadows every other consideration.

He secured the mounting of his regiment, took it to the front, and had the supreme satisfaction of riding at its head into burning Richmond the day after the abandonment of the city by Lee. A few weeks later he broke down again, this time completely, was obliged to leave the regiment and return to Boston reduced to a skeleton, a mere wreck from fever, exposure, and hardship endured for four years. He received the brevet of Brigadier-General, and in June, 1865, was mustered out of the service. He had served his country well in the field. He had been a good soldier, courageous and self-sacrificing, active and earnest in the performance of every duty. It was a wonderful experience, educating, expanding, strengthening, and as he grew older he seemed to value it more and more. The memory never grew dim, the teachings of that terrible struggle of the nation for life never faded. His service in the war was to him a precious possession and such in truth it was to all who had fought through the four years as he had done.

While absent on sick-leave during the winter of 1864-65, he became engaged to Miss Ogden, the second daughter of Edward Ogden, of New York, then living in Newport. There he passed the summer of 1865 and there he was married in November. Immediately after the wedding he went with his wife to Europe. His father was still Minister to England and he was able to rejoin his family in London. He travelled also on the Continent, and the journey restored his shattered strength. His opportunities in England were of course exceptional, but Charles Adams felt, as he was apt to feel, that he did not make the most of them either there or elsewhere.

The condition of his health no doubt interfered, but it seems probable that he made more of his opportunities at that time than he was ever willing to admit and it is certain that he saw and learned much.

In September, 1866, he returned to Boston and it is not surprising that the prospect which he faced seemed at first unpromising as well as uninviting. He came back to a world and to conditions greatly changed from those which he had left five years before. From a high military command, from a position of responsibility and importance, he now returned to the obscurity of civil life, to his abandoned profession for which he had no love, and with no definite place, no settled and necessary work ready to absorb his time and satisfy or occupy his energies. He went back to his office and then, facing with clear courage and good sense the indifferent world about him, he set to work to establish himself, to make his place and to find and do something worth doing.

He made a wise if quick choice by turning to the railroad system, to use his own words, "as the most developing force and largest field of the day." He started with an article upon "Railroads" in the *North American Review*. Clients did not come to his office, but articles upon railroads flowed out into the magazines and reviews. Gradually the steady work began to tell, although it was not apparent as the days went by. Slowly but surely he was awakening his public to the vast importance of the railroad system growing and spreading rankly over a continent without either regulation or control. He made it apparent that this necessary servant upon which the development of the country depended was becoming a dangerous master. He demonstrated the need of action in the public interest. He became an authority upon his subject.

The patient labor told. The "aptitude" in writing had found a field and brought in its harvest. In 1869 he delivered a Fourth of July address before the Grand Army Post at Quincy, which attracted much attention. In the same month the law establishing a railroad commission in Massachusetts, which he had been largely instrumental in passing, went into effect and he was appointed one of the commissioners. On the first day of that same July, so memorable to him, appeared his article entitled "A Chapter of Erie," which had a widespread and deep political and economic effect at the moment and without which the history of that time could not now be properly written or thoroughly understood. There had been a "railroad commission" in Rhode Island and "railroad commissioners" in New Hampshire since 1844 and statistical returns of railroads in Massachusetts since 1836, but nothing had yet been accomplished in the direction of regulation or control. The Massachusetts Railroad Commission of 1869 was the first effective commission and was the foundation of the system of railroad commissions with large powers which spread to all the States and culminated in the Interstate Commerce Commission of the United States. This beginning of the great system of Government regulation of railroads in the interest of the public was the work of Charles Adams. The idea, the theory, the principles, were all his, and the first practical demonstration, for he served ten years as railroad commissioner, was his also. It is not going too far to say that no single man produced by his own unaided thought and effort so great an effect upon our economic development, with all its attendant political manifestations, so far as it was involved in transportation by rail, as did Charles Adams when he brought about the establishment of the Massachusetts Railroad Commission and through the practical work of the Commission, as well as by his writings, educated the public to a belief in Government regulation and supervision of the vast system of railroads which was growing up in the United States.

The " Chapter of Erie " was the crowning stroke in the work which he had been doing by his writings for nearly three years. It is difficult now even to imagine such a situation as is depicted in this remarkable article. Physical violence, corruption of legislatures, corruption of courts, stock-gambling, robbery of the public and the stockholders, set off against a background of vulgar display and coarse vice, all these foul things were there, not concealed but flaunted openly and flagrantly, with a cynical disregard of public morals and public opinion. The people had looked on, disgusted and helpless. They saw the various villainies as they passed one by one, but they neither understood nor appreciated what it all meant until the isolated events were knit together into a single connected story powerfully and skilfully told by Charles Adams. Then they knew what had happened, then they realized the danger which threatened them, then and there the revolt against railroad domination began. The foresight displayed in these articles is as remarkable as the grasp of facts and principles. But even their author could not foresee how far the movement, so beneficial, so necessary in itself, and as he conceived it, would travel in the next fifty years. From being a peril and a corrupting force in politics, the railroads have now become the helpless subjects of Government commissions and too often their victims. The general result has been of the utmost value politically and in a less degree economically. Many evils have been cured, many wrongs redressed, much good has been accomplished, while serious harm has also been done by the crude and violent methods pursued in certain instances. The unfortunate stockholders have suffered under both systems. As in all revolutions — and the movement begun by Charles Adams in 1867 was nothing less — the achievement of great good, the reform of grave abuses brings with it suffering to guilty and innocent alike and the final expiation is often vicarious. Two meaner and more injurious tyrants than Louis XIV and Louis XV it would be difficult to find. They both had exceptionally long reigns and died quietly in their beds. For their sins Louis XVI, harmless, dull, and kindly, went to the guillotine. Those who rightly feel that the treatment of our railroads by law, by Congress, by legislatures and commissions, is often harsh and unjust will do well to read the *Chapters of Erie* and consider the doings of Gould and Fisk. They may not find there an abstract justification of all the mistakes and extreme measures of the present day directed against the railroads, but they will certainly discover an ample explanation of how those measures came to pass.

Just at this time, when he was bringing the labors of nearly three years to practical fruition by the establishment of the Massachusetts Railroad Commission, Charles Adams left Boston and made his home in the ancestral town of Quincy. He had been absorbed in a great state and national question, the transportation system of the United States, and he continued that work for many years to come. But he now added to it the affairs of the town in which he lived, affairs as purely local as one could conceive, but which he contrived, before he was done with them, to carry in their influence not only outside the bounds of the township, but far beyond the borders of Massachusetts.

With his elder brother, John Quincy Adams, who was not only a man of marked ability, but an accomplished speaker and personally very popular, he entered upon the field of town affairs. The general condition of the town was not good and there was ample opportunity for reforms in various directions. Many were effected, and for twenty years the two brothers not only led but largely managed the town. The methods of doing business in town meeting were wholly reformed and became a model. The debt was extinguished and the tax rate kept at a moderate figure by wise, economical, and effective expenditure. During these twenty years Charles Adams was a member of the school committee, a trustee of the public library, a park commissioner, and a commissioner of the sinking fund. He was constantly active in town work and never defeated when a candidate for office.

The best-known part of that work was the reform of the methods of teaching and administration in the public schools which he started and carried through. The result became famous as the "Quincy System," which was studied and investigated by teachers and educators everywhere. It was largely followed and imitated and in this way had a wide influence upon education in the United States. Hardly less important, although less generally known, was the result of his work as trustee of the public library and as park commissioner. With entire justice he says in his autobiography that the public library given by Thomas Crane and the Merrymount Park which he himself gave to the town are permanent memorials of his work in the affairs of Quincy. No man could ask for better records of disinterested and unpaid public service than these. He also left a full account of his labors in Quincy in the last of his *Three Episodes of Massachusetts*

History. And yet perhaps his best monument, quite impalpable and incorporeal, is the demonstration which he and his brother gave of the fine results which can be obtained by men of energy, ability, and public spirit working through the direct democracy of the town meeting, properly applied to suitable purposes, when the same energy, ability, and honesty exerted through the forms of city government so commonly end in failure and so rarely achieve more than a partial and often merely evanescent success.

During these years of life in Quincy the work as railroad commissioner went on steadily and Mr. Adams's reports, including that which he prepared as special commissioner on the Troy and Greenfield road, were all important contributions toward the solution of the general transportation problem. The most interesting and far-reaching of these reports was that of 1877, as courageous as it was able, which dealt with the grave questions raised by the prolonged strike of the engineers on the Boston & Maine Railroad. Mr. Adams advocated investigation and publicity as against compulsory arbitration, and it is interesting to note that the very able Roosevelt Commission, called into being by the great coal strike more than twenty years later, adopted and enforced his views. In publicity and investigation, as the best method of dealing with the most serious troubles of this character, Charles Adams never lost faith.

The work on the Massachusetts Railroad Commission, together with his writings, inevitably led to wider fields. In 1878 he became chairman of the Government Directors of the Union Pacific and after going over the lines drew the report. In 1879 he resigned from the Massachusetts Commission and became chairman of the Board of Arbitration

of the Trunk Lines. In 1882 he was chosen a director of the
Union Pacific, and two years later was elected president of
the company. This was a most responsible position and as
burdensome and trying as it was important. The company
was involved with the Government, the worst of all possible
handicaps; it was unpopular in the territory it served and in
very bad financial condition. During the first five years of
his presidency Mr. Adams did much for the road. He put
the finances in order, improved alike the service and credit
of the road, and paid off the floating debt. But he could not
bring the relations with the Government to a settlement and
that was the most serious obstacle to complete success. He
had proved himself efficient and capable and if he had gone
out at the end of five years all would have been well for him.
But, as he himself says, he made the serious mistake of remaining a year and a half longer, struggling in vain for the
Government settlement which always fled as he approached
it. During those fateful eighteen months the clouds in the
business world which culminated in the great panic of 1893,
were gathering darkly upon the horizon. At that time Charles
Adams was deeply involved in other and extensive enterprises of his own, and as conditions constantly grew worse
both the road and its president suffered from them. At last,
in 1890, he wrenched himself free, not without large personal
sacrifice, and his twenty years of railroad work came to an
end, leaving with him at the time a bitter sense of failure.
But the failure, if it was such, was in reality confined to the
last year and a half in the Union Pacific, when the general
financial situation, continually growing worse, brought ruin
to many men and many enterprises. The eighteen preceding
years were a success in the largest sense, because during those

years he did a work toward the solution of the vast railroad question, informing and educating public opinion, which stands out conspicuous in the history of the time and which was one of his best and most enduring achievements.

Yet the work in Quincy, the labors as railroad commissioner, then as a member of the Arbitration Board, as director and president of the Union Pacific, together with large business affairs in which he was privately engaged, although they would seem beyond the strength of any one man, by no means comprised all the public service rendered at that period and later by Charles Adams. In 1872 he went at the head of a commission authorized by the Massachusetts Legislature to visit the Vienna Exposition and drew the report of the commissioners. In 1892 he was appointed chairman of the preliminary and advisory commission to prepare a plan of parks and public reservations for Boston and its vicinity. The result was a scheme for a park system probably unequalled in extent and in far-sighted conception by any great city of modern times. Greatly to the surprise of Mr. Adams the report was accepted and he was made chairman of the commission created to carry the plans into effect. He served until 1895, and then, feeling that his work in this direction was completed, he resigned. The preservation of the Blue Hills and of the Middlesex Fells by including them in reservations was largely due to his efforts, and he justly felt that he had accomplished much in saving those regions of remarkable natural beauty not only for the public of his own day, but for the generations yet unborn. Those, who in the long days to come will find enjoyment and happiness in the regions thus preserved from the ravages of the spoiler, may not know to whose hand they owe the precious gift, but none the less the hills and woods and lakes thus saved are a great and lasting memorial to the man whose disinterested and far-seeing labors made them a permanent possession of the people of Massachusetts.

In 1897 Charles Adams was appointed chairman of a Massachusetts commission to investigate the relations between street railways and municipalities. For this purpose he visited Europe to inquire into the different systems in operation there and in Great Britain, and on his return he drew the report upon which general legislation was based and enacted. In 1903 he served as chairman of a special commission to apportion the cost of maintenance of the parks and reservations among the several cities and towns included in the system.

During this entire period he was also active in another and very different field. In 1882 he was chosen an overseer of Harvard College and served there four terms of six years each with an interval of one year in 1895. His deep interest as an educational reformer, so strikingly shown in the schools of Quincy, he now turned to the methods and modes of teaching in the great university. In 1883 he delivered the Phi Beta Kappa address entitled "A College Fetish," which was directed against the classics, and not only attracted much attention, but excited abundant criticism and discussion which Charles Adams always enjoyed. From that time forward, for nearly a quarter of a century, he was most active in all the affairs of Harvard, concluding his many years of service by an elaborate report on the English Department which was followed by important changes in the English courses of the university.

As one comes to the end of this long list of activities in

public service and with public results, supplemented by business interests enough in themselves to absorb the entire mental and physical strength of a man of more than average vigor of mind and body, one pauses in surprise at the force, energy, and capacity for work which made it all possible, and yet even this was not everything. Through all there ran the "aptitude" for expression in writing, and not content with the articles in magazines and newspapers or the elaborate reports dealing with the educational, economic, and railroad reforms upon which he was engaged, the "aptitude" reached out and turned to the inviting fields of history and biography, subjects for which Charles Adams, quite unknown to himself at first, possessed another strong gift which was his both by nature and inheritance. In 1874 he was asked to deliver an historical address at the celebration of the two hundred and fiftieth anniversary of the settlement of the town of Weymouth, next neighbor to Quincy. He knew but little of Weymouth; nothing of its history. After a brief hesitation he accepted and delivered the address on the 4th of July, 1874. His work as an historian had begun. The Weymouth address was followed by his election as a member of the Massachusetts Historical Society, lightly accepted at the moment, but which was destined to mean so much to him in a future then long distant. The Weymouth address, however, did much more than this. It led him insensibly into the pleasant paths of historical study and investigation. He came, perhaps without realizing it, well equipped for the new pursuit. From the earliest beginnings in the days of the college and the law office he wrote easily and well. He seems never to have passed through the severe struggle necessary to most men when learning to express themselves in writing with force and lucidity. Yet the old saying that easy writing makes hard reading does not apply in his case. All that Charles Adams wrote is eminently readable. He had no faith in the elaborate, no patience with what was dry or obscure. He was strongly of Martial's opinion:

Non scribit, cujus carmina nemo legit.

One might agree or disagree with his opinions, but no one found difficulty in either reading or understanding what he wrote. Rarely rhetorical, his style was always clear and effective. The humor of a situation when he described it did not escape him if it was anywhere present, nor did he ever fail to see the pathos or the tragedy when either existed or the remote results of the events of history or of the deeds of men. He had also another quality in a high degree of excellence which is very essential to the historian. This was the power of developing and weaving together a closely connected and interesting narrative from a mass of complicated and disorderly facts and of intricate, widely scattered details. In the *Chapters of Erie*, which were the first of his writings to attain to book form, in a volume of essays by himself and his brother Henry, this power is made very manifest. The literary quality in this respect is as admirable as the substance of the attack upon the infamies of the Erie Railroad management. From a wilderness of details, from masses of testimony, judicial orders, and newspaper reports, he drew forth a clear, succinct, coherent, easily understood, and also keenly interesting story. The ability to do this implies not only patient and untiring industry, but skill and proficiency in the difficult arts of selection, compression, and omission. To the work of the historian Charles Adams brought this

ability, and the thoroughness of research and the mastery of
details were as conspicuous as the easy and vivacious manner in which the results of his labors were finally stated upon
the printed page. Following the lead of the Weymouth
address, he extricated from the confused and too often
broken records of the seventeenth century, the story of the
earliest English settlements of Massachusetts Bay, which
was first printed privately in 1883 as *Episodes in New England History*, and later, in 1892, in two volumes entitled
Three Episodes of Massachusetts History. There is much in
the records of those times which seems petty if carelessly
regarded. The figures on the scene are for the most part
obscure men, moving dimly on the edge of a vast, untrodden
wilderness. Yet when looked at, as Charles Adams looked
at them, with a discerning gaze, it is apparent that adventure and romance were both present and, when they are, the
names and importance of the heroes are of secondary consequence, for romance and adventure do not depend upon the
worldly position of the actors in making their appeal to human imagination and human interest. Isolated and alone
these early wanderers to the New England coast might well
have had no other charm than this, but as it happened they
were also founders of a State, beginners of great things, fac-
tors in world events, and their connection with the larger
history of their own time and of the future was brought out
by Charles Adams in a way which makes the deeper meanings
of these Pilgrims and adventurers clear and emphatic to all
who read their story as he told it.

This work went with Charles Adams through all the period
of railroad and business activity and was a resource and comfort in the disappointments and trials which came with the

successes in practical affairs. During the last months of his presidency of the Union Pacific, when all the many anxieties of the road and of his own business interests were culminating, he none the less managed in some way, not easily comprehensible, to write the biography of his old friend Richard H. Dana, in whose office he had studied law. Just as he left the railroad and regained once more the freedom from the care and responsibility which the presidency of the road had brought upon him, the book was published. There is nothing in its pages to suggest the wearing conditions under which it was composed, an indication of a rare capacity for self-abstraction and for applying the mind to the subject which the will commands. It is a wholly admirable piece of work, vivid, interesting, one of the very best of American biographies. It merits more than the credit of an important contribution to our history; it is also an addition to our literature.

From this time forward the "aptitude," finding its truest field in history, gave to Charles Adams his principal interest and his chief occupation, one which was entirely congenial. There were five hard years to be passed through while he dealt with the burdens which the railroad and his own affairs, involved in the great business depression between 1893 and 1897, brought upon him. He gave up Boston and Quincy and established himself upon a large estate at Lincoln. There his time at last became his own and he turned to history and historical studies, where, in the midst of other and very different labors, he had already done so much.

During the twenty-five years which followed his retirement from the presidency of the Union Pacific, he published, in addition to many noticeable and much noticed addresses, historical and otherwise, *The Life of R. H. Dana* and *The*

Three Episodes of Massachusetts History, already mentioned; *Massachusetts; Its Historians and History*, in 1893; a memoir, all too brief, of his father, in 1900; a volume of *Studies: Military and Diplomatic*, in 1911, and in 1913, in book form, the lectures delivered at Oxford and later at Johns Hopkins University entitled *Transatlantic Historical Solidarity*. This last volume represented part of the study he was making with his usual thoroughness and industry of the diplomatic history of our Civil War. He had gathered an immense mass of original material for this purpose and was constantly accumulating more, upon which he was occupied at the time of his death.

In addition to all this original production, with its wide historical research, he found time to edit for the Prince Society in 1883, during the railroad period, Thomas Morton's *New English Canaan*, in 1894 the Winthrop-Weld tract on *Antinomianism in New England*, and later gave much assistance in the preparation of the Historical Society's monumental edition of Bradford's *History of Plymouth Plantation*, which appeared in 1912. This edition of Bradford, suggested by Mr. Adams in 1898, was but one of many things that he did for the Society which filled a large place in his life for twenty years. He was chosen a vice-president in 1890 when he left the Union Pacific, and in 1895 he was elected president to succeed Dr. Ellis. He came to his new duties, as he had come to all the positions he had ever filled, with an abundance of fresh ideas and in the spirit of the reformer. He not only worked for and helped the Society in every possible way, he not only brought to it and expended in its service unbounded energy and enthusiasm, but he enlarged its field, increased its usefulness, and made it more of a power in history, literature, and in the community, than it had ever been before. The bane of all learned societies, historical, antiquarian, or scientific, is the tendency to see only the trees and not the forest, the houses and not the city. They are too apt to forget that one fact is gossip and that two related facts are history. All persons of healthy minds love gossip, whether oral or written, if it is clever, humorous, and suggestive. That is an attribute of human nature and is due to the fact that good gossip has the quality of the story, the touch of romance, the appeal to the imagination. But it is a perilous mistake to suppose that all gossip, good or bad, dull or amusing, that all facts, simply as facts, are of value. The result of this error when indulged in is the heaping up of unread pages of facts of no value at the time of their existence or at any subsequent period. Mere age does not give a fact importance. Something more is needed, and the tenderness which we all feel for that which the centuries have spared should not blind us to its intrinsic worth or worthlessness, which is the only real question to be determined. Diamonds and pearls are no doubt to be found now and then on the rubbish-heaps of the past, but the mounds are none the less rubbish as they were from the beginning, and their final resting-place should be not the printed, gently preserving page, but the fire or the dust-bin, even if a precious stone, happily rescued, should have once glittered among them.

With this vice of collecting valueless facts purely because they were old, and then encumbering not only shelves but the limited time of finite humanity with endless volumes of printed paper, Charles Adams was very familiar and equally unsympathetic. This in itself made him peculiarly fit for the president's place in an historical society. But he did much more. He carried the work of the Society out of the Colonial Period, the seventeenth and eighteenth centuries, where it had been too much and too long confined, and brought the nineteenth century, and especially the period of the Civil War, within the scope of its communications, investigations, and monthly consideration. Not content with this extension he led the Society into still wider fields of history by his own addresses and essays, which ranged from the battle of Salamis to the current events of the day and which greatly enlivened and adorned the volumes of the *Proceedings*. His generous gifts to the Society were never lacking, but the greatest gift of all was his own untiring energy and enthusiasm; the way in which he asserted, developed, and maintained the position of the Society as an influence and power in literature and historical research.

The removal from Quincy to Lincoln proved in all ways fortunate. He genuinely enjoyed the country life and the new occupations which his estate afforded. He became a benefactor, too, of his new town as he had been in the old home of his family. Journeys to Europe were interspersed as the years went by, and in 1905 he purchased a house in Washington and thenceforth passed his winters there. That change, too, was a fortunate and a happy one. He liked Washington. The varied society, the people from all parts of the United States and from foreign lands whom he met, interested and amused him. The climate was more genial than that of Massachusetts and there were few days when he could not walk and have his daily ride, which he kept up steadily until the very end. These last twenty years were, I am sure, very happy ones. The cares and anxieties of his railroad and business life were all behind him. The crushing burdens which came after he left the Union Pacific were disposed of and lifted from his shoulders. He was constantly occupied with work which he keenly enjoyed, work worth doing, and which he had the satisfaction of knowing was well done, and the natural "aptitude" had at last full and unrestricted opportunity. His physical and mental vigor remained unimpaired to a degree which made it impossible to realize the number of his years. He was spared the trials of gradual decay which age so often brings. He escaped the fate which above all others he would have dreaded and resented:

> To hang
> Quite out of fashion, like a rusty mail
> In monumental mockery.

In the full tide of activity and work, instinct with interest in life, he was seized with pneumonia; a few days of illness and the end came on the 20th of March, only two months before his eightieth birthday. To him was given the good fortune, which usually comes alone to youth untimely taken, of leaving in the lives of those who knew and admired and loved him, as well as of those who were nearest and dearest to him, a gap which never can be filled.

In such fashion this career so crowded with work, with public service, with achievements of many kinds, came to the inevitable close. What shall be said of the man himself who had a career so striking and who in such a vivid and earnest manner lived the life of his time, who exercised so much influence upon the community of which he was a part and in various ways upon the thought and the development of his country? How shall we approach any attempt to judge him and his work? Charles Adams would have been the first to agree with Drummond, of Hawthornden, "That there is nothing lighter than mere praise." In his admirable biographies, in all his historical writings, when he deals with those who have played their part upon the stage of life and then have gone from among us, he never treads the beaten paths of eulogy and undiscriminating panegyric. He would, I am sure, resent any failure to follow his own precepts and example, when those who honored and admired him came to speak of him after his work was done. As we may learn from his autobiography, he judged himself far more severely, far more harshly one may often say, than any dispassionate critic would think of doing. Rarely does he express satisfaction with anything he did. Constantly does he point out where he had failed to reach the standard he desired, and the censure of himself for lost opportunities recurs, often quite unjustly, as it seems to me, again and again. His aims were very high, very large; like most effective men he fell short of his own ideals, like most men who make anything he made mistakes. But he overrated the number of lost opportunities and he underrated his own successes. He was very modest in his judgment upon all that he did himself, but it must be confessed that he was equally modest in his judgment of other people, an attitude often mistaken for self-satisfaction when in reality it implies nothing of the sort. This was eminently true of Charles Adams, who was wholly free from small conceits and petty self-complacencies. No one can read his autobiography and fail to see that so far as he personally was concerned he was humble-minded; but when he analyzed or criticised any man, whether that man was historical or contemporary, he dealt with him as he dealt with himself — unsparingly, rarely with any illusions, but always as fairly as he could. He fully intended to be simply just in judgment, for malice, jealousy, or uncharitableness had no existence in his nature.

In reviewing his life one is struck most by the extent and variety of his activities and filled with wonder that any man had the really enormous energy, both mental and physical, necessary to undertake and to accomplish so much. He felt himself that he had attempted to do too many things and had expended his efforts in too many directions. As a rule, no doubt, the greatest reputations and the greatest results, both in fame and accomplishment, have been obtained by the concentration of a man's powers upon a single object; but this in no way detracts from the effectiveness of the work or the credit due to one who has had a large measure of success and of high usefulness in many different fields of thought and action, as was the case with Charles Adams. His energy may have spent itself on too many objects, but it was never fruitless, and to whatever subject he turned he left his mark and a deep impress behind him. His varied interests and incessant labors in many directions were very different from the mere restlessness which flits here and there, touching everything without adorning anything, and effecting nothing. His labors may have been, they were, indeed, very diverse, but they were never in vain.

Next to the extent and variety of his activities that which is most arresting is the fact that in all he undertook he never entered upon the one field for which, by strong inheritance as well as by natural capacity, he would seem to have been most peculiarly fitted. Statesmanship, politics in the largest sense, diplomacy, were with him bred in the bone, were an instinct rather than an inborn tendency or inclination. Yet he never made any effort toward a public life in the ordinary and restricted sense. He certainly never sought, it seems as if he never even desired, public office, either political or diplomatic, although by inheritance and natural endowments he was so remarkably suited for both. He took a deep interest in politics and was entirely conversant with them both at home and abroad. He understood all political questions thoroughly, far better than most of those who are immediately engaged in them. He was intensely patriotic, profoundly American; he performed all the duties of a citizen at all times, but he never became a public man himself in the accepted meaning of the term, although he demonstrated by his life that public service of the highest kind could be rendered without holding public office. In the work he did he influenced public thought and the development of his country; he left in our great railroad system, in education, in our park systems, in our history and literature, substantial results, monuments of labors far more beneficent and enduring than those achieved by most men who have official titles appended to their names, in catalogues and dictionaries. He held strong political views and never hesitated to express them at elections great and small. He was an independent in politics, not the kind which always votes against and opposes one party without admitting that they belong to the other, but a genuine independent, voting for and supporting the candidacy and the principles which he believed under existing conditions were best for the public welfare. His opinions and views were sharply and publicly expressed in all contests over public questions of any importance and had a wide influence because of his real independence and entire sincerity. Those who differed from him never questioned his disinterestedness or the complete absence of self-seeking, which was so marked in all he did. Strongly as his opinions were held and expressed, he always could put himself in the other man's place, understand his position, and do him justice without an air of self-righteousness or any touch of illiberality. And yet, despite this knowledge of politics, this inborn aptitude for public affairs, as I have just said, he never sought or held any public office dependent upon political elections or political appointment. Those which he accepted came to him without any political reason and solely because he was the man above all others in the town or State fitted to perform a particular and important public service.

The reason that he never sought the higher public offices, that he never tried to take the place which seemed in all ways to belong to him in the broad and inviting field of national politics at home, and the still wider field of international politics abroad for which he was so especially adapted, is to be found, I think, in what he himself calls at the outset his "individualism." At a later day, in a very interesting address at the Hawthorne centenary, he said, "I am, also, naturally inclined to be otherwise-minded, and a bit iconoclastic." This is what he meant, when describing his boyhood, by "individualism," more clearly and expressively stated; and here is to be discovered, I think, the cause of his entire abstention from any effort to follow in the footsteps of his father, his grandfather, and his great-grandfather, which had carried them to the summits both in public service and in history. To be "otherwise-minded" both naturally and in practice leads, in the case of a man of original thought and high ability, to much achievement on his part and to a strong and stimulating influence of great value to the community. But this quality, like all marked attributes, has, if not its defect, the necessity of sacrifice in some other direction. It makes it difficult for its possessor to work with other men on a large scale. In the many commissions upon which Charles Adams served his relations with his colleagues were always pleasant and harmonious in the fullest sense. But these colleagues were few and his leadership and superiority, so far as their especial work was concerned, were entirely and readily acknowledged. When he was brought into relations with larger numbers of colleagues and associates with whom it was necessary to act in furtherance of a common purpose, as in the case of the Union Pacific, we have but to read what he says in this connection of the financial magnates and business men with whom he came in contact in order to realize the difficulties he found in the management of varying opinions and in taking joint action where many men were involved. In politics this necessity for coöperation, not only with many others but with large bodies and groups of men, is greatly increased, to a degree in fact surpassing that of any other form of human activity. Politics are carried on, among English-speaking people at least, through the instrumentality of parties. Parties are composed of thousands, of millions of men, indeed, who are agreed upon certain general principles and certain broad policies, but who of necessity differ widely among themselves as to details, often of a very serious character, and also as to those who are to be selected to represent and lead the party. To attain success not only are much patience and a readiness always to subordinate the lesser to the higher and larger purpose demanded, but also a willingness to compromise details in order to obtain united action, as well as to accept at times not merely a half loaf, but even a quarter or less with a view to an ultimate result and to a further advance in the future. These sacrifices of individuality Charles Adams did not care to make, felt, perhaps, that he could not make them. He preferred to exercise his influence and his powers for the furtherance of the great and useful ends he sought, in other ways, and he therefore shunned or at least never tried to enter the wider and more conspicuous fields of public life and service, for which by inheritance, training, and talents he was so remarkably adapted. But if his individualism, in his own opinion, prevented his entrance upon the field which seemed so peculiarly his own, it was at the same time the source of his power, of his influence, and of his success in the many others where he played a most distinguished part. For his "otherwise-mindedness," to use his own homely and most picturesque phrase, was, it must always be remembered, a quality far removed from the empty love of facile paradox. We have had of late years, if not here, at least in England, a group — it might almost be called a school — of paradox-makers who have achieved a now fading notoriety and who have certainly ardently admired each other. In the trick of paradox, no doubt, some cleverness has been shown and some passing amusement excited. But at bottom the whole business is shallow, and, like all tricks constantly repeated, becomes tiresome. A paradox is merely an inverted platitude or truism. If a string of platitudes wearies, the same collection inverted, after the short-lived novelty of inversion wears off, becomes even more intolerable, because the truism is, as a rule, true, while the paradox is not, and in the long run truth is a better companion than falsehood. If a man stands on his head in the street, he is sure to attract momentary attention, but he is less desirable, less easy to live with, and far less useful than those who pass by about their business in the normal and unnoticeable position of the human biped. With the professional paradox in all its tiresome futility and melancholy vacuity, the "otherwise-mindedness" of Charles Adams had no relation whatever. Still less had it any resemblance, not even the most remote, to cheap cynicism or to an artificial pose. He saw with clear vision what was defective, what was wrong, as he believed, in his own times and in his own country, but he did not on that account hold up with factitious admiration some long dead century, or some foreign country as an ideal where all was perfect, for he knew that such perfection existed nowhere and that the bygone century and the foreign country had their defects and their wrongs, which, if not worse than those of his own time and of his own land, were certainly quite as bad. He was not a pessimist, and professional pessimism had, for him, no attraction On the other hand he had no patience with "the barren, optimistic sophistries of comfortable moles," for the instinct of the reformer was strong within him. He saw life steadily and saw it whole, he knew that it was a tangled web in which the strands of evil and good both mingled, and to him it seemed a duty to tear out the one and preserve the other. This he could not have done had he not sanely recognized the existence of both.

The "otherwise-mindedness" of Charles Adams was in reality independent and often original thought as to all the conditions which he met. Whether it was in education or railroad systems, in literature or politics, in life or history, his instinct was to question the accepted system or the accepted view, and if he thought it harmful or erroneous he set himself to correct it. This spirit of questioning, of divine discontent, which is not satisfied with mere ineffective snarling, but which seeks always a practical result, is the spirit which has saved the world from stagnation, which has lifted man from the shell-heaps and the cave-dwellings to the place which for good or ill he occupies to-day. This was the spirit of Charles Adams. He always expressed his views or opinions with uncompromising vigor so that every one took notice of them and no one failed to understand them. When convinced that he had made a mistake he admitted it with the same uncompromising clearness. I have been reminded more than once by his confession of some error, of the story of Dr. Johnson, who replied, when a lady asked him why he had wrongly defined the word "pastern," — "Ignorance, Madam, pure ignorance." The same blunt sincerity, the same absolute honesty of mind, was eminently characteristic of Charles Adams. He stated his opinions with all the force of absolute conviction, and he was equally direct and outspoken if he was satisfied that he was mistaken, or if further reflection or new facts led him to change his mind. Disagreement he was sure to arouse and intended to do so. But whether he went too far or not, whether he was wholly right or measurably wrong, in practical affairs he wrought improvements and brought progress; in history, if he did not always change the accepted opinion, he caused men to review and reconsider their judgment in the interests of truth. In whatever he did throughout his long, active, and distinguished career he was always a stimulating and uplifting influence. To his questioning spirit backed by his energy, his love of practical results, his readiness to understand the positions of other men from whom he differed, he owed his success and all that he accomplished for his State and country, for American letters and for American history. He underrated his own measure of success, as it seems to me, but he judged himself and his career in a singularly dispassionate way. At the close of his autobiography he says:

Finally I want to say that preparing this résumé has been for me a decidedly profitable use of time. It has caused me to review, to weigh, and to measure. As a result of that process, I feel I have no cause of complaint with the world. I have been a remarkably, an exceptionally, fortunate man. I have had health, absence of death, dissipation, and worthlessness in my family, with no overwhelming calamity to face and subside under; and the world has taken me for all I was fairly worth. Looking back, and above all, in reading that destroyed diary of mine, I see with tolerable clearness my own limitations. I was by no means what I in youth supposed myself to be. As to opportunity, mine seems to have been infinite. No man could ask for better chances. In a literary way, financially, politically, I might have been anything, had it only been in me. The capacity, not the occasion, has been wanting. It was so in the army; it was so in railroads, in politics, and in business; it was so in literature and history. In one and all my limitations made themselves felt; most of all, in the law. On the other hand, my abilities, as ability goes in this world, have been considerable; never first-rate, but more than respectable. They have enabled me to accomplish what I have accomplished; and I have accomplished something.

. . . In other directions also I have, perhaps, accomplished nothing considerable, compared with what my three immediate ancestors accomplished; but, on the other hand, I have done some things better than they ever did; and, what is more and most of all, I have had a much better time in life — got more enjoyment out of it. In this respect I would not change with any of them.

This brief extract, which will be read in the future with its context, as it ought to be if it is to be fully understood, seems to me very illuminating. It shows to any one who will consider it carefully that Charles Adams was, as I have said, essentially humble-minded as to himself and that he was disposed to underestimate his own success and achievements. But it also shows that he was in the highest degree honest-minded. He meant to give himself full credit even when he judged himself most harshly. He hated shams, he looked truth and facts squarely in the face, and he shrank from neither. Boasting was as alien to him as repining. These are very noble intellectual qualities. There are, indeed, none finer, none which should more command the imitation and respect of men.

With these qualities of mind in Charles Adams the moral qualities fully corresponded. The highest sense of honor, the most absolute moral integrity, were so completely his, so accepted by all as a matter of course, that in his life no one thought it necessary even to allude to them; but when we speak of him in commemoration they must find their place upon the printed page for the benefit of those who will only know him there. He was a man of the highest courage, both moral and physical, and of the purest patriotism. He served his country in the field through four years of war. There he might have paused with the consciousness that the duty and the debt which all men owe their country had been fully paid. But for that debt and that duty there was for him no full payment possible. He continued to render public service in many ways until the day of his death.

In the same fashion he sought to serve his fellow-men, not only in the wide sense of the public, but the individual man and woman. He was generous, he liked to be helpful. He was a good friend, although he made few professions, and so loyal that he found disloyalty hard to comprehend. Under a manner somewhat brusque, sometimes abrupt, was concealed one of the kindest, most affectionate hearts that ever beat, and how tender his sympathy could be those to whom it went out know well.

The uppermost thought, the keenest feeling, in the minds of all who knew him is pervaded by the sense of personal loss and of personal sorrow. One lingers reluctant by the closing door which shuts him out from the present and leaves him with his great ancestors as a figure in our history. As we turn away, this final word may at least be said. The world is torn with war, tortured with pain and anguish, oppressed with dark forebodings. Many dangerous and difficult questions confront our beloved country. But the fact that we as a people can still bring forth, can still honor, still be influenced and helped by a man of the character, ideals, and aspirations of Charles Adams, must give us hope in the present and confidence in the years that are yet to be.

The Horatian lines, so old, so familiar, so beautiful, come unsought to the memory because they can be said of Charles Adams without reservation and in all the simplicity of truth:

> Justum ac tenacem propositi virum,
> Non civium ardor prava jubentium,
>   Non vultus instantis tyranni,
>   Mente quatit solida, neque Auster
> Dux inquieti turbidus Adriae,
> Nec fulminantis magna manus Jovis:
>   Si fractus illabatur orbis
>   Impavidum ferient ruinae.

Charles Francis Adams
1835-1915
An Autobiography

❧ Charles Francis Adams ❧

AN AUTOBIOGRAPHY

I

YOUTH AND EDUCATION

SHAKESPEARE causes Falstaff to tell Chief Justice Gas-coigne, in a certain familiar interview, that he "was born about three of the clock in the afternoon, with a white head, and something a round belly." [1] No character of that period lives for us now quite so distinctly and in the flesh as Shake-speare's creation, and we must skip a hundred and seventy-five years before coming to another, this time one who really lived, moved and had his being, but who to-day is as much a presence in the world of the past as Sir John Falstaff. That battle of Shrewsbury in which Shakespeare makes Falstaff figure occurred July 21, 1403; so it is fair to presume that Falstaff, had he come into the world at all, would have made his appearance in it at "about three of the clock in the afternoon" of some day in the year 1360 — there or thereabouts. Michel de Montaigne, the succeeding vivid individuality referred to, has recorded the exact hour when he was born, "betwixt eleven and twelve o'clock in the forenoon, the last of February, 1533." [2] It so happens that, owing to the fact of my father's keeping a diary, I can fix the exact hour of my birth as definitely as did either Falstaff or Montaigne. I came into this world in a house on

[1] *2 King Henry IV*, i, 2.　　　　[2] *Essays*, Book i, ch. xix.

Hancock Avenue, as the narrow footway on the right-hand side of the statue of Horace Mann, west of the State-House grounds in Boston is still designated, between nine and eleven P.M. of the 27th of May, 1835. My father and mother had passed the winter at the house of my grandfather, Peter C. Brooks, on Pearl Street; but, on the 11th of May they had moved up to Hancock Avenue, their own house, with a view to the approaching event. In my father's diary of that period there is a reference which fixes another and, to the generality, far more interesting date. Quincy granite was then in great vogue. On the 27th of April my father went out to Quincy, and up to the Old Granite Railway in Milton, on business connected with leasing some quarry lands, and he there "observed some beautiful specimens which are in process of sculpture for the new hotel of Mr. Astor in New York." These were the familiar Astor House monoliths, until recently so conspicuous a landmark in the architecture of Broadway.

The period of childhood, and school and college days of any man, no matter how considerable, are not a profitable field on which to dilate; and yet, after all, as Wordsworth has said: "The child is father of the man," and, for the autobiographer, if he only knows how to deal with them, the recollections of early life and education, told in the light of experience, carry about as useful lessons as any of riper years; if, indeed, they do not carry some far more useful. As the twig is bent, the tree inclines; I know this has been so in my case, and my youth and education now seem to me to have been a skilfully arranged series of mistakes, first on the part of others and then on my own part.

During all my earlier years my father and mother were

living very quietly in Boston and Quincy, and there they
continued to live until, in 1859, my father went into active
public life. I was then twenty-four years old. Previous to
that great, and blessed, break, they were always at home,
never even going to Europe — not a small thing in those
days — and, until, in 1853, I went to college, I lived at home.
It was just the sort of bringing-up I ought not to have had.
The Boston life of those days was simple, and, in many respects, not bad; but it was distinctly provincial and self-
complacent. Until 1842 my father lived on in the Hancock
Avenue house. He then moved to the house he subsequently
occupied as a winter residence during forty-five years, No.
57 Mt. Vernon Street, nearly opposite the head of Walnut
Street, a vamped-up dwelling, the purchase and occupation
of which were highly characteristic of the man. Bought
by my grandfather, Peter C. Brooks, for his daughter, my
mother, the house had been built in the early part of the
century, and in the way then usual. Subsequently it had
been re-modelled, and a little elementary plumbing and
heating apparatus forced bodily into it; but, unfortunately,
it contained one large and handsome room on the second
floor into which the sun poured, and which occupied the
entire front. The only really desirable room in the house,
my father fixed on it for his library regardless of other considerations. So the house was bought for my mother, and
in it I grew up. That house threw a shadow across my whole
early life. I well remember my disappointment at its aspect
the first time I ever rang the door-bell — a boy of seven.
And when, forty-seven years later — my mother having
died and the house having been emptied of everything — I
crossed the threshold for the last time, and turned the key

in the door, I walked away with a distinct sense of relief, thanking God that chapter was closed. I have not a single pleasant recollection associated with No. 57 Mt. Vernon Street. There hangs about it, stretching through a memory covering long years, a monotonous atmosphere of winter gloom.

It was not so with Quincy, our summer, as well as im-memorial family home. Quincy was associated in my mind with spring and summer — bright skies, open windows, green fields, singing birds, the blue bay with white sails dotting it, and a distant view over a country rolling into great whale-back hills, with the State-House dome on the horizon. Boston was gloom personified, frost, snow and discomfort; short days and long school-hours; wet, cold feet, and evening lessons. In those days — 1840–1853 — Quincy was by no means a bad place in which to grow up. A Massachusetts country town, it had not altogether outgrown the colonial period, it still savored of the past. The famous Quincy granite quarries had been opened some years before, and already, physically and morally, had worked the place mani-fest injury; but their far-reaching destructive influence was not made fully manifest. In point of fact, though it would hardly now be imagined, Quincy was in a natural way more richly endowed than any other region adjacent to Boston. Lying on the seaward slope of the Blue Hill range, without being a seaboard place it stretched for miles along the shores of Boston Bay, with the rocky and picturesque Squantum headland at one extremity and the Great Hill and Fore River at the other. The hills at the west and north offered residential sites of the choicest character, since gutted for the stone that underlay them, and now converted into an abomination of desolation. The passage of ten thousand years could not restore a trace of the natural advantages in that region obliterated since my boyhood.

The Old Colony Railroad, connecting what was originally the Plymouth Colony with that of Massachusetts Bay, was not constructed until I was ten years old; and up to as late as 1850 Quincy was practically what it had always been — a quiet, steady-going, rural Massachusetts community, with its monotonous main thoroughfares and commonplace connecting streets, both thoroughfare and by-ways lined with wooden houses, wholly innocent of any attempts at architecture, and all painted white with window blinds of green. With the exception of the workers in the quarries, not yet developed into a purely mining community — with all the term implies — the place was still peopled by those of the original stock; for the foreign and more particularly the Irish element had not yet reached the self-asserting point. Later Quincy became to a large extent a bed-room annex to the Boston ware-house; but in my boyhood period it was still largely agricultural, while its leading industry was the making of boots and shoes, almost every house along the main street having a small one-story annex, from which on any summer's day could be heard the incessant tapping of the hammer on the lap-stone. The factory and the machine-made shoe were as yet unknown or in their earliest stages of development. In the centre of the town, where the roads to Plymouth and Taunton branched, stood the meeting-house and the town-hall; the "tavern," as it was called, also was here located, with the big, shady elm-trees in front of it. From it the daily stage-coaches started for Boston over the "pike," or went down Plymouth way; while, in summer, on the porch and in their shirt sleeves, sat the red-faced, big-bellied, village topers and loafers, as well known as the town-pump. The blacksmith's shop on the main street, the tannery "down in the Hollow," and the oxen-drawn stone-teams were objects of deep interest, as my brother John and I, red-headed and freckle-faced urchins of six and eight years, trudged daily through the village to and from school. Since then what they are pleased to call "the march of improvement" has done away with that whole phase of more placid existence. The mass of mankind in Quincy as elsewhere is now doubtless much better housed, better taught and better served than it then was; but the place I as a child loved so well no longer exists. It has been transformed into a conventional, commonplace suburban community, progressive and well to do, but wholly devoid of individuality. So, no more than its everlasting hills or the islands in its bay are the present inhabitants of Quincy suggestive of the Quincy of my boyhood. The hills have been stripped, and gutted or built over, made common and vulgarized, or devastated and turned, as I have already said, into a mining horror, while the islands have lost their green, whale-back outlines under an eruption of summer hotels and seashore cottages. As to the population, no one knows me now as I walk the once familiar streets; and I recall no faces. With local feeling, traditions also are gone. As I pass to-and-fro in Quincy I now seem to wander with ghosts.

Going back to the old days, my grandfather with his family lived in what we knew as "the old house, down the hill," while we occupied "the house on the hill," built by my father two years after I was born. There we passed the summers, from late May to early November, until we children grew

up. Then the house no longer sufficed. We were crowded
out. My grandfather died in 1848, and my grandmother
occupied "the house down the hill" only one or two summers
afterwards. In 1850, I think it was, my father took possession; and there in June, 1889, my mother died, just one year
more than a century after John and Abigail Adams first
took possession in 1788, after their return from Europe and
our first English Mission. We were all fond of "the old
house," and pleasant recollections cluster about it. Still
belonging to the family, it is now (1912) occupied by my
brother Brooks; and I know of no other case in all my New
England acquaintance of a fourth generation still living
under the same roof-tree, covering an unbroken occupancy
of considerably over a century.

My earliest recollections of that house are associated with
my grandfather and his family, consisting of my grandmother, his daughter-in-law, "Mrs. John," and his grand-
daughter, the only surviving child of his second son, John.
As to my grandfather, he was during the whole period I
remember him an old man, absorbed in work and public
life. He seemed to be always writing — as, indeed, he was.
I can see him now, seated at his table in the middle of the
large east room, which he used as a library, a very old-
looking gentleman, with a bald head and white fringe of
hair — writing, writing — with a perpetual inkstain on the
fore-finger and thumb of the right hand. He was kind and
considerate to his grandchildren, and seemed to like to have
us in that library of his, walled in with over-loaded book-
shelves; but his was not a holiday temperament. Always
unaccompanied, he used to wander about the ragged, unkempt old place — with its pear and cherry trees, and old-

time orchard — hatchet and saw in hand, pruning and
watching his seedlings; and he would take grave, sedate
walks — constitutionals — invariably along the highway,
and apparently absorbed in meditation; but he never seemed
to relax; nor could I imagine him playful. In his library he
was always at work, or nodding in his chair. Though in detail different, my father was in substance much the same.
To their own great misfortune, neither of them had any real
taste — no innate love — for innocent outdoor amusement;
that is, they did not care to get near to Nature whether in
the woods or on the water. They were, moreover, both of
them afflicted with an everlasting sense of work to be accomplished — "so much to do, so little done!" The terrible
New England conscience implanted in men who, inheriting
its traditions, had largely outgrown Calvinistic theology.
They were, in a word, by inheritance ingrained Puritans,
and no Puritan by nature probably ever was really companionable. Of the two, however, my grandfather was incomparably the more active-minded and interesting. His
was a truly inquiring and observing disposition; and, moreover, he had a fairly pronounced taste for social life. His
chief difficulty lay in a tendency to introspection, which was
almost morbidly developed by the journalizing habit. His
diary was his daily confidant; and he grew to desire no other.

The "old house" stood on the Plymouth road facing
south, in comparatively low ground; but in 1837 my father
built a country home on "the Hill" — President's Hill, as
it was called, Stoneyfield Hill in Provincial days — in what
had previously been John Adams's cow-pasture. The two
residences were perhaps an eighth of a mile apart, though
in full view of each other; and, from the gallery of my father's

house — portico, we called it — my grandfather used daily to time the rising and the setting sun. Now, seventy years later, I can see him standing or sitting, watch in hand, noting the earliest and last rays of the summer day. There is nothing of that period I more vividly recall. A somewhat solitary man, he was to me, hardly more than a child, an attractive as well as a great one. He impressed my imagination.

It was not so with my father. He was built on more rigid and narrower lines. He was even less companionable. He was never the companion of our sports and holidays. To us, it would, as I now see, have made all the difference conceivable had he loved the woods and the water, — walked and rode and sailed a boat; been, in short, our companion as well as instructor. The Puritan was in him, and he did n't know how! In reading his diary, for instance, I came across two entries which tell the whole story — they are as a calcium light cast upon him, and his relations with his children. They are from the record of 1843, and as follows; my sister, his eldest child, being then a girl of about twelve: "Took a walk with my daughter, Louisa. We went along the road to Quincy Point, until we reached a street that has been lately opened and called North Street, from which we struck into another called South Street, which comes out below Mrs. Miller's house. It is curious, and illustrative of my little inclination to ramble, that, so long as I have lived in Quincy, I have never before to my knowledge been in this pretty little road." Yet South Street is one of the oldest and most picturesque — at least it was so then, and long after — it has now, eheu! gone the way of all the rest — it was, I say, one of the oldest, the most picturesque, and to

me the most familiar roads in Quincy; and almost within
sight of his house. Yet at thirty-six he did n't know of its
existence! So the same year, but two days later. My brother
John and I, that summer, were at a sort of small boarding-
school, at Hingham — of which, more, presently — and we
were brought home every Saturday, to pass Sunday. The
autumn was come, and with it the smelting season; the
only kind of sport in which I ever knew my father to en-
gage. He used now and then to take us down to Black's
Creek, as it was called, where was Greenleaf's wharf, half-
a-mile or so from the house. So he now made this entry of
30th September: "The weather was charming. I idled
away the morning on Mr. Daniel Greenleaf's wharf, with
very little success. Perhaps this consumption of time is
scarcely justifiable; but why not take some of life for simple
enjoyments, provided that they interfere with no known
duty? My boys came home from school and joined me. We
remained until dinner time."

There you have it! Hereditarily warped, he had no conception of the idea that in idling away that soft, kindly
September day in companionship with his two boys just
home from school, and all close to Nature, he was saving
one day at least from utter loss — making of it the very
best possible use that could be made! And so he had to excuse himself, to himself, for this scarcely justifiable waste
of time! The thought of it even now saddens and irritates
me — the difference to me would have been so great. I
have suffered from it all through life. The twig was bent
wrong. I ought to have been brought up in closer touch
with Nature and its enjoyments. I should then have acquired aptitudes — sailing, rambling, the playing of games,

the genuine love of outdoor life — which I never did acquire, and the lack of which I lament more and more every year I live. I would to-day give much to feel at home on a boat or a bicycle. I have since sailed a great deal, and bicycled somewhat; but it was in both cases too late! I never got so as to feel really at home when handling sheet and tiller, or when on a wheel. And so the most important as well as enjoyable branches of education for me were neglected or abjured in youth, and only partly made good by my subsequent fortunate army experience at over twenty-six. But my father saw no good whatever in athletics; and he had a prejudice against the gymnasium. As to my army experience, altogether the most beneficial of my life educationally, until long after the event he simply deplored it as to me ruinous. What was in truth my salvation, developed, as he at the time persuaded himself, all my most objectionable tendencies. In his case, two hundred years of ancestral swaddling clothes could not be burst. The loss has been great, and, in my case, the injury sustained was irreparable. It was never, except in part, made good.

This was educational error number one; and, before I get through, the list will be long! My father had the old New England sense of duty in religious observances. The Sabbath and church-going were institutions. All through my childhood how I disliked Sunday! I was glad when Monday came; for me it was n't "black Monday," for it was six days before another Sunday. I remember now the silence, the sombre idleness, the sanctified atmosphere of restraint of those days, with their church-bells, their sedate walk and their special duties. We children had to be brought up strictly in the way we should go; for then we would not depart from it when we were old! Would n't we! The recollection of those Sundays haunts me now. We always had a late breakfast — every one did; and we dined early — roast beef always for dinner; and I got a dislike for roast beef which lasted almost to manhood, because I thus had to eat it every Sunday at 1.30, after a breakfast at 9. Then came the Sunday hair-combing and dressing. After which, Bible reading, four chapters, each of us four verses in rotation. Then a Sunday lesson, committing some verses from the Bible or a religious poem to memory. I especially remember the Sermon on the Mount and Pope's Messiah; and these were the hardest lessons of the whole week, those we all disliked most; and so distasteful were they that they have left on me to this day a sort of aversion to the Bible and to Pope. Then came the going to Church. Lord! that going to Church! Twice a day, rain or shine, summer and winter. In town [Boston] we went to that dreary old Congregational barn in Chauncy Street, — the gathering place of the First Church of Boston — where my uncle, Dr. Frothingham, held forth. And, by the way, only the other day I heard a good story of Dr. Frothingham. It came from Mr. Stetson, with whom I was associated in the Commission to award cost, etc., of the Metropolitan Park System. He was the son of old Caleb Stetson, of Medford, who married my father and mother more than ninety years ago. He mentioned a turn of speech of Dr. Lunt's, our Quincy pastor, who once remarked of my uncle Frothingham, in a grand burst of expression: "Dr. Frothingham is a man of gentle and saintly life; I picture him as a sanctified isle in the midst of a wild and Godless sea."

Dr. Frothingham may have been all that. He certainly

was a man of very sweet and gentle character; but, as a preacher, he recalls to me only a slow, somewhat soft and diffuse delivery in that superheated, roof-lighted, somnolent barrack, where I passed so many weary, penitential hours in those winter months in "the forties" and the "early fifties." The old meeting-house was removed in 1868, I think; and I well remember going there on the Sunday when services were held in it for the last time [May 10, 1868] in order that, as I went down the familiar steps on leaving, I could say to myself: "There; that is behind me. Never, never again, shall I enter those doors, or sit in that pew."

Such was my Boston church-going. That at Quincy was not so bad; and yet bad enough. Dr. William P. Lunt was a natural orator. He looked the preacher; and his voice was rich and full. The church too was more cheerful, and the summer air used to steal in through the open windows. But the only portion of the service which ever commended itself to me was that closing prayer, which I knew by heart — and can repeat now — and then the benediction — and the hateful services were over! I was free then to hurry home, to get out of my Sunday into my week-day clothes, and I could go and play; for Sunday was now done, and would n't come again for six days! Those New England Sabbaths actually embittered my youth. It required the drastic war education to emancipate me from them. Educational mistake number two!

Fortunately for me, the railroad did not get into Quincy until 1846, and I was then eleven years old; so I did have a few years of child life really in the country. The common-schools my father did not care to send his children to; and I have always been glad of it. I don't associate with the laborers on my place, nor would the association be agreeable to either of us. Their customs, language, habits and conventionalities differ from mine; as do those of their children. I believe in school life; and I believe in the equality of men before the law; but social equality, whether for man or child, is altogether another thing. My father, at least, did n't force that on us. So, as children, we went to the small private schools, were taught in a way by the clergymen of the Episcopal Church, or, what was quite as well for us, were not taught at all. But that school question got serious; and, in 1843 — I being then just eight — John and I, by a happy inspiration, were sent to Hingham, to be boarded and schooled by a young man named Wilder, who took in four other boys, two named Eldridge, from Boston, and two others, sons of George Bancroft, the historian, both of whom subsequently I was with in college, the younger being in the same class with me.[1] I remember the first week at Hingham well. How homesick John and I were! We were only eight and nine years old, and had never been away from home; and we were as miserable as boys usually are under such circumstances. But that summer ought to have taught a lesson to my parents and to us. John and I always afterwards agreed in looking back on the months at Hingham as the one bright, pleasant, joyous summer of our school-days. It stands out from among the others, in white. We did n't learn anything; but we were with other boys, and we bathed, and rambled, and were up to boyish mischief. Forty years and more afterwards I used often to ride through Hingham on my way to our summer seaside resort, the Glades, in North Scituate, and I always liked to go by that house,

[1] John Chandler Bancroft (H.U. 1854) and George Bancroft (H. U. 1856).

looking up at the window of the room in which John and I slept.

And here was educational error number three; an error I never have been able sufficiently to deplore, for it deeply affected my character, my physical development, and my subsequent existence even to this day. As a developing boy I peculiarly needed the influence and atmosphere of boarding-school life. I should have been compelled to rough it with other boys. Of that I stood in great want, and that for several reasons.

And, in the first place, though in no way remarkable, I see now that I was, and am still, individual. I don't see things, and take things, quite in the usual and average way. I did n't when a boy; and the best and most useful education I ever had was when undergoing constant attrition after I went to college, and, subsequently, in the army. I look back on it with deep thankfulness, as well as sincere pleasure. I needed more of it — all I could have of it! Not by nature daring — physically, on the contrary, inclined to be shrinking — having a positive inaptitude for games and athletic exercises, disposed to be studious in a way, I grew up as a child during the period of my grandfather's greatest political prominence; and its light was reflected on me at school. I was the grandson of John Quincy Adams; and not quite as other boys. This I felt. There was therefore in me a dangerous tendency, which needed correction sadly, and which a boarding-school life would have strongly tended to correct. Moreover, I would so much have enjoyed it; just as I enjoyed the mere taste I had of it at Hingham. It might have made me "a good fellow." At any rate, it would have taken me away from home, and home influences and surroundings; and these, in my case were bad, or, rather, not what I needed. But I never did go to boarding-school, and the plastic period was passed in immediate contact with home and amid a most miscellaneous collection of books, in which I sedulously hunted up everything that was pernicious, as well as much that was good. Here was educational mistake number four!

In my boyhood nothing whatever was done to amuse children. They might amuse themselves, or go unamused; that was their affair! That was before the day of games and sports; and at Quincy we had few horses, and no boats. I did not realize it at the time, but my vacations and intervals of leisure were dreariness personified. We bathed in Black's Creek, and that was all; and, curiously enough, bathing — diving and swimming — is the one activity which has stood by me ever since. It has been my delight; and in it I have excelled. That, I did acquire when young; and the pleasure I have had in that one out-of-doors sport has caused me to realize how infinite, how irreparable has been my loss in not acquiring other muscular aptitudes while so doing was possible. And there I struck a natural defect which a different education would have strongly tended to counteract. I am inclined to be what is known as muscle-slow — that is my muscular system is not elastic. I think I have somewhere remarked in writing on this; and when learning to ride a bicycle, at over sixty, an appreciation of the fact first dawned on me. This ought to have been corrected in my youth by practice at all sorts of games — skating, fencing, boxing, riding. Unfortunately — most unfortunately, for me — my father did not at all believe in that sort of training. Sports and games he held in horror; almost as much as for

young men just out of college he held Europe in horror, because a classmate of his — Alleyne Otis — after graduation
chanced to go to Europe, and came home an ass, and
remained an ass all the long continuing days of life. My
father did n't realize that Alleyne Otis was born an ass; and
was, though as yet not effusively so developed, an ass when
he went to Europe, as well as when he came home. So he
failed to discriminate between individuals; and, laying down
one rule for all, his theory was that the proper thing for
every young man was to get to work as soon as he could
scrabble through college, begin to make a living, marry, and
become, as he would express it, "a useful member of society." Any exceptionalism or individuality he regarded with
aversion. It was a snare and delusion; so, in my case, he
uniformly, and, in fact, all through life, diagnosed wrongly,
and took a mistaken course. He meant well; but he was
neither sympathetic nor observant. With him boys were
alike, and one hat fitted them all; while Europe was merely
another term for demoralization. As I look back on his course
towards me, well as he meant it and thoroughly conscientious as he was, I should now respect myself a great deal more
if I had then rebelled and run away from home, to sea or
the Devil. Indeed, if I had had in me any element of real
badness, or even recklessness of temperament, it would have
been fatally developed. But I was n't bad or a dare-devil;
and I was born with a decided sense of obligation to myself
and to others.

But, in looking back on that early home and school educational period since I began this writing, and considering
the light that period throws on the man's subsequent life, I
confess to a sense of bepuzzlement. I find myself observing

and studying myself at a distance of nearly seventy years, and trying to make myself out. My observation in life leads me to believe that nearly every human being has an aptitude; that is, there is something that he or she can do better than all other things. One in a hundred, again, has a remarkable aptitude; and, in one in a thousand, this aptitude is developed into something extraordinary. It then amounts to natural insight, and constitutes genius. Now a perfect system of education, if it could be devised, would be one which, while developing to the fullest extent all the faculties, would allow free play to the special aptitude. But this is just what our American school system fails to do, and does not aim at. In that system a child is — a child! and all children are cast in the same matrix. Thus the average child gets along with a tolerable degree of comfort; but the child with an individuality experiences much the fate a child with large feet would undergo if all children's shoes were made on one last.

In my case, it so chanced that I was individual without any specially pronounced aptitude or exceptional capacity. In reading one of Montaigne's *Essays* the other day I came across the following, which seemed very applicable to me. He was writing of his own childhood, and he said: "I had a slow wit, that would go no faster than it was led; a tardy understanding, a languishing invention, and, above all, ineradicable defect of memory; so that it is no wonder if, from all these, nothing considerable could be extracted." For me, as I now see it, the absolutely ideal training would have been that described in *School Days at Rugby*. I ought to have been sent away from home and been rubbed into shape among other boys; I should have been made to undergo a

severe all-around discipline; I should have been forced to
participate in all sorts of athletic games; I ought to have
been rounded into shape as much like other boys as a school
life could round me. The radical error in my case was that
I was kept at home, and brought up in an uncongenial day-
school. I do not hesitate to say that these mistakes of childhood have gravely prejudiced my entire life.

At ten years of age I did have the good fortune to be sent
to a private day-school kept by a Mr. David B. Tower. He
was a very portly, good-natured man, coming from the
Cohasset family of that name, and a good teacher. For some
reason, Tower saw, or thought he saw, something in me; and
to him I am, to this day, under great obligation. He encouraged me; and did all a man could to cure my lamentable want of capacity for verbal memorization. At his school
I rapidly gained in confidence, and began to feel some faith
in myself. Unfortunately, it was a day school, kept in a room
in the Park Street church-building, and I was at home in
the evenings and Sundays; and such play as I had was in
the streets of Boston. I needed the atmosphere of boarding-
school life.

Instead of getting it, I was, at the age of thirteen, sent to
the Boston Latin School. Of this institution my father had
a very exalted opinion. He had gone to it himself, when
brought home from Europe in 1818, and been under Master
Gould. For some reason, it suited him; perhaps in contrast
to the school he went to in England, and the antiquated
systems of teaching to which he had there been subjected —
systems about as absurd and illogical as those pursued in a
State's prison. In any event, however, the Latin School —
the "famous Boston Latin School," as it was then, and has

since been, called — became a kind of fetish with my father, and to it in due time all his sons were destined to go, as a matter of course.

It may have worked well with my father under Dr. Gould, but it did n't work well with his sons under Mr. Dixwell — that I can assert with confidence. The school building was then in Bedford Street — a street has since been laid out over its site. The school building was a cold, dreary, granite edifice, of the stone-mason style of architecture in vogue about 1840. It was pulled down about thirty years ago; and I rejoiced to see it go! It effaced to a degree a hateful memory. I was at the Latin School three years; my brother John was at it five. I loathed it, and John loathed it worse than I. Not one single cheerful or satisfactory memory is with me associated therewith. Its methods were bad, its standards low, its rooms unspeakably gloomy. It was a dull, traditional, lifeless day-academy, in which a conventional, commonplace, platoon-front, educational drill was carried on. I absolutely languished there, and, for that reason, my judgments might be deemed harsh; but one day, only a few years ago, I found myself seated at table next David P. Kimball, who was always at the Latin School at the head of the class before mine, and who, subsequently, was first scholar in my class at Harvard. I got talking with him of schools, for he had in life been a successful man, and our relations were kindly. So I said to him: "Well, David, I hardly need ask you, I suppose your sons all went to the Latin School." He turned on me, and vindictively snapped out, "Latin School! I would n't send a dog to the Latin School!" I certainly felt that way; but I never got on there, and always gravitated towards the foot of the class; David

Kimball, on the contrary, was at the head, and a favorite prize-taker. All the same, on that subject we were one. My single pleasant association with the Boston Latin School was — leaving it! Under the system there in vogue in the days of Dixwell and Gardner, I don't see how any good results, as respects scholarship, individuality or character, were reasonably to be expected. It was a conventional, mechanical, low-standard day-school and classical grind-mill. I left it sixty years ago, and I think of the period I spent there still as the dreariest, the most depressing and the most thoroughly worse than profitless of my life. I have not a good word to say of it; and like John Randolph and the sheep, I would go a long distance out of my way to give it a kick.

Sending me to the Boston Latin School was educational mistake number five: and a far-reaching one!

Then came in rapid succession mistakes numbers six and seven — serious both, **very** serious! As I plainly did n't get on at the Boston Latin School, my father, in 1851, concluded to take me away. I ought then to have gone to Exeter or Andover, been there fitted for college, and gone in the regular way. Instead of that, largely at my own solicitation, my father put me under the charge of Francis W. Palfrey, the son of his old friend Dr. John G. Palfrey, whom, in reality, he wanted to aid. The intention was good; the choice bad — absurd. Frank Palfrey graduated that year, and, with me, he was far more of a companion than a preceptor. With quick faculties he was a fair scholar; but he greatly lacked judgment and sobriety, and his and my thoughts were far more intent on parties, social life and dissipation than on our studies. It was a singularly unfortunate arrangement.

More unfortunately still, I liked it; and, for some unaccountable reason, instead of entering college at the regular time and in the usual way, I stayed out a year, and entered sophomore, in 1853. It was a great blunder; and I have never ceased to regret it. Had I been really fortunate, I would, in 1853, have failed to pass my examinations for the advanced standing, and been thrown back on the class of 1857. A severe mortification and disappointment at the moment, this would, in reality, have been for me a piece of great good luck; for the class of '57 was a remarkable class in many ways, and especially for its class feeling and spirit. It contained, too, an unusual number of agreeable and interesting men, many of whom have since attained distinction, and with whom I grew to hold close relations; while, on the other hand, the class of '56 was noticeably lacking in all these respects. It was as a class distinctly unnoticeable — a low average; and, in subsequent years, the chief distinction it achieved was contributing two inmates to the State's prison.

None the less, my college life I look back on with pleasure, and a moderate satisfaction. I blundered through in a way, committing, I may fairly say, as I see it now, about as many mistakes as I easily could; but, after all — studied from a distance in time — it was the period of freedom and germination. I was boyish and silly, but I did begin to develop. Acting on tradition, and influenced by my brother John's example, I did not live in the buildings and in the full atmosphere of college life; and, during the two last and best years, I had my brother Henry to room with me, though he was two classes after me. This was bad for both of us; but I did learn by experience, and preserved him subsequently from the mistakes into which I had fallen. When I graduated, I persuaded him to live in the buildings, and by so doing, having a chum of his own class, to identify himself absolutely with college life and the associations of Holworthy. He did so, and it saved his college course.

It was at Harvard that my aptitude, such as it was, began to develop; and to that I owed most of the satisfaction I derived from college life. I had always been a reader; and I now began to take to writing. Every man of any intellectual activity has, I presume, been conscious of certain periods of germination — times of receptivity. If a book then chances into his hands, he reads it in a way which thereafter acts as a milestone on the road of life. He has developed a new sense; the seed has fallen in soil ready to germinate and make it bear fruit. I perfectly well remember in the winter of 1848 my father returning from a journey to Washington, and bringing in his hand a paper-bound copy of Harper Bros.' cheap reprint of the first volume of Macaulay's *England*, then just out. I was thirteen; and of Macaulay I had never even heard the name. Boy-like, I picked the book up, and began to turn over its pages. I can see the room and the day now — the dining-room in the Mt. Vernon Street house, the fire in the grate, the hair-covered rocking-chair in which I sat, the table, set for dinner. I took the book up, and almost instantly got absorbed in it. Though I did not the least in the world realize it, I then and there quickened, my aptitude asserted itself. The only trouble afterwards was that, being a mere aptitude and not an overpowering call, this tendency, or inclination, never dominated me to the exclusion of all else. It was just the ordinary case of a facility in a certain direction, existent, but not strong enough to dictate a line of life action.

Nevertheless, in college the tendency developed, and I was one of the recognized litterateurs of my time and class. In the Pudding Club, I was Secretary, Poet and Odist, and my success as such was marked. I knew it, and felt it. I wrote for the *Magazine;* there the articles — on Whittier, Hawthorne, Charles Reade, etc. — are yet, bound in my voluminous *Miscellanies.* This was the one great and gratifying feature of my college life, the sense of growth. For the rest, it was very, very pleasant; but it did n't amount to much. A great miscellaneous reader, I was no student, and had no "call." I got through my course without any trouble; securing no rank, but avoiding all difficulties. I was not wise in my selection of studies; but I had no sort of encouragement to wisdom. For instance, I had rather a fancy for Greek. With no aptitude for language of any sort, I was conscientious; and, in my own way, studiously inclined. Those were the days of Professors Felton and Sophocles, and the methods of instruction in Greek at Harvard were simply beneath contempt. It was taught in thorough school-boy fashion — neither philosophically nor elegantly; we were not made grammarians, and we were not initiated into a charming literature. We blundered along in class-readers, a parcel of half-taught school-boys. I came within an ace of being a fair Greek scholar. The slightest encouragement or assistance would have made one of me. But Felton and Sophocles threw me off the track; and they were, both of them, admirably calculated so to do. In my sophomore year, merely as a self-imposed task, I read the *Iliad* through, from the first line to the last. I got so that I could read it at sight — a hundred lines an hour. A very little more, and I would have acquired the faculty of reading

Greek as a living language — as I read French and German. The methods of instruction in use killed the possibility. Absolutely without inducement to keep on, I weakly desisted; and, to my infinite and lasting subsequent regret, the half-acquired faculty fell into disuse; and now I can't even read the Greek characters. Again, with a faint aptitude, I had neither call nor encouragement. It has been so with me all through life.

In those years I kept a diary. So doing was enjoined on me by my father; and I kept it from my Latin School days until the time I went into the army, in my twenty-fifth year. Later on I kept the volumes sealed up in a package, with directions that they should be destroyed in the event of my death. A few years ago — some ten or twelve — I opened the parcel, and looked through the volumes. I did this during my Sundays, passed in the house at Quincy while living in Boston — very charming Sundays they were, too; pleasant to pass, pleasant to look back on. That was in my busy, Union-Pacific period. Starting early, before the family were down, I used to walk out to Quincy — always by the old Plymouth road and over Milton Hill — and pass the quiet, delightful morning hours, reading undisturbed, in my sun-lighted library. Then as the day grew old and the light failed, I would start back, and walk home to Boston, through Neponset and by Massachusetts Avenue. Those were the pleasantest days I then had in my whole winter life. Those, I would like to re-live.

During those days I exhumed the sealed package, and, thirty years later, read over that old diary. The revelation of myself to myself was positively shocking. Then and there I was disillusioned. Up to that time — and I was then about fifty-five—I had indulged in the pleasing delusion that it was in me, under proper conditions of time, place and occasion, to do, or be, something rather noticeable. I have never thought so since. Seeing myself face to face through fifty years cured me of that deception. I felt that no human being who, between fifteen and twenty-five, so pictured himself from day to day could, by any possibility, develop into anything really considerable. It was n't that the thing was bad or that my record was discreditable; it was worse! It was silly. That it was crude, goes without saying. *That* I did n't mind! But I did blush and groan and swear over its unmistakable, unconscious immaturity and ineptitude, its conceit, its weakness and its cant. I saw myself in a looking-glass, and I said—"Can that indeed be I!" and, reflecting, I then realized that the child was father of the man! It was with difficulty I forced myself to read through that dreadful record; and, as I finished each volume, it went into the fire; and I stood over it until the last leaf was ashes. It was a tough lesson; but a useful one. I had seen myself as others had seen me. I have never felt the same about myself since. I now humbly thank fortune that I have almost got through life without making a conspicuous ass of myself.

But to go back to college days. "Tell me who your friends are, and I will tell you who you are." That is an unfailing test; and, going back, I must confess that my college friends were of a very miscellaneous character. One thing I can, however, surely say of them, that, edifying or otherwise as influences—idle or studious, sedate or dissipated—and I was intimate with all kinds—they were the brightest and most attractive men in the Cambridge of my time. Stephen G. Perkins was, perhaps, the closest of my friends. He was afterwards killed at the battle of Cedar Mountain, in the summer of 1862 — a lieutenant of the gallant Second Massachusetts Infantry; and I say of him now, nearly forty years after his death, what General F. C. Barlow, of the class of '55, said of him to me many years ago — Stephen Perkins was, on the whole, the man of "the choicest mind I ever knew." He was manly, simple, refined; and he had withal fine perceptions and a delicate humor. He always impressed me with a sense of my own inferiority, and his friendship was a compliment. He loved to talk; but in a quiet, reflective and observant way. He was mature and self-respecting; one who thought much, and looked quite through the acts of men. I read of his death one day when in camp at Hilton Head, and I felt I had lost something never to be replaced — a friend of college days. He lies buried, I believe, in the Georgetown cemetery; and "green be the turf above him!"

I cannot spare time to run over the names of the others. Some of them were from the South; and they also, most of them, died in the war. Not a few were very dissipated in college, and their dissipation ended them. Others were the exact opposite; and not a few achieved eminence — Phillips Brooks, Frank Barlow, Edward Dalton, H. H. Furness. Taken altogether, it was a goodly company, and it almost reconciles me to the image I saw of myself in my diary, that it was given me to walk as an equal in such a throng.

Meanwhile, I was not popular in my college days; nor, indeed, have I ever been so since. My brother John was. He had a very charming, ingratiating presence and manner, when in the mood, and a far greater social aptitude. He was essentially "a good fellow," as the term went, and a charming companion. I wanted to be; but it was n't quite in me. Never quiet and natural, I was inclined to be always acting a part; and I did not act it well. Moreover, *gauche*, I was singularly lacking in what is known as tact. I had almost a faculty for doing or saying the wrong thing at any given time; and I was always painfully self-conscious. This made me shy; and the world, as usual, set my shyness to the account of pride. Not a bad fellow — indeed, at heart, a very good fellow, anxious to be friends with all the world and liked of every one — I never could overcome my pre-natal manner, and learn to do and say gracious things in a gracious way. It was so in college; it has been so ever since. It was congenital — hereditary and in the blood; or, as James Russell Lowell remarked in some familiar letter of his printed by one in long subsequent years a greatly prized friend of mine — Charles Eliot Norton — "the Adamses have a genius for saying even a gracious thing in an ungracious way!" I well remember Norton's aspect of unconcealed embarrassment when I referred with keen appreciation to this passage in the volume he had edited, and expressed my sincere gladness that he had not editorially omitted it. It was so keen and true!

Yet, recurring to college days, at Cambridge, I was not actually unpopular. I belonged, and belonged easily and of right, to all the clubs and all the societies, literary and social; my difficulty, I suppose, was that I was always thinking too much of myself, and not enough of others. Certainly, the first impression I made on people was not altogether a favorable one. And, here again, the child was father of the man.

As to my college course, and what I then did, I have never

quite been able to make up my mind. I was studious in a way, for I followed my aptitudes and inclinations, and they led me to infinite reading and much writing. Was this better than to have studied for college rank? — for of that I had none. I was not even in the first half of the class. On the whole, in my case, I think the course I pursued was best. I broadened. The nutriment, and there was lots of it, passed into my system all the same — it entered into the grand, in the sense of final, result. I at least did not idle away my time. As contrasted with my father, my awful college diary compared with his of the same period of life — all of which I have been over — shows that I then was not half the man he was at the same age; but, a better fellow, I had much the more enjoyable time. The mistake in my case lay in not understanding myself, and cultivating persistence in some plan. As it was I just browsed about as fancy led. As I have said, the simple fact was, that, an ordinary man, I had no strongly pronounced aptitude; and, accordingly, felt no distinct call. Still, I look back on my Harvard days with pleasure, as a period of rapid development and much enjoyment. It compares brightly with what went before; and, educationally, was second in importance and value only to my subsequent army experience.

It came to its predestined end in 1856, just as I attained my majority. That was the year of the Buchanan-Frémont campaign, the year in which the Republican party assumed national proportions. I had been brought up in an atmosphere of politics. My earliest recollections were associated with my grandfather's triumphs in the conflicts of the House of Representatives, and I was impressed in imagination by the circumstances of his death and the outburst of

popular feeling elicited by it. I remember now most vividly
his funeral on that March day in Quincy, the eloquence and
impressiveness of Dr. Lunt's funeral discourse, with the
coffin lying before him, the solemn appearance of the familiar and crowded church, and the booming of the minute-
guns from the hill, on which I afterwards lived, as the body
was slowly borne from tabernacle to tomb. I also remembered in a vague way the bitter disappointment of the election
of 1844, and the war with Mexico which followed. In the
canvass of 1848 my father took me with him when he went
to Buffalo; and, while the Convention was in session, Charles
Sumner, who was there but not a delegate, took me to Niagara,
where, a few days later, my father joined us. He had then
been nominated for Vice-President, on the ticket with Van
Buren. In those days we saw a great deal of Mr. Sumner,
and I felt for him an admiration closely verging on affection.
He was very kind and considerate to us children, taking a
deep interest in us, and being very companionable. He was
at that time thirty-seven, and certainly a striking and most
attractive personality. The world was all before him; he
was kindly, earnest, enthusiastic and very genial. A constant guest at my father's house, he exercised a great influence over me, and one very elevating. To him, as he was at
that period and later, I feel under deep obligation.

Those were the days of the Free Soil party; but I threw
my first vote in 1856, and as a Republican. Thus I was from
childhood a part of the anti-slavery agitation. I grew up
in the atmosphere of it; and always at school I was in the
small minority, my schoolmates being almost without exception the sons of Whigs, and as a rule devoted adherents
of Daniel Webster, between whom and my grandfather it

was tacitly recognized there was no love lost. The very name of my grandfather was to the Webster Whig gall and wormwood. It is strange how tense enmities endure and are handed down. Even now, well on in a new century, the tradition of the bitter controversies which marked the commencement of the last century prevent the public recognition of those of my name. Their prominence and the great character of the service they rendered, no one pretends to deny; no memorial thereof exists.

But politics, and why I never found my way into political life, will come up naturally later on and in other connections. I must first dispose of Harvard, and college life. The course I ought to have pursued at Harvard is now plain to me; and I almost wholly missed it. I should have followed Greek and Latin *as literatures;* taking the almost wholly worthless prescribed courses under the dead-alive methods of instruction then in use, but acquiring the faculty of sight reading by chamber practice. This I now see I was on the point of doing, and could easily have done. It would have been a most useful training for the practical work of after life; unfortunately, as I have said, I met with no one to incite me to that educational line, and I had not sufficient force to strike out a path for myself. I should then, next, have compelled myself to take some of the more elementary mathematical courses, simply for the mental discipline they afford. Having no mathematical aptitude whatever, I never could have attained any rank in those courses, or figured otherwise than as a dolt in the recitation room; but that would in the desired result have "cut no ice," as the expression goes. What I needed was the regular mental gymnastics — the daily practice of following a line of sustained thought out to exact results, more or less remote. Such an intellectual discipline I needed above all else; and, moreover, I could easily have acquired it; for, in subsequent life, I have more than once puzzled myself and somewhat surprised associates by reasoning out abstract formulas on general principles applicable to all cases of a similar character. Had I in college been trained, or trained myself on these lines, so doing would have contributed materially to my effectiveness in practical life. Finally, I should have settled myself systematically down on the development of my aptitude — the art of literary expression, and would naturally have done so. In this last respect, however, I was not wholly wanting; it came about by gravitation.

This subject is one which has since interested me greatly, especially of late years; and I have reached some conclusions peculiarly my own. At Harvard there was quite a sufficiency of elective courses in my time; and, since then, they have been multiplied out of all reason. And yet what would for me have been the most valuable of electives for purposes of mental training has never been proposed — a course in chess! Gravely to suggest it even would give rise to a look of surprise — probably a smile. Yet what is it but the German *kriegspiel* adapted to civil life vocations? In playing chess, you must have a defined plan of campaign and follow it up intelligently and consecutively; you must watch your opponent and understand and meet his play. You must measure yourself against him. All this I have been doing after a fashion throughout my life; yet I never went through any special training in preparation for it. A course in chess would have been for me — *kriegspiel!* So, also, for others. Why not sometimes educate through amusement?

Beyond all that, however, the difficulty then lay, as it still lies, with the Harvard system. It was and is, in my judgment, radically wrong; and the more satisfactory results can never be secured until an organic change is worked in it. Without knowing what the matter was, I suffered under the system still in vogue in the middle of the last century as a student; and now (1912), well advanced in another century, I distinctly saw it as a member of one of the governing boards to as late a period as 1906. I then set forth my experience and conclusions drawn therefrom in a Phi Beta Kappa Address — my parting word as an Overseer — delivered before the Columbia Chapter. That address is in print, and I still (1912) adhere to the conclusions therein set forth. In one word: the educational trouble with Harvard in my time was the total absence of touch and direct personal influence as between student and instructor. The academic, schoolmaster system prevailed; and, outside of the recitation room, it was not good form — it was contrary to usage — for the instructors and the instructed to hold personal relations. Our professors in the Harvard of "the fifties" were a set of rather eminent scholars and highly respectable men. They attended to their duties with commendable assiduity, and drudged along in a dreary humdrum sort of a way in a stereotyped method of classroom instruction. But as for giving direction to, in the sense of shaping, the individual minds of young men in their most plastic stage, so far as I know nothing of the kind was even dreamed of; it never entered into the professorial mind. This was what I needed, and all I needed — an intelligent, inspiring direction; and I never got it, nor a suggestion of it. I was left absolutely without guidance. I might blunder through, and, doubtless, somehow would blunder through, just as I did; but if I could n't work my problem out for myself, it would remain unsolved. And that was the Harvard system. It remains in essence the system still — the old, outgrown, pedagogic relation of the large class-recitation room. The only variation has been through Eliot's effort to replace it by the yet more pernicious system of premature specialization. This is a confusion of the college and the university functions, and constitutes a distinct menace to all true higher education. The function of the college is an all-round development, as a basis for university specializations. Eliot never grasped that fundamental fact; and so he undertook to turn Harvard College into a German university — specializing the student at eighteen. He thus made still worse what was in my time bad enough. He instituted a system of one-sided contact in place of a system based on no contact at all. It is devoutly to be hoped that, some day, a glimmer of true light will effect an entrance into the professional educator's head. It certainly had n't done so up to 1906.

A better considered and more intelligent system will doubtless in due time evolve itself; but when, or how, remains to be seen. I only now know that so far as producing the ideal results on individual minds standing in crying need of direction, the system in use was very bad fifty years ago, and I have every reason to believe that the system now in use is yet worse. In my time, its methods were mechanical; it turned out nothing individually artistic. I see now that I was myself a very fair bit of clay for the wheel had the potter had an eye and a hand for his work. I might have been shaped into something rather good. As it was, I was tumbled into the common hopper, to emerge therefrom as God willed. No instructor produced, or endeavored to produce, the slightest impression on me; no spark of enthusiasm was sought to be infused into me. In that line, I owed far more to Charles Sumner than to all of the Harvard professors put together. And it was exactly the same with my father before me. From the recitation room I got as nearly as I can now see almost nothing at all; from the college atmosphere and the close contact with a generation of generous young fellows containing then, as the result showed, infinite possibilities I got much of all that I have ever had of quickening and good. So, after all, I owe a great debt to Harvard.

Leaving Harvard for good and all in June, 1856, I was, as all well-disposed young men of narrow vision and common-sense direction from outside then were, full of the idea of "getting to work," as the cant term went. Some of my friends, including Stephen Perkins, went to Europe. Perhaps I should have done well to go with them; but on that point I am not clear. Indeed, I doubt. I was not a mature young fellow, with a native sense of dignity and responsibility. I did not have the social faculty; I failed to impress others with a sense of my being "a young man of promise." So, if I had then gone abroad, apart from a pleasant experience and a stock of memories, I doubt if I should have brought much back with me. I was not only young, but immature.

II

LAW AND POLITICS

BUT now came educational blunder number seven; and
another bad one. Having no particular sense of a special
vocation, I almost as a matter of course turned to the law.
It went without saying. Doing so, I ought to have entered
the Harvard Law School; passed through the full course
there; and then gone into the office of some law firm in active
practice. Cambridge was, however, associated in my mind
with dissipation and literary idleness, and I was "full of
high purpose" — I wanted to buckle down to real work!
So, through my father and his political associations, I got
myself taken into the office of Dana and Parker; and there
I reported myself as a student in September, after my graduation in June. I made a mistake in not going to the Law
School, and taking hold of the profession I meant to follow
in a thoughtful, sensible way; but, if I was going into any
office at all, I made no mistake in selecting that of R. H.
Dana and F. E. Parker. They were two men with whom
personal contact was in itself an education. That Mr. Dana
impressed himself deeply upon me, I long afterwards showed
by becoming his biographer; and, in my *Life of Dana* [1] I set
forth my opinion of F. E. Parker. His classmate, T. W.
Higginson, has also spoken of him in his volume entitled
Cheerful Yesterdays; and, though Higginson and I were very
differently constituted, we set much the same estimate on
Parker. On the whole, as I never could have been a lawyer

[1] II. chap. 2.

and must, under any circumstances, have drifted out of
what was to me a most unattractive calling, perhaps it was
quite as well that I passed that educational period not at
Cambridge, but in Court Street. I was at least in daily contact with active life, and rubbing up against men of high
character and marked ability.

During these years my brother John and I lived at home,
and were a great deal in society, that is, as young men of
the party-going, dancing set. Of Boston society, as it then
was and, I believe, still is, I can say little that is pleasant.
It was a boy-and-girl institution, the outgrowth of ten generations of colonial and provincial life, about as senseless,
unmeaning and frivolous as could by any possibility be
imagined. It was essentially a Sammy and Billy, a Sallie
and Nellie affair; very pleasant and jolly for young people;
but, so far as the world and its ways were concerned, little
more than a big village development. In fact, I may say
that in the course of my life I have tried Boston socially on
all sides: I have summered it and wintered it, tried it drunk
and tried it sober; and, drunk or sober, there's nothing in
it — save Boston! The trouble with Boston socially is that
it is an eddy, so to speak, in the great world-current. With
powerful formative traditions it has a keen self-appreciation.
For strangers, well introduced, it is a delightful city; for a
life-long resident it is curiously conventional and *borné*.
Not only are the social circles sharply divided, but the ages
do not mix. The old people and the young stand apart; and
Billy and Bobby and Sue do not feel at home in company
with outsiders of distinction, or their domestic elders. It
has always been so. In Boston, the salon has ever proved
impossible. We go to formal dinners, and we pass our even-

ings at home. The young people frolic and dance; the old retire, or are retired — shelved! And so, of my early Boston social life I have little to say save that it was not improving; but still I had a very good time — a time brought to an abrupt close in 1861, when I was swept away by the torrent of war.

My great friends during those years were my brother John — with whom my relations were the closest possible, for we lived together — my former tutor, Frank Palfrey, and Arthur Dexter. Both of these latter were men of ability; but the former had a curiously frivolous vein running through his composition, which interfered greatly with his success and standing; while Dexter, though really a man of superior order, was, for himself, most unhappily compounded. There ran all through him a false strain. In many respects brilliant, he lacked persistence and character. He perpetually rang false. I knew him intimately for many years; but our ways gradually parted. He died early in 1897; we had long before become almost strangers. But at this period (1856–1861) we saw a great deal of each other; and, on the whole, I derived benefit from him. In the summer, my brother John and I lived at Quincy, where we began to take great interest in tree-planting, and he, then and later, forested Mt. Wollaston. Meanwhile, my aptitude was showing how little real force there was to it, for it was lying almost wholly dormant. I wrote continually — diaries, letters, abstracts of books I read, and, now and then, an attempt at a review article; but there was no systematic effort; and I really did not in any degree realize what careful, thorough, painstaking work was. The fact is, I was simply slow in maturing. At last, in the early months of 1861 — during the winter which followed the election of Lincoln — I braced up, and, one day, went out to see Russell Lowell, then a professor at Harvard and editor of the *Atlantic*, and asked him if he would let me write an article for that magazine on a semi-political topic. He was then living, with his wife, at Mrs. Upham's lodging-house. He received me very cordially — for he was then a man of only about forty — and I lunched with the two, talking very fast, and, I am afraid, airing my views somewhat ingenuously. He encouraged me to make the attempt; and so I set to work and wrote my first well-considered, carefully prepared and laboriously copied-out magazine paper. I have written many such since, but that one — "The Reign of King Cotton" in the *Atlantic* for April, 1861 — marked in me a distinct stage of development. I was getting my bearings. It proved quite a success. It caused me to be recognized as a young man of somewhat nebulous promise.

Meanwhile, as a lawyer I was not proving myself a success. I showed just what I was by getting myself admitted to the bar after about twenty months of desultory reading, and decently prepared for practice in my own eyes only. George T. Bigelow was then Chief Justice of the Supreme Court of the Commonwealth; or became so shortly after. I knew Judge Bigelow well, we being neighbors at Quincy, and I was on terms of intimacy with his family. One day, without consulting any one, I took it into my head that I would be examined for entrance at the bar; and, what followed shows the loose way in which admissions were then granted. I asked Bigelow to examine me. He ought to have asked me a few questions as to my length of study, etc., and then, in a good-natured, friendly way advised me to wait a while longer. Instead of that, however, he told me to come at a certain time into the Supreme Court room, where he was then holding court; and he would examine me. I did so, and the clerk of the court at his direction handed me a list of questions, covering, perhaps, one sheet of letter paper. I then sat down at the clerk's desk, and wrote out answers to such of them as I could. I remember well that on several of the subjects in question I knew absolutely nothing. A few days later I met the Judge on the platform of the Quincy station, and he told me I might come up to the court room and be sworn in. I did so; and became a member of the bar. I was no more fit to be admitted than a child. The whole thing illustrated my supreme incompetence, and the utterly irregular way in which admission to the bar was then obtained. At the same time I rather imagine that Bigelow's personal knowledge of me had something to do with it. He had confidence in my coming out all right; if he did, he certainly acted on his faith.

This must have been somewhere in 1858. Anyhow, I at once left Dana and Parker, taking with me not much law but many pleasant memories; and I have often since, with some sense of humiliation, tried to imagine what the keen-sighted, incisive Parker thought of me and my proceedings. I would even now like to know; for in my whole life I have since met no man who saw into the true inwardness of persons and things as it was given to Francis E. Parker to see. In my case, however, it made not much difference. I was not cast for a lawyer; and I rather imagine Parker fully took the fact in. I never took to the law; and I am sure the law never came my way. However, I tried, establishing myself first with my brother John, and later in a gloomy, dirty den in my father's building, 23 Court Street; and there I sat for the next year and a half, trying to think that I was going through an apprenticeship. I did n't realize it, but I was a round peg trying to get into a square hole. Still, my father was satisfied. He, now, was in Congress, and the home had been broken up; much to my satisfaction. I liked the irresponsible, Bohemian life; though I did n't know it, I was tired of conventional Boston. My father saw it all, however, in a wholly different light. In his eyes I was passing through a very critical period in a way which promised much; I would soon acquire steady business habits, and settle down into a respectable and useful member of society. But now, great events were immediately impending.

In '59, I think it was, we had the "Concord muster." All of us young men were then in the militia; and a most useful preliminary training it afterwards proved. We were drilling the whole time. I was a member of the City Guard; and then adjutant of the First Regiment of Infantry; and then a private in the Fourth Battalion. In this way I picked up the manual, and learned how to march. Moreover, after my father went to Washington in the autumn of '59, I went on there to pay him a visit, and I saw something of the Washington world, and the great movement of events. I was now twenty-four, and began to get a little into the touch of society. I by no means lacked self-confidence; but I was also self-conscious, and lamentably deficient in that nice social faculty which, in a place like Washington, so tides a young man along. None the less, I availed myself to a certain extent of my opportunities.

I remember very well the Senate and House of that time. Neither body impressed me. The House was a national bear-garden; for that was, much more than now, a period of the unpicturesque frontiersman and the overseer. Sectional feeling ran high, and bad manners were conspicuously in evidence; whiskey, expectoration and bowie-knives were the order of that day. They were, indeed, the only kind of "order" observed in the House, over which poor old Pennington, of New Jersey, had as a last recourse been chosen to preside, probably the most wholly and all-round incompetent Speaker the House ever had. It was altogether indescribable, and I remember my father laughing until he had to wipe the tears from his eyes over an account I gave of the usual procedure of the body of which he was a member, in a letter I wrote to the Milford *Gazette*, a paper in his district. I had then the *cacoëthes scribendi*, and it found a rather injudicious and somewhat risky vent in newspaper correspondence; but I redeemed my lack of judgment by a strong sense of boyish humor. "It is n't very respectful," said my father, "but it's dreadfully true." "Of all the disorderly bodies I ever saw," I wrote, "the present House of Representatives, under its efficient presiding officer, is by many degrees the most disorderly. When nothing of interest is before the House, it is simply a general hubbub. When anything of interest is going on, the performances usually resolve themselves into a concerted piece by any six members at once, with at intervals a general chorus of the whole House. Then, indeed, confusion does become confounded, and Speaker Pennington rides upon the storm; not, indeed, directing, but, with uplifted voice and gavel, acting rather as *maestro*, or grand conductor, to this thnndering song of the nation."

That House was an angry, quarrelsome body, full to overflowing of men who subsequently became "Confederate Brigadiers." Among them I specially recall Roger A. Pryor, of Virginia, who "petered out" during the Rebellion, and subsequently came North and quietly took to the law in Brooklyn, New York, then a pronounced fire-eater, a typical Southerner of that period. I remember him at one of Buchanan's receptions, a rather tall and lank Virginian, stalking about with a lady on each arm. In shabby black, of course, and ugly as a stone fence, with tallowy, close-shaven features, and prominent high cheek-bones, his eyes had a hard, venomous look, while his flowing locks, brushed carefully back behind his ears, fell well down over his coat collar, innocent of the shears. He was representative of a large class — men who were just spoiling for a fight. They had it, too! and, before they got through, had a belly-full! But never on this earth did human beings more richly deserve the complete, out-and-out thrashing that those men then coveted, and afterwards had.

None the less *tempora mutantur, et,* etc., etc., even as respects that community and those very men. Long subsequently, as a result of my two addresses on General Lee, that at Chicago in 1902, and that at Lexington in 1907, I became a very popular character in Virginia; and the change of sentiment was manifested many times and in ways very gratifying to me. Even Roger A. Pryor assumed a pleasant personal aspect. I first met him face to face in New York, December 9, 1911 — just fifty years later. He was then manifestly a very old man, softened by experience and domestic affliction, for he had lost a most promising son, already professionally far advanced. It was at a reception given by the New York Genealogical Society to old John Bigelow, who died just one year later. I had agreed to read a paper on the occasion, and Judge Pryor came expressly to hear me. I recognized him, sitting on one of the front benches, the moment I came into the room; and at once went and introduced myself to him. He was plainly gratified; and so was I at seeing him there. On both sides, all the old feeling was gone. In the quieter rays of a setting sun, I like to think it was so!

Of H. Winter Davis I saw a good deal that winter. He was a man of very different type; the extremely gentlemanly representative of the Baltimore "Plug-uglies" as they were called. He died a few years later, having become an extremist among the Union men. I don't know what his game was; but, with him, I imagine it was all a game. A man of medium size, very boyish in appearance, with thick, dark curling hair, cut short, a small moustache and a dark complexion, he had a quiet manner and was extremely careful in his dress. I heard him deliver from the floor of the House one of the most effective, if not the most effective speech I ever listened to. That day he followed Lamar, of Mississippi, whom, long afterwards, I knew much better. Lamar at that period looked the Southern college professor — lank, tall, bearded, long-haired and large-featured. Of both of these men — Davis and Lamar — my brother Henry has much to say in his volume *The Education of Henry Adams*, and his means of observation were far better and closer than mine.[1] This was not so with some others. John Sherman was a case in point. He was then by far the most noticed man on the floor of the House, having been suddenly brought into much prominence in the long struggle for possession of the Speaker's chair. Then in his first vigor,

[1] His account of Henry W. Davis is in *Mass. Hist. Soc. Proceedings*, XLIII. 660.

John Sherman was a young-looking man of the Ohio type, tall and slender, with black hair and beard, keen eyes and a large nose. His face was expressive of character and decision, and he had the reputation of being a fighter in every sense of the word. I saw something of him in 1860–61 — much more years later — and he edified me by telling me on one occasion that, in politics, "he made it a rule always to act with his party; on great matters from principle, and on small matters from policy." He certainly followed his rule throughout his public life; and he was more than forty consecutive years in position at Washington. I heard of his death (1900) while passing through Chicago.

The Senate was, however, in 1860–61 far the more interesting body; and I then made very fair use of my advantages. Seward was the leader on the Republican side; though, as one looked down from the gallery, the only man, I remember, whose face and bearing, whose figure and the air of large refinement about him, seemed to me impressive was Mr. Sumner. He certainly always offered a notable exception to the prevailing commonplace, and coarseness of fibre, both mental and physical. Douglas, of Illinois, was very much in evidence, "a squab, vulgar little man, with an immense frowsy head." Mason, of Virginia — afterwards my father's vanquished opponent in England — also attracted my attention from the first, "a large, handsome man, not unpleasant to look at," as, dressed ostentatiously in a grey suit of Virginia homespun, he appeared to own the Senate-chamber. Of Senator Fessenden, of Maine, I at that time saw a good deal, calling on him at his hotel-room on Sunday afternoons, when he evidently was gratified at my attention and glad of company in his boarding-house solitude. He impressed me as a man of natural refinement and decided force — every inch a Senator. He talked to me of my grandfather, with whom he had served in the House, and, for whom, as did all those men — his contemporaries — he expressed a keen admiration. Fessenden left on me, however, a sense of a dreariness and solitude in life, as I found him always sitting there in that forlorn private "parlor" of a Washington boarding-house hotel, as Washington hotels then were — unkempt barracks, spotted along the north side of Pennsylvania Avenue, from the Capitol to the Treasury. They all had the third-rate, Southern-slouchy aspect and atmosphere. That may have been a period of high thinking; it was certainly one of plain living; and there was in Washington a noticeable absence of the more ordinary elegancies of civilized life; its luxuries were undreamed of. The "mess" and the Southern boarding-house were in order, and accepted. They knew nothing better; but Senator Fessenden's old-time hotel — furnished sitting-room with its bed-room attachment, devoid of any pretence of life's amenities and attractions — impressed me with a sense of neither domesticity nor taste. I suppose, however, it compared fairly well with what he was then accustomed to at home, in Maine; but in all respects the Washington of that period was in strange contrast with the Washington of this. The Civil War marked the dividing line.

Recurring to Fessenden and what he told me of my grandfather, Jefferson Davis was on that topic the most outspoken of all I met. I do not, indeed, with the exception of Joshua R. Giddings, remember any public man of that epoch who seemed to feel such a genuine sense of appreciation for J. Q. Adams as Jefferson Davis, and he repeatedly put himself on record on the subject. Davis, by the way, impressed me that winter more agreeably than any Southern man I met. I did not see him again until, in May, 1885, I called on him at his house at Belvoir, near New Orleans; but to me he was a distinctly attractive as well as interesting personality. Of medium height and spare of figure, he had an essentially Southern face, but he was very much of a gentleman in his address — courteous, unpretending and yet quietly dignified. A man in no way aggressive, yet not to be trifled with. I instinctively liked him; and regret extremely that it was not my good fortune, then or later, to see more of him.

Physically, Washington was then curiously unkempt, the wide, half-built, unpaved streets being alternately oceans of mud or deep in dust. A dirtier city materially — "Nigger" — it would not have been easy to imagine; while, socially, it was quite innocent of "style." Among those in public life very few had houses of their own, and those of such as had them were unpretentious — modest to a degree. There were a few private carriages, but no equipage. The entertainment was of the simplest. The social element was altogether Southern in sympathy and in expression; and, as a young man, I am forced to say that the inducements to flirtation sometimes extended by certain of the young ladies were of a nature not usual in more conventional centres — they were of the jolly-girl brand. My now destroyed diaries bore witness to the fact that on more than one occasion I did not know what to do, or which way to look; and ignored what I did not dare reciprocate. Miss Harriet Lane then presided over the White House; and, of wholly another sort, she did it very well. Young, handsome, dignified and imposing, she bore herself as became her position, having, beside a London experience, a well-developed natural, social faculty. I was presented to her at one of the White House receptions of that very simple and most democratically unconventional period when the White House entertainments, conducted absolutely without rule or regulation, were thronged by people of both sexes, dressed each one as his or her means or fancy directed. As respects Miss Lane, I was deeply impressed by the fact that, the next time I met her, she addressed me by name. It was close upon forty years later. I then once more found myself in the same room with her. She was now an elderly lady; a white-haired, childless widow, living in Washington; she was pointed out to me at a wedding reception, and I "tried it on," going up and expressing my disbelief in any possible recollection of me on her part. But the old social faculty was there. She at once called me by name. Through what process she instinctively worked the problem out or by what mental action she divined, I do not know; but that she should have remembered both face and name is not supposable. It was an instance of the exercise of a social faculty which I never possessed in any degree, and the absence of which has been in my case a badly felt handicap throughout life in many ways. Few things do I envy the possession of in others more than the faculty of remembering faces or placing names.

Subsequently, during the first winter of my later Washington life, I saw a good deal of Mrs. Johnson, and our relations became exceptionally friendly. The fact that I had been part of the *ante-bellum* Washington of her White House days constituted a sort of bond of kindliness between us. Hence her death a year or two later was for me an appreciable loss — Washington became the poorer because of her decease. There are frequent and admiring mentions of Miss Lane, as she then was, in Hawthorne's *Our Old Home: English Sketches*, and Mrs. Johnson could certainly have counted me among her obliged admirers. She is a gracious memory.

My two winter visits to Washington in 1860 and 1861 were my only social experiences outside of Boston until after the war. They were of great educational benefit to me, something I of all things needed. I there came in contact with men, and distinguished men; and I met women, and not girls. In Boston there was no political element in social life; and no foreign element. In Washington, you met interesting men and some clever women; and conversation sometimes rose above the level of society small-talk.

Meanwhile, at the law I was in these years doing absolutely nothing, making no progress. Regular in my habits, I was constantly at my office; but business would not come my way; and, naturally, I got discouraged. I kept writing, if I did not publish; but — I am sorry to say it, though I see it clearly now — I had not the native force to break through the barriers, and strike out in some line for myself. I remained a round peg in a square hole. I would now give much, if I could look back on some virile action of my own at that time; an attempt, even though it had been a failure. It simply was not in me; and I went along, stupidly adhering to the old precedents and traditions, just as if I were not a young man, with a great, untried world all about me. I was quite lacking in both aggressive initiative and correct forecast.

In the summer of 1860, however, came the monitions of great impending change; though I quite failed to read the signs aright. In the long, hot summer of 1860, as we were getting into the swing of that lurid, red-painted political canvass which proved the prologue to the war, Governor Seward one day turned up in Boston, coming from the eastward. Just defeated at Chicago, Seward then showed a real bigness. Nursing no sense of disappointment, he came out in large, earnest support of the cause, and its exponent who had been preferred to him. With a clear eye, though that of an astute politician, to the unknown and unforeseeable future, he was carefully cultivating relations with my father, seeing in him I imagine a much-needed New England political counterpoise to the distrustful and impracticable Sumner. He had, I think — going back to what took place in "the forties" — sized my father; and, almost alone of the public men of the period, he had "sized" him correctly. So now he turned up suddenly in Boston; singled my father out for special notice; and came out to Quincy to pass a day. Seward was then at the highest point of reputation and political prominence he ever attained. As a political factor he was of the first class; and he now proposed to my father, that he and I — I having met him in Washington — should join him in an electioneering tour through the Northwest in the coming month of September. I eagerly caught at the idea, and prevailed on my father to fall into it. We went, and it proved a considerable episode in my life. I saw the West for the first time, and moved among men.

During that summer also I saw a good deal of Charles Sumner, and very pleasantly. We none of us in the least suspected it; but for the old intimacy it was the beginning of the end. He was then in great spirits. Physically, he had recovered from the Brooks assault, and was in the full swing of political movement. In June he had delivered in the Senate his long and carefully prepared, but most unphilosophical, speech entitled by him the "Barbarism of Slavery." This effort of his had long been fore-shadowed and was loudly heralded; but I am glad to say that, my great personal admiration for Sumner *non obstante*, my mental vision was not now obscured. Of this speech I at the time wrote: "I have steadily stood up for it, and defended and endorsed everything in it; yet, in my heart of hearts, this speech is heavy proof that Sumner is not nearly so great a man as I had supposed and hoped. He had a great chance; and he was not equal to the occasion. After being stricken down as he was, with four years of subsequent illness, he should have risen in the Senate-chamber grand and magnificent; — something more than mortal, above revenge or spite, he should not have 'poured forth abuse as from a cart,' even on institutions. He should have dealt only in great principles, not in newspaper paragraphs and book clippings; he should have said that which would have offended no man, and yet would have touched and appealed to all. This he has not done. His speech is a farrago of newspaper items collected with toil and codified with reflection, but not marked by good temper or pervaded by inspiration. It is the able *ex parte* argument of an ordinary mortal, and by no means the crowning effort of a great genius." I have not since read, and never again shall read — as, I opine, will few others — that bitter, railing indictment of June 4, 1860; but I imagine I was not far wrong in this contemporaneous estimate of it.

A few days later, however, I came across Sumner characteristically and pleasantly; and in a way curious for me now

(1900) to notice, looking over my diary of that time, having wholly forgotten the incident. It had a noticeable bearing on the address I had just been delivering at Madison, showing how I revived in the summer of 1900 an historical parallel which I had worked out in detail forty years before, and then retained no faintest recollection of. My entry of July, 1860, was as follows:

"For the last two years I have been industriously laboring on a parallel, covering the slavery question, between my grandfather and Calhoun. This last week my thunder has been stolen, and rolled louder than I ever could roll it, and that by no less a person than Charles Sumner, of the United States Senate. In a political address in New York last week, he began with that parallel exactly as I had thought it out; and, when I had read what he said, a vague impression came across me that I had one day at Washington, while dining with him at home, run the parallel, and stated the relative influence of the two men on our own time. My father presently came into the office, and I spoke to him of it. He remembered the conversation perfectly; and advised me for the future to be more careful of my gems, if I did n't want to have them stolen. My only desire was to give his dues to my grandfather, so I can't say I care much for the thing; but I think Sumner might have done it rather better; and, if ever I now carry out the parallel, as I certainly meant to do, I shall be said to perfect only, and not originate."

Queer coincidence! There is the parallel, to-day, in Sumner's *Works*.[1] I have looked it up since coming across this diary entry of my own; and forty years afterwards in the Madison address, I harked back to my own old inspiration,

[1] I. 193, 323.

and, for the first time, presented my grandfather's record. And, now, what do I care for Sumner?

But my diary record did not end there. Just a fortnight later (July 29, 1860) I went on as follows:

"Sumner dined here yesterday, and came out evidently primed on some subject. I met him at the [Quincy] station; and, as we walked over the hill home, out it came — 'We must have an edition of my grandfather's political speeches — this year — at once!' I read him an extract of a note I had had from Mr. Giddings, a day or two before, in which he [Giddings] speaks approvingly of the parallel in Sumner's Cooper Institute speech. On hearing it Sumner laughed loud, and smote me on the shoulder with immense delight. He seemed greatly amused at the idea of my own idea coming back to me in this way, through him, with the stamp of approval from J. R. Giddings. After dinner, he went off again on the subject of the speeches; his parallel had provoked discussion and comment, had been ridiculed; he knew he was right; but where were his authorities? We must have an edition of the speeches at once, we must get those at least between hard covers! My father thought the time had not yet come; my grandfather, when brought forward as a character in history, had best be brought forward as a whole, etc., etc. I cannot agree with him, except in part. A man's historical character must rest on evidence; and it seems to me the evidence on which my grandfather's ultimate position in the history of his time must rest cannot too soon be brought before the public. A collection of his political speeches and reports, if published now, would be of interest as bearing on the questions of the day, and be read and referred to now more perhaps than at any future time. I have no idea, however, that such a collection will be issued, and my grandfather must wait yet a while for justice."

This I now (1912) find rather an interesting record of a talk. In less than two years from that time, emancipation under the war power was a living question, and my grandfather's utterances were rummaged up. Fourteen months later, Sumner himself was working up the partial record on the subject, which now appears in his *Works*;[1] for which he was indebted to a communication from me in the Boston *Transcript* of September 11, 1861. On the 1st of January, 1863, Lincoln's proclamation took effect; and only now, forty years later, has an incomplete record of my grandfather's enunciation of the doctrine of emancipation under the war power been put on file.[2] Sumner was wholly right. An edition of those speeches was in the summer of 1860 greatly needed; and they would have appeared in the very nick of time. I ought to have brought them out. He meant to incite me so to do. Again, I was not equal to the occasion offered me.

At this period, however, I was seeing a good deal in an intimate way of some men of considerable mark; and I am glad to be able to say that, in this respect, I did appreciate my privilege. I think, also, I stood fairly well in their estimate. I was very much younger; I did not realize how much, or have a correct sense of my own position, failing properly to subordinate myself. But I was twenty-five, and ought to have matured more than I had. R. H. Dana was then forty-five, and absent on his trip round the world taken to escape a break-down, threatened from overwork and the utter disregard by him of all sanitary rules. Had I been awake to

[1] VI. 19–23.   [2] 2 *Mass. Hist. Soc. Proceedings*, xv. 436.

my opportunities, I would have gone with him; but, in fact, so doing never even occurred to me. I was accomplishing nothing at home — eating my heart out in a clientless office, and wasting my time in ball-rooms; and here was an opportunity never to be had again, and I simply did not see it! It has been so all through life — unequalled chances missed; that with Dana in 1860 one of the most educational and maturing. Sumner I saw much of; he was then in his fiftieth year. Seward was ten years older, and at his best. Dr. Palfrey, occupied with his history, was older yet; born in May, 1796, he was in his sixty-fifth year, one year younger than I now (1900) am. My father was fifty-three. I was a young fellow, eager and aspiring; intensely interested in politics; in a social way healthily frivolous; and trying to follow a profession for which I had no natural aptitude. In fact, I was blindly seeking for my bearings.

I find in my diary, which was little more than an empty record of aspirations, comments on current events and social dissipations — many of the last distinctly the reverse of creditable, for I was, I do not regret to say, a very human youth — a few, a very few, notes of conversations, etc., not wholly without interest still. For instance, Seward was then rapidly establishing himself in the estimate of all of us as the Republican leader — the philosophical politician, statesman and guide of the party of the future. I shall revise and review this estimate presently, in the full light of fifty years later; but, in the summer of 1860, he certainly bore himself well. In a short speech he made on his arrival in Boston at this time, he took occasion to declare himself a political disciple of J. Q. Adams — which, except in theory, he distinctly was not — and while at Quincy, sitting on the piazza and puffing at his everlasting cigar, he talked freely about himself, J. Q. Adams, and public life. My brother John reminded him of a remark he (John) heard him make the previous winter in Washington to the effect that no man should continue in the Senate more than twelve years; and, observing that he had said this before Lincoln's nomination, inquired if he was of the same mind still. "Yes," said Seward, "I still think so. I shall have been in the Senate twelve years; and, in that time, I have seen Benton die a vagrant, pining to get back there; Calhoun die, chagrined, disappointed, ambitious and unsatisfied; declaring almost in his last words in the Senate that he would not speak to me; Clay die, eating his heart away, and naming the Committee of the Senate which was to carry him home to Kentucky, designating Hamilton Fish, so as to cut me off; and I am clear that unless a man can come out on some new course in this country, appear in some new character, as did J. Q. Adams, he must fail as those men failed. As compared with J. Q. Adams, Calhoun was a man of talent and originality; but he was visionary; whereas Mr. Adams, equal to him in other respects, was a practical statesman. Calhoun, for instance, wrote a book about the Constitution in which he advocated a dual executive and a balance of power between the free and slave states, than which what could be more absurd. But to imitate J. Q. Adams was not possible for most men, because there were few who, like him, loved combat for combat's sake, and who could thus fight through a long life. For himself, he [Seward] thought it much more difficult to retire gracefully from public life than to keep in it. It was different in Great Britain. There Palmerston had been in Parliament perhaps forty years; but in Great Britain the same man might be King many times, and there was a variety in Parliamentary life which Congress did not afford." While driving into town, where he was to take his train home, I asked him about Webster, Clay and Calhoun, with all three of whom he had sat in the Senate. He said that, in his judgment, Calhoun was the most eminent of the three; "but," he added, "they are all over-rated men; for they converted the Senate-chamber into a mere intellectual arena for their own struggles. Calhoun had undirected, original eloquence; Clay had a fiery, brilliant imagination; Webster, brute intellectual force. Calhoun's logic was not sound; he led and did not follow it, using it to support a pre-conceived theory."

My diary records that, when we got to town that day and were waiting on the platform of the station for the starting of the train, we found there only a very few enthusiastic souls to look at the famous New Yorker, "and I could n't but agree with one or two of them that a more unpromising looking subject for a great man than Seward did n't stand on the depot platform at that time. Small, rusty in aspect, dressed in a coat and trousers made apparently twenty years ago and by a bad tailor at that, lolling against the partition as he talked with my father or those about him, with a face and head in no way striking, who would have put his hand on that man — small and insignificant — as the first statesman in the country?"

The very next day Dr. Palfrey chanced to dine with us at Quincy, on his way to Plymouth, where he proposed to spend a few days in walking along the shore, to familiarize himself with it in connection with his history. Sumner came out the day after, a curious contrast to Seward, with his fine presence and lofty carriage, his careful, well-arranged dress, and his deep, rich voice. Sumner was always a distinguished-looking man; he had a bearing and presence. He was then in excellent spirits, "but evidently disgusted at not being more completely backed up by his party in the matter of his recent speech, the 'Barbarism of Slavery.'" He does not doubt the success of the party; but fears for its principles, if those composing it continue so timid in support of them. He talked much of Seward, and of the necessity of his taking the lead in Lincoln's Cabinet. He told us that Seward was much mollified now; but, on his pressing on him that necessity towards the close of the session Seward had exclaimed that "not all the angels in Heaven nor all the demons in Hell could induce him to subject his name for ratification to the votes of twenty-four men on that side of the Senate — indicating the side on which the Democratic Senators sat."

My journey that autumn through the West in the train of Governor Seward was a noticeable episode in life, and had on me a most invigorating effect. I was then somewhat run down in bodily health, as well as mentally demoralized. Worn out waiting for that legal practice which to me never came, I was in great need of change. I was in fact stagnating. We — that is, my father and I — left Quincy on Monday, September 3d, joined Mr. Seward's party at Kalamazoo, Michigan, on Friday; went with him to Chicago, Milwaukee and Madison; thence to Dubuque, where my father left the party, and went home. We got to Quincy, Illinois, by rail from Mendota; then crossed Missouri to St. Joseph, in 1860 the extreme western end of the railroad system. We went by steamboat from St. Joseph to Leavenworth; and from Leavenworth we drove by ambulance to Lawrence. Returning over the same track, we puffed up the dreary Missouri one dull, rainy day late in September, back to St. Joseph, whence we crossed to St. Louis by rail. From St. Louis we went by way of Springfield to Chicago; and at Springfield Mr. Lincoln came into the car, accompanied by Senator Trumbull, of Illinois, to pay his respects to Governor Seward. From Chicago we went to Cleveland, and thence to Buffalo. My journey ended at Auburn, where I passed a Sunday at Governor Seward's house, getting home on the 9th of October; and a very discontented, homesick young barrister I was when I found myself once more back in my dismal, clientless office!

During this, to me, most memorable trip Governor Seward evinced a uniform kindness and consideration which were extraordinary, and are now unaccountable. It was a singular party; and one not altogether to be commended to a young man. Next to Seward the principal character was General James W. Nye — "Nye of Nevada"; and he was a character! He was then a man of only forty-six, a coarse, genial, humorous, New York lawyer, stump-speaker and politician. He had with him his daughter, a pretty, bright girl of only seventeen, with whom I became very intimate during the trip; though I never saw her afterwards until she recognized me in a railway car twenty-five years later, and sent her husband to ask me to come over to where she was sitting, and renew our acquaintance. The General was excellent company, and full of stories and experiences, for he had seen all phases of life; but his conversation was by no means always edifying, and he was a decidedly free liver. Indeed, the consumption of liquors and cigars during that trip was out of all cess. I, however, was young, and in no way encumbered with scruples. Seward smoked the whole time; indeed my diary of the trip from Mendota to Quincy — a night journey by rail — says: "The early morning sun shone on Seward, wrapped in a strange and indescribable Syrian cashmere cloak, and my humble self, puffing our morning cigars in a baggage-car, having rendered ourselves, as he expressed it, 'independent on this tobacco question.' " When it came to drinking, Seward was, for a man of sixty, a free liver; and at times his brandy-and-water would excite him, and set his tongue going with dangerous volubility; but I never saw him more affected than that — never anything approaching drunkenness. He simply liked the stimulus, and was very fond of champagne; and when he was loaded, his tongue wagged. He was a very considerate, delightful travelling companion; and, so far as accomplishing work was concerned, his faculty was extraordinary. Seeing him the whole time I never could understand where, when or how he then prepared the really remarkable speeches he delivered in rapid succession.

That of 1860 was my first trip into the great region west of Niagara. I have since been over the same ground too often to try even to take account of the times, and it has become monotonous, even terribly tedious; I was young in 1860, and it was all new and fresh — my first taste of travel. Travelling was, however, in its most commonplace and uninteresting estate; for the stage-coach and ambulance had disappeared, while the railroad appliances were crude, and toilet accommodations in their infancy. The picturesqueness of travel was gone; its comforts had not come. There were, for instance, no private cars, and the most that any railroad company could do was to put an ordinary day-coach at Governor Seward's special service. This was quite frequently the case; but the eating-houses were wretched, and the hotels overgrown taverns. The single picturesque episode I saw was by night, on the upper Mississippi. It was the wooding-up of river-boats by torch-light, and a genuine spectacle — the flames of the pine-knots blazing up from the great side braziers lighting the tree-clad shores and the red shirts of the hurrying roustabouts. But apart from this, and the constant racing and manœuvring of the river-boats to get the lead of each other, the travel by water was decidedly tedious, far more so than that by rail, which, in its turn, was bad enough.

Kansas was the most interesting of the regions we visited. It was just after the "border-ruffian" excitement, and the Territory had not yet become a State. Kansas, the always either bleeding or starving, had ceased to be a bone of contention between the sections, the slave interest silently admitting itself defeated; but the scenes of the border-ruffian outrages were pointed out and their memory was still fresh. Kansas was in 1860 but sparsely settled, and the unfortunate inhabitants were suffering under a prolonged and very destructive drought. There seemed no end to their misfortunes. I believe there was not at that time a mile of railroad west of the Missouri; so our journey beyond the river, made by ambulance, was delightful as a variety. The river was, I remember, so low that we forded the Kaw at Lawrence, the water not rising to the horses' bellies. I did not go beyond Lawrence.

I have spoken of the meeting between Lincoln and Seward at Springfield, as our party was passing through Illinois, on the way from St. Louis to Chicago. My diary contained an account of it. It was the first time I ever saw Lincoln; afterwards I heard him deliver his inaugural; was presented to him at a White House reception; and, finally, as an officer of a cavalry regiment in the Army of the Potomac, passed in review before him once in Virginia. Save that once at Springfield, I never really spoke to him. We went through to Chicago on the regular train, nor did they give Governor Seward a car for himself; when we got to Springfield the train was quite full, and our party were occupying seats as ordinary passengers. "Mr. Lincoln and Judge Trumbull," my diary records, "came on board the train. Judge Trumbull I had met before in Washington, and again in St. Louis the previous day; but 'old Abe' was a revelation. There he was, tall, shambling, plain and good-natured. He seemed shy to a degree, and very awkward in manner; as if he felt out of place, and had a realizing sense that properly the positions should be reversed. Seward too appeared constrained." Judge Trumbull, between whom and Seward the true senatorial ill-will and cold distrust existed, did the introducing, we all standing in the aisle of the car; for no arrangement had been made for stopping the train, and we none of us left it. There was no demonstration; not a pretence of a reception. It was exactly as if a couple of ordinary business men had come down to a station to meet some travellers passing through, and exchange a few words during a five-minutes stop. "Governor Seward, with his usual thoughtfulness on such occasions, introduced Mr. Lincoln to all the members of the party, and to me among the others. The only remark Lincoln made to me was — 'A son of Charles Francis Adams? I am glad to see you, Sir'; but at the same time I saw a look of interest. Lincoln's face is a good one, and he has proved his skill as a debater; but, if I could judge from a passing glance at a moment when the man was obviously embarrassed, I should say that his eye never belonged to a man great in action; it is neither the quick sharp eye of a man of sudden and penetrating nature, nor the slow firm eye of one of decided will; but it is a mild, dreamy, meditative eye which one would scarcely expect to see in a successful chief magistrate in these days of the republic. *Mais nous verrons.*"

A few days later, on our way from Chicago to Cleveland, we ran across another prominent public man of that period — a statesman of the American and western type. It was characteristic — characteristic both of the individuals and of the times; though, of course, I am no longer in touch, I doubt if it could happen now. Governor Seward went from Chicago to Cleveland by night, and I had my first experience of the sleeping-car as it had at that time been developed. It was a singularly crude, tentative affair, constructed on the pattern of the canal-boat cabin; that is, with a tier of permanent berths on each side of the aisle, practically three shelves, one above the other, as I remember. Anyhow, after smoking in the baggage-car — the only pretence of a smoker — we wriggled into the recesses respectively assigned us; and actually fell asleep, though fully dressed. When we got to Toledo, I was suddenly waked up by a sound of loud cheering, and looked for a midnight reception, for the country was then throbbing with excitement. "Instead of a reception I heard some one rush into the car, and inquire in a loud voice, 'Where 's Seward!' The Governor's berth was pointed out, the inquirer stating that he was Mr. Douglas, and he at once rushed up to it, thrust the curtains aside, and exclaimed, 'Come, Governor, they want to see you; come out and speak to the boys!' To this Seward replied in a drowsy voice, 'How are you, Judge? No; I can't go out. I'm sleepy.' 'Well, what of that?' said Douglas; 'they get me out when I'm sleepy.' Seward, however, simply said he should n't go out; to which Douglas replied, 'Well! if you don't want to you shan't,' and withdrew. All this time it never entered my head that the intruder was no other than 'the little Giant' of Illinois, then and in that way conducting his Presidential campaign. He had a bottle of whiskey with him, and, as he left the car, he stopped to take a drink; and, next morning, I was told he was plainly drunk." He had been having a Democratic meeting at Toledo, and the cheering was incident thereto. I asked Seward about it. He simply said that it was Douglas's "idea of political courtesy; but he [Seward] did n't mean to let Douglas exhibit him to his [Douglas's] followers, just to make a little political capital for himself. So far as Douglas himself was concerned, Seward told me that they had always been on the most friendly terms. I remarked that Douglas's conduct on the floor of the Senate did not always square with that fact. 'No,' he replied, 'but Douglas always did what you refer to for political effect. Personally, we have always been on the most friendly terms.'" So, on this occasion, Douglas, a Presidential candidate, had, more than half drunk, rushed into that car at midnight, whiskey-bottle in hand, to drag Seward, the Premier to be, out of his sleeping-berth, to show him in a railroad station to his (Douglas's) political heelers!

Our last campaign meeting was at Buffalo; where, I remember, when brought forward as I perpetually was —

generally under the idea on the part of the audience that it was my father — I made my chief oratorical success of the trip, really getting out of a very false position quite well. Saturday, the 6th of October, we got to Auburn; and it was really pleasant to see Governor Seward as we approached the journey's end. It suggested to me poor old Walter Scott when he drew near to Abbotsford on his return from Italy shortly before his death. So Seward now showed a great deal of genuine, kindly human nature. "He seemed to enlarge, and to dwell with real affection on every object along the road. He told me of the country, and gave me the names of the lakes and bridges; and, when we stopped at way stations, he would get out of the train, and look about with a homeish air, exchanging greetings with almost every man he met. He seemed to know the whole country-side. At Cayuga, the local bar-keeper seemed to know him well, and, with a grin, produced four pike, fresh from the Lake. 'Ah!' said Seward, 'just what I want!' and, paying for them, he turned them over to me. At Auburn, where we arrived about nine o'clock, a noisy throng was waiting for him on the arrival of the train. It was not a reception, but merely a friendly welcome home. They rushed about him and would let him do nothing for himself, until he, greatly pleased, was hustled into a coach, and so ended his journey at his own door."

Seward, in fact, never appeared so well as at home, in Auburn. He was there really and unaffectedly simple. He walked the streets exchanging greetings with every one; and, as he sat at home in his office, every one came in without form or ceremony, and to every one the same welcome was extended. It was, too, all genuine — the relations were kindly, unaffected, neighborly. His family relations were admirable. With his wife and daughter, he was affectionate, considerate, unselfish. At Auburn he really left on the stranger an impression of individuality approaching greatness. On the whole, looking back at that experience, I think I must have acquitted myself more creditably than my diary — now destroyed — would lead me to suppose. Certainly, Seward and Nye bore with me pleasantly, and I saw and talked with them on terms of great freedom. My diary contained many long memoranda of conversations, but they would have no value; so I do not preserve them. One entry only seemed to carry a lesson — and not in any way a novel one—in connection with what has since occurred. "At breakfast General Nye asked me about my grandfather's diary, when would it be published, etc.? Seward seemed to think it a dangerous experiment; and expressed a hearty concurrence in my remark that the great thing concerning that diary was 'Who was to edit it?' For on the editor must depend the great question of extracts, and the light in which the diarist would be shown. 'Nothing,' said he, 'is so dangerous to the reputation of a public man as a diary. Look at Evelyn.[1] A most respectable man; a Secretary of State for Charles II, and see what a picture he has left of himself: "Got up this morning and put on my best mulberry suit, which cost me ten pounds, and went to the office; coming home saw a crowd collected, and, on enquiry found it was to witness the execution of Sir Henry Vane; he had a large boil on his neck, which he particularly requested the executioner not to touch; about fifty persons in attend-

---

[1] Pepys was intended, and Seward has made up his quotation to suit his purpose. Some of it may be found in Pepys' account of the execution of Sir Henry Vane, in *Diary* (Bright), II. 263.

ance"; and so on. How would I appear if I had kept a diary, and recorded all my cursing and swearing on the 19th of May last?'"—a closing reference to the Chicago Convention of 1860 and the nomination of Lincoln.

As between Evelyn and Pepys, it must be conceded, the future Secretary was a trifle mixed; nor was his selection of an example of frivolous diary-keeping exactly happy, for there are not many eye-witness records of events more interesting than Pepys' account of the execution of Vane.

Of the rest of the memorable Presidential canvass of 1860, it would be useless here to say more. It still stands out in my memory with awful clearness; and for me it was distinctly educational. It was a demonstrative campaign, and, in recalling its events, a lurid glare seems reflected from the light of innumerable torches against an ominous gathering of heavy lowering clouds. Nor is this a case of present imagination casting a shadow backwards; it was an actuality. The campaign of 1860 was essentially a midnight demonstration — it was the "Wide-awake" canvass of rockets, illuminations and torch-light processions. Every night was marked by its tumult, shouting, marching and countermarching, the reverberation of explosives and the rush of rockets and Roman candles. The future was reflected on the skies. But of the tremendous nature of that future, we then had no conception. We all dwelt in a fool's Paradise. It is a source of amazement now to realize our own shortsightedness; for, however much people may since have educated themselves to believe that they foresaw everything, and looked for exactly what afterwards took place, it is all pure self-deception — cases of wisdom after the event. We were, all around, of an average blindness. I know it was so

in the case of Seward and my father; as it was absolutely so
in that of Sumner. We knew nothing of the South, had no
realizing sense of the intensity of feeling which there prevailed; we fully believed it would all end in gasconade. We
fell into the rather serious error of under-estimating our
antagonist. For instance, here is my diary entry made ten
days after the election — the 18th of November, the election having been on the 7th: "After election came its results
— its effect on the South. Hardly were the returns in, when
there came mutterings of secession from the Slave States,
which swelled immediately into a shout. This, however, is
an old story; and we take it philosophically. The only difficulty is that it has led to a money pressure, and may result
in a panic. The South is in a bad way; for it has got to face
a financial and a political crisis at the same time, the one
aggravating the other. My own impression is that the experiment of secession is about to be tried; and I hope it will
be, for the country is weary of the threat. My impression
also is that the experiment will cost the States which try it
about ten millions of dollars, and that it will fail ignominiously. We shall see! Meanwhile we are calm; and, but for
the money pressure, I believe every one would say: 'Let the
experiment be tried.'" Two months later I wrote: "Politically, the world is busy. My letters from Washington
[which have disappeared since] will some day be of value;
but it is strange how the back is proportioned to the burden.
A few months ago the word 'Disunion' threw us into a cold
tremor; but now, the secession of a State is an event of
hardly importance enough for a paragraph in a newspaper.
At last the Northern spirit is roused, and I think there will
be trouble before we back down. The action of the seceding

Slave States has put them wholly in the wrong; and, day by day, my impression is growing that the crisis is past, that it is mostly sound and fury in the South, that the victory is going to rest with us, and that there will be no fight."

All this was, however, pure self-deception — whistling to keep the courage up. In truth it was a wretched time. Terribly anxious, we watched the daily papers with feverish interest, snatching at every straw. For instance, on the 9th of February I wrote: "Tuesday [four days previous] a great sense of relief passed over the whole community as it heard that Virginia had, almost unanimously, spoken against disunion. In the morning we got a few returns, enough to give us the general complexion of the result; and, I confess, my heart went up into my mouth, as I read those returns, for I felt that the tide of secession was at last turned, and I felt confident, and still am confident, that the ebb will be no less rapid than was the flow. Decisive news reached us in the afternoon. I was skating on Jamaica Pond, all by myself, when I noticed the throng of skaters flocking together on the further side of the Pond, and almost immediately they began to shout and cheer with all their souls. Some one had come out bringing a paper with fuller and final returns. The tears almost stood in my eyes; and I skated off to be alone, for I realized that the crisis was actually passed."

III

WASHINGTON, 1861

THAT winter I went on to Washington on the 18th of February, and remained until the 13th of March, staying over Lincoln's inauguration, of which I was a witness. An intensely interesting period, we all in a way realized its nature. And yet I now wonder at our lack of prescience and general incapacity, North and South, to realize even in a remote degree the imminence as well as magnitude of the impending catastrophe. Something would surely happen to avert it! We did n't know what — we could n't even suggest a "something"; but we clung to the childish belief all the same. Consequently, neither as a whole nor as individuals did we make any preparation. Perhaps it was just as well; and yet there was the flag flying over Fort Sumter, with the eyes of the whole country directed that way! Still, I cannot now but wonder at my own purblindness; for I was at the time in position to know fairly well what was going on, being in close contact with prominent men, and an interested if not a keen observer. Of course I had no share in events or influence over them — no one that I know of did. We were, as I now see, drifting — drifting into an inevitable and close impending war; but this we could not realize, and every day brought with it reports, doubts, hopes and fears. My record of that period was quite complete, what with diary and letters, and has now an historical value of the lesser sort; for it shows what the plan, so far as they had one, of Seward and my father was, as they groped their way along. My

father and Governor Seward had by this time been brought
into close coöperation. Their policy was simple, and, as I
still see it, eminently sensible — though based on an entire
misapprehension of the facts, and fore-doomed to failure.
Their scheme was to divide the South, by conciliating the
northern tier of Slave States, including Virginia especially;
and, holding them loyal until the tide of reaction, setting in,
should drive the seceding States into a false position from
which they would ultimately be compelled to recede. All
winter the immediate effort had been to gain time until the
Government had been transferred to the newly elected
Administration. This essential point had been practically
assured through the Virginia election. The peaceable inauguration of Lincoln was now practically certain; the next
question was as to the policy he would adopt when he became President. The working theory of my father and of
Seward was that the less extreme Slave States — notably
Virginia — were in a condition of senseless panic from fear
of something terrible intended — some invasion of their
constitutional rights, they did not well know what; but, if
Lincoln could be safely inaugurated and his Administration
set quietly in motion without any overt act of force having
taken place on either side, it was not unreasonable to hope
this groundless fear would gradually subside, and a strong
and rising Union reaction could be anticipated. The question would then settle itself, without bloodshed; and once
for all. Wholly mistaken, as the result showed, it was still,
at that stage of trouble-development, the only sound theory to work on, at any rate until the possession of the
Government was secured. Meanwhile, Lincoln's attitude
was wholly unknown. His every movement was jealously

watched; his utterances closely followed. In Washington, the Republican party was divided between the extremists and coercionists — of whom Sumner and Chase were the exponents; and the conciliators and opportunists — of whom Seward and my father were chief. With which side would Lincoln be allied? That, North and South, was the question.

That winter I saw in Washington a great deal of Seward, and I still think he was then at his best — truly a statesman. The secession movement had by its force, volume and intensity taken him by surprise. Failing correctly to appreciate conditions, he had shown that he was not a statesman of the first order; but still his attitude, bearing and utterances were statesmanlike. Awaiting final developments, he was conciliatory, patient, and, outwardly, cool and confident. He had formulated a policy based on the careful avoidance of a collision and bloodshed until there had been ample time allowed for reflection and the saving second-thought. The course of subsequent events showed that he was wholly wrong in basing any hopes on this misconception of the real attitude and feelings of the South; but, on the other hand, they also showed that the day of compromise was over, and that the attitude of conciliation, while it might gain valuable time, endangered nothing.

In point of fact, as was found out in the following April, Seward was laboring under a total misconception of the real facts in the case and of the logic of events. If, however, he had been endowed with the prophetic gift and read the future as an open book, I do not now see that his policy or line of conduct at this juncture would have been other than they were in any essential aspect. It was a period of crystallization, North and South; and any attempt at decisive action on either side would have been premature and disastrous. A more far-seeing statesman would, perhaps, have occupied himself, very quietly, in the work of preparation, observing the course of events and — biding his time! But this again was, practically, the course pursued; the Executive Government was still in the old hands — untransferred; Congress was composed largely of future Confederates; and whatever was done had to be done through the States. So, even now, I cannot see any error or weakness in Seward's attitude and policy. My father acted in close harmony with him; totally misapprehending, he also, the nature of the situation, and wholly failing to realize the intensity of the forces at work. Since the election, Lincoln had hitherto maintained a Sphinxlike silence. He was still at Springfield, while Seward, understood to be the coming Secretary of State, had found himself compelled to formulate such a policy as he might, without any means of knowing the mind of his future chief, or forecasting his policy and action.

Thus when, in February, 1861, I reached my father's house there, the situation in Washington was about as chaotic as was possible. I see it all now; then it was inscrutable to the best informed or the wisest. The simple fact was that the ship was drifting on the rocks of a lee shore; nothing could save it; this, however, was something none of us could bring ourselves to believe. We still clung to a delusive hope that the coming change of commanders would alter the whole aspect of the situation, and we would work clear. Meanwhile, where and what sort of a man was the new commander? That conundrum was foremost in all minds. Abraham Lincoln was an absolutely unknown quantity; and yet he was the one possible *Deus ex machina!*

The President-elect had left Springfield on the 11th. In the interim his silence had been broken; he had been doing a good deal of talking. The whole value of my record of those days lies in its giving the spirit of the passing time, the daily fluctuating hopes and fears of a critical and most exciting period.

I reached Washington on the afternoon of Tuesday, the 19th of February. My father's house on K Street Northwest, near Pennsylvania Avenue, was full; so I was quartered in lodgings at Jost's, on Pennsylvania Avenue — the place, by the way, where Russell, of the London *Times*, lived shortly after, and from the windows of which he observed the condition of Washington's main thoroughfare in the days succeeding Bull Run. My brother Henry was acting as secretary to my father, and he also was living at Jost's, where he met me on my arrival. A little later on he wrote his own contemporaneous account of these events; and this account I, just fifty years later, communicated to the Massachusetts Historical Society;[1] and what I there said forms part of the present record.

My own narrative, however, begins at my meeting him on that Tuesday afternoon in February, 1861. It ran thus: "I don't know why, but Henry's very presence seemed to exercise a depressing influence on me. Hardly daring to put to him a question, I prepared for dinner. We all sat down [at my father's house] but, somehow or other, while the talking was fast, all present were evidently blue as indigo. Evil was in the air; and I felt it. I finally got a clue to the trouble in a feminine outburst on the mention of our President-elect's name, and it became at once apparent that his

[1] *Proceedings,* XLIII. 656.

recent peripatetic oratory on his route to Washington had by no means served to elevate him in the estimation of the Adams family circle. Little was said, however, until dinner was over; when, at last, my father gave mouth. Temporarily, it then appeared, the fat was all in the fire. He did not hesitate to say that, ten days before, the whole game was in Seward's hands; but now it was surrendered again to the chapter of accidents. The difficulty was wholly owing to Lincoln's folly in not consulting with his official advisers, but saying whatever came into his head. Thus he was dividing his party deplorably — destroying the chance of union in action. Seward's position had thus been made lamentable; for, with his strength exhausted, he was surrounded by opponents, friends and foes; and here now was Lincoln, without consultation or understanding with Seward, and with no apparent regard for the policy indicated by him, showing an ignorance as complete as lamentable of the position of public affairs, fomenting dissensions and jealousies already too formidable. Jeopardizing, in fact, the only hope of the country's salvation. The present indications were that the extremists — the Sumners and Greeleys — had prevailed, and that Seward had been thrown overboard. In which case, my father did not hesitate to say that he expected war within sixty days."

> His prophecy on the whole
> Was fair enough as prophesyings go;
> At fault a little in detail, but quite
> Precise enough in the main; and hereupon
> I pay due homage.

In point of fact, and as afterwards appeared, Seward was not thrown over, and Lincoln had not joined the extremists;

but we did have war in exactly fifty-three days from that talking. My record then goes on: "Later in the evening I had quite a long talk to the same effect. He [my father] told me that a few days before Governor Hicks, of Maryland, Andrew Johnson, and Cassius M. Clay had offered to answer for their States on the basis of the propositions of the Committee of Thirty-three; and that Mr. Rives, of the Virginia State Senate, had told him that, upon those propositions, they could carry every Virginia district in the spring election; but, in consequence of the developments of the last few days the whole aspect of affairs had changed, and Seward was at that time more depressed than he had been previously during the whole Winter—in fact no man in Washington then knew where he was standing. I walked home, blue enough. The very knowledge of the military preparations going on all about gave me in the darkness a feeling almost approaching fear. In my letters I had all winter long noted the sudden and violent transitions from extreme exultation to the depth of despair; but I had not learnt from experience. I now felt as much in doubt as if this had been my first experience of a panic, and asked myself in vain — Where is it all to end? The issue seemed made up, and the result in the worst possible hands — those of the Virginia Convention. We sat in Jost's discussing the gloomy aspect of affairs until long after midnight; but, though I felt that my nerves had received a considerable shock, I did not notice that my night's sleep was troubled."

I had gone on to Washington in company with Arthur Dexter of Boston (H. U. 1851), a grandson of Samuel Dexter, Secretary of War in the Cabinet of John Adams, and then on intimate terms with my family generally. Two days after

our arrival we went together to the Capitol, and I sent in
my cards to Mr. Sumner and Governor Seward, not having
seen the last since I left his house at Auburn, in the previous
October. "Sumner came out almost immediately, greeting
me most cordially, and at once invited us round to the cloak-
room. On the way we passed a rather tall, strongly built
man, with black hair and a swarthy complexion, who,
Sumner said, was Andrew Johnson, of Tennessee, and immediately introduced me to him. Mr. Johnson shook hands
with me, and at once referred to the fact that he had formerly
sat next to my grandfather in the House of Representatives,
occupied his seat during his first illness, and seen him fall in
his last. Mr. Johnson's manners are quite gentle, though
slightly formal. He has a deep, black eye, and, with his
somewhat neat black clothes and clean-shaven face, looks,
physically and intellectually, like a strong man. While
talking with him, I turned round and my eyes fell on Seward,
just coming out of one of the side doors in the lobby. There
he was, the same small, thin, sallow man, with the pale,
wrinkled, strongly marked face — plain and imperturbable
— the thick, guttural voice and the everlasting cigar. Yet
it was immediately apparent that his winter's cares had told
on him, for he looked thin and worn, and ten years older
than when I had left him at Auburn. I went into the cloak-
room, and sat down with Sumner; but, seeing Wilkinson, of
Minnesota, in the Senate-chamber, I sent in for him. The
conversation soon turned on the one topic of the day, and
for the first time I realized that I was in Washington, and
how intense was the excitement and how bitter the feeling.
It was immediately apparent that all these men had been
brooding over the questions at issue and dwelling on them

till their minds had lost their tone, and become morbid. They were in fact now the last men in the country to be entrusted with responsibility. The conversation was long, interesting and excited. Wilkinson was riding the high blood-and-thunder horse; but, after uttering one or two excited platitudes about Major Anderson and 'the traitors,' and looking somewhat surprised when I remarked that 'all that might do very well for the hustings but would n't go down with me,' he subsided." I ought, by the way, to say here that, while in the Northwest with Seward in September, I had seen a great deal of Wilkinson, and quite intimately; and had "sized him up." He was no grave or potent Senator to me; and he knew it well enough. But to return to my diary. Wilkinson subsided; but "not so Sumner. I had heard that he was excited, but his manner and language amazed me. He talked like a crazy man, orating, gesticulating, rolling out deep periods in theatrical, whispered tones, — repeating himself, and doing everything but reason. He began by remarking in a deep, low voice and with earnest gestures that 'the session was drawing to a close, and the only question of real practical statesmanship before it had not been touched and would not be touched — that was the treatment to be accorded to the seceding States — the only question of true statesmanship.' I suggested that this question was not at all a new one; that secession was but another name for revolution; and, accordingly, it was but the old question of the treatment of revolution, and nothing more! This idea seemed rather to stagger him, and he passed on to talk of what he called 'the compromisers' — meaning Seward and my father. In less than five minutes, however, he was back on his old topic of 'the one true question of real statesmanship'; and this he kept reiterating, each time more excitedly until our conversation came to a close. I soon saw that reason was out of the question, and the only course for me was to hold my tongue, letting him run down. Still, I could not resist the temptation now and again to put a spoke in his wheel; but it was not possible to throw him off the track, he merely gave a bump and a jerk, and went on fiercer in his utter disregard of logic and policy. His attack was on Seward and 'the compromisers'; 'he had thought of this matter in the daytime, and lay awake over it whole nights; it was all clear to him; to him, his path was as clear as day,' and then he reverted with a jolt to 'the one question.' 'Seward,' he went on, 'did not realize the true position of affairs; he had been demented all the session, and the film had not yet cleared from his eyes. He was demoralizing the North. If he had but held firmly to his position, and refused all parley with secessionists, all would have been well. An appeal should have been made to the loyal, Union-loving feeling of the border Slave States, and all would have been well.' 'Seward,' he said, 'had read to him his speech, and to him only of the Senate,' and he then proceeded to orate; with intense feeling and animated gesticulation, he described how he 'had pleaded with him, he had prayed him, besought him, implored him by his past record, his good name, his memory hereafter' to omit certain passages. Had he done so, 'assuming the pure ground of his party, the whole North would have rallied to him; — but now — too late! — too late!' Then he would reiterate: 'I am sure — I am certain — I see my way so clearly; such a glorious victory was before us; right was with us, God was with us — our success was sure did we only hold firmly to our principles.' Once I lost my patience, and attempted to stop the conversation as not likely to lead to any good result; but at this he got angry, and said that I was discussing, not he; that I began it; and then he went straight on, for, evidently, he could think of nothing else. It was very painful. The man talked so without reason, and almost without connection; and yet he gave me distinctly to understand that he alone could now guide affairs; that Seward was a mere politician vainly trying to deal with great issues. I was disgusted, shocked and mortified; the more because of Dexter's presence, who entertains for Sumner a pet aversion. Finally Seward came out; and what a relief it was! Thin and pale, but calm, gentle and patient, he was as philosophical as ever, as pleasant and companionable; and I now realized his position. With a formidable enemy in front and such allies around — foolish, positive, angry — it was a general-of-division in battle, his reserves used up and waiting for reinforcements — praying for night or Blücher. And meanwhile, Lincoln, his Blücher, was perambulating the country, kissing little girls and growing whiskers! We talked for a few moments only, as he was quite busy. He said that half the men there — indicating the Senate-chamber — were intent on pulling the house down, and he was merely trying to prevent them; that he was very much occupied, for the women and children of the whole South were writing to him, and looking to him for protection.

"As we walked home, we passed the artillery. It was the first time I had seen them. Washington is almost in a state of siege. Every morning and evening I hear from my room the bugles and drums of no less than three companies quartered almost within a stone's throw of us."

Such is a copy made in 1900 of my contemporaneous record of a very noticeable talk, and one the painful impression created by which at the time it took place is still vivid in memory; for it was disillusioning. Even now I can see Sumner's eyes gleaming with something distinctly suggestive of insanity, as he rolled out his oratorical periods. He was plainly off his balance, nor did I ever again feel towards him as before. Of my record, made at the time, I forgot the existence. The deluge of the Civil War had swept over my recollection, obliterating every trace of it, until in 1900 I had occasion to recur to it. It then threw additional light on a subject I have twice had occasion to discuss — once in my *Life of Dana*, and again in that of my father. I shall have to discuss it once more. In my *Dana*, I see, I gave to Mr. Dana at the time an account of this conversation almost exactly as I now find it in my diary.[1] Since doing so I have frequently tried to make out some theory which would afford a reasonable explanation of Sumner's attitude. What policy did he propose? What course of action was it that was so clear to him? — that would result so immediately in a glorious victory? It is most unfortunate that when then in Washington I was not a little older, and did not have a good deal more tact and objectiveness. Had I been so blessed, I might have learned and recorded — for I was industrious enough with my pen, recording indeed at great length — many things now of interest. Sumner's brain was at that time super-heated, his nervous system over-loaded. When he got in that condition, and in February, 1861, he was so almost continuously, he seemed surcharged with rhetoric. His voice vibrated with a tremulous depth, he orated, he laid down the law. Had I

---

[1] *Life of Richard Henry Dana*, II. 252.

only had the sense to invite him to do so, he would have disclosed the heart of his mystery. As it is I have had to piece together a plausible hypothesis.

I understood the position of Wilkinson at that crisis. It was as simple as it was senseless. He wanted to fight "the traitors" then and there, regardless of conditions. That the machinery of government was still in the hands of the old régime, that we had neither army nor navy, that a precipitate act would bring on a premature crisis — none of these things did he take into account. He was just mad; and he wanted to get at the "traitors." The course he suggested was not sensible; but it could be understood. Not so Sumner. What curious hallucination did he then have in his head? What was he driving at when he orated and reiterated his "one question of true statesmanship, which had not even been touched"? What was that proposed mysterious treatment of the seceding States? This question has interested me, because it was here that my father broke with Sumner, and their intimacy ceased for good. After that, I never met him again on the old footing. Either he had become perverted or I had developed. Possibly both.

When I wrote the *Life of Dana* this problem did not occur to me. When Sumner discoursed to me in Washington, Secession was in my thought simply Revolution; and, so, a very simple thing. It, later, became such in Sumner's mind, as in every one else's. But how was it with him at the earlier period — the intensely interesting educational period which immediately preceded the crisis? What did he have in mind when declaiming to me and Dexter that morning in the Senate ante-chamber? As the result of much puzzling and piecing together I think I afterwards reached a correct solution of the psychological puzzle. That Sumner was an agitator, a rhetorician and a theorist — in a word, an egotistical doctrinaire — is well understood. As such he was devoid of hard common sense and true sagacity of insight. He saw every situation through his feelings, often over-excited, and he evolved his facts from his inner consciousness. His mind had dwelt on the issues which now presented themselves, waking and sleeping, until he had ceased to be a reasoning being; and his friends at times feared for his sanity.[1] His mission was to denounce Seward, and, if possible, force him from public life. He openly declared Seward ready to sell us out. In February, 1861, he was actually haunted with fear of some compromise. In point of fact the time for compromise was past; *that* any clear-sighted, well-informed man should have seen, and ceased to concern himself with the thought of it. Sumner still regarded it as the one great danger. The policy he had in mind — concerning the results of which he felt such absolute certainty of conviction — was in reality based on an hallucination and a complete misapprehension of the facts of the situation.

His idea was that the Republican party should take what he called a lofty moral stand. Firm, absolutely unyielding, it should use no word of conciliation, much less make any suggestion of compromise. It should, on the contrary, go straight forward in its course; and then came in his utter inability to comprehend the slave-holding character and the situation in the South. He fully believed that "firmness," as he called it, was all that was necessary; in its presence they would yield, like petulant, passionate children, prone to violence. He looked upon the whole slave-holding class as

[1] *Life of Dana*, II. 258.

a combination of ruffianism and bluster, whiskey-drinking and tobacco-chewing. In dealing with them "firmness" was essential; by them, any word of concession would be construed into an indication of fear or symptom of weakness, and do infinite mischief. When, in June, 1861, Russell, of the *Times*, got back to Washington from his trip through the Confederacy he pronounced Mr. Sumner as "ignorant of the whole condition of things below Mason and Dixon's line as he was of the politics of Timbuctoo."[1] So in February — three months previous — he derived his confidence from the wholly imaginary condition of affairs, evolved from his own inner consciousness. As he implied in his talk with me, he believed fully in the existence of a strong Union sentiment — a really predominating sentiment — in all the border Slave States. That sentiment he considered was "debauched," as he expressed it, or, more properly, demoralized by any word of conciliation. Those entertaining it "besought us" not so to weaken them. If, on the contrary, the "slaveocracy" was met with absolutely unyielding firmness the people now cowed by it would assert themselves, and the "slaveocracy" would yield. But how about the seceding States — those below South Carolina and bordering on the Gulf? There was where his question — "the only question" — of "true statesmanship" came in; and there was my cause of mystification. He never intimated to me, but his solution of that difficulty was "to let them go," he "would not lift a finger to retain them." We would be well rid of them and their slavery. This explanation of his theory never suggested itself to me at the time of our conversation, and I only became aware of it recently in reading Russell's *Diary*[2] and Yarnell's *Recol-*

---

[1] *My Diary*, II. 121.   [2] I. 80.

lections,[1] but it accounts for all he said in the talk I have narrated. His theory was that, in presence of a display of absolute firmness at Washington, the border States would, in the end, adhere to the Union, and the Gulf States, after a sufficient exhibition of bluster and rhodomontade, resulting in their secession, would come back into the Union on our own terms. So, let them go; there need be no war. Only be "firm" and it would in the near future be a complete and glorious triumph; only Seward's and my father's weakness now jeopardized it. No sillier figment ever gained footing in agitator's imagination; *that* subsequent events demonstrated to him. The supposed Union sentiment did not exist in the border Slave States; it was both the intention and in the power of the extreme Slave States to precipitate a conflict; the possession of the National Capital would, as he well knew, be in dispute. Such, however, was in February, 1861, the policy which Charles Sumner felt absolutely certain would afford a plain and easy way to glorious and permanent victory!

As I look back on it — recalling those days of doubt and pain — we were all wrong; a band of men — anxious, excited, blind or blind-folded — some passionate and vindictive; ready, ripe for blows, all groping their way to a dreaded result; but Sumner was the most wrong and the blindest of the whole throng; though by all odds the most certain in his own clearness of vision and knowledge of the facts. Seward and my father were in his belief wrong; for they fixed their eyes on the change of administration, and looked no further, confidently believing that a reaction would then set in, and reason reassert itself. Seward so told Russell, of the *Times,*

---

[1] Yarnell, *Recollections,* 8.

speaking with perfect confidence only five days before Sumter: "the States would come back at the rate of one a month."[1] The "compromisers," as Sumner called them, referring always to Seward and my father, but who in reality were Crittenden and the supporters of his East-and-West line project, were so very wrong as to call for no comment; for the Southern extremists — let alone the Northern Republicans — would not consider it, and were intent on a separate, slave-holding nationality, and nothing short of that. The day for compromise on that basis was wholly past. On the other hand, the Northern extremists were wrong, for they, after the manner of my friend, Wilkinson, wholly underestimated their enemy. On the whole, therefore, up to this point — the change of administration — Seward and my father were the coolest and wisest counsellors. They were wrong in their understanding of the ultimate and fundamental facts of the situation; but their error implied no consequences. They proposed to get possession of the machinery of the Government; that was absolutely essential. That secured, they counted on a sullen but undemonstrative attitude on the part of the seceded States, and a strong and increasing reaction in the border States; and, if in this they proved mistaken, a policy of another character must then be shaped to meet events as they developed. In such case the true course could not yet be foreseen. That was the only statesmanship possible in the situation as it then was; and the event fully justified it.

Unfortunately for Seward, following this wise policy until the close of April, when he then at last found his hopes vanishing; when, plainly, no reaction in the border States was

[1] *My Diary*, I. 103; II. 113.

to be longer hoped for, and the problem of the Southern forts pressed for an immediate solution — could, indeed, no longer be deferred — then, one day, Seward lost his head. He found himself fairly beyond his depth; and he plunged! The foreign-war panacea took possession of him; and he yielded to it. Then, once for all, he showed himself unequal to the great occasion; his limitations became apparent. The fact is, as I now see him, Seward was an able, a specious and adroit, and a very versatile man; but he escaped being really great. He made a parade of philosophy, and by it I was very effectually deceived; but it was not the genuine article. It was, on the contrary, something else — stuff of a very flimsy texture. Seward was not well grounded either in learning or in the facts surrounding him — did not have a strong, firm grasp. He was, after all, as men instinctively felt, more of a politician than a statesman. Perhaps my own impression could best be conveyed — looking back on him now through the perspective of forty years — by saying that he was an adroit politician and pseudo-statesman, having in him a dash of the philosopher. He was patient, good-tempered, tolerant, and a great believer in his countrymen and their institutions. Sumner, on the other hand, I knew better. He was a very considerable historical figure — the most considerable in Massachusetts during my time. As I have already said, a theorist, agitator and rhetorician, a doctrinaire with no real insight into men and conditions, Sumner was a tremendous egotist and woefully lacking in plain common sense. Strange to say, by no means a bad politician, he was no statesman. Intolerant to the last degree when any issue he had at heart was involved, he was as a Senator great, and, in many respects, ideal. He was there essentially a round peg in a round hole; and he filled the hole, also, though by no means a small one.

To return, however, to myself and the narrative of 1861. My father was more fortunate than Seward. Absolutely right and wise in his course up to the change of administration, he then ceased to have any connection with the conduct of home affairs. When the reaction he had so confidently counted on failed to develop, and a new policy had to be devised, he was wrong in his inclination; for he failed to see that the time for action had at last come, and the issue must be met. He favored the abandonment of Sumter. His horror of civil war was such that I find myself at a loss to fix the point at which he would have made a stand. I am not at all sure he would not have concluded that a peaceable separation was best. This, however, is and was a mere abstract proposition. A peaceable separation, involving as it did the border States and the National Capital, was out of the question. Had my father remained in public life in Washington, he would have found his course marked out for him in his own despite, as did the others. On one point, however, I am clear: he never would have been a victim of Seward's foreign-war delusion. No more so in Washington than he was in London.

I left off on the 21st of February. On the 22d, a dull, murky day, Henry and I dined at Arlington, with the family of General Lee. He was not there, and I never had even a glance at him; though, possibly, I may have seen him one day shortly after, as I was riding away from Arlington after a morning call. If I did, he was going up the Avenue in a carriage, just returned from Texas; and he looked at my sister and myself from the window — curiously — a military, handsome man, with a short, grey beard. The dinner at

Arlington was interesting, and I remember it well. One of General Lee's sons[1] had been a classmate of Henry's at Harvard. A daughter, Miss Agnes, I thought extremely attractive. We had some young officers of artillery there. A few months later we were all arrayed against each other; and I fancy there must have been fully half-a-dozen future generals and colonels about the Arlington table that day.

The following evening I went to a reception at Mrs. Eames's, then the salon of Washington. I there met J. J. Crittenden and Governor Morehead, of Kentucky, both in Washington in attendance on the time-consuming, but otherwise futile, Peace Conference. "As good specimens of the Kentucky gentleman as one often meets; large, with white heads, stout, burly figures, and those elaborately polite but very formal manners so common with Southern gentlemen. I had more or less talk with both; and, I must say, I was more impressed by their appearance than by what they said. They seemed possessed with the Southern idea that cotton is all in all; and they actually told me that the South neither wished nor intended to be more prosperous than now, or to produce anything but cotton; 'they were, Sir, the most prosperous people on the face of the Globe, Sir,' etc., etc. And this is much the sort of stuff now talked in Washington by most Southern men."

On the 25th I was in the gallery of the House. The report of the Committee of Thirty-three was under discussion. I took a deep interest in the fate of the recommendations contained in that report, being as purblind as all the rest in regard to the small importance of all things then under discussion; and those opposed to them were having recourse to

[1] William Henry Fitzhugh Lee (1837–1891).

dilatory tactics. So I recorded that I was made "almost crazy by the indecision and lack of force of the old owl of a Speaker [Pennington]. The fate of the country seemed hanging in the balance, and the dolt had not force to drive business ahead. As I fidgetted in the galleries, I groaned in spirit: 'Oh! for one hour of Banks!' Finally, despairing of action, I turned my steps homeward. On the way I saw Governor Seward, and joining him, walked up the Avenue. He was rather more neatly dressed than usual, and seemed quite cheerful, as he walked along, holding his light bamboo cane by both hands in front of him across his legs, watching everything that went on in the Avenue, and talking incessantly. I left him at his door, going to dine 'with some friends' at Willard's — of course, the President-elect."

During this visit to Washington I made my first acquaintance with that Virginia country, with which I was destined shortly after to become so drearily familiar. In fact, I never approached such a knowledge of Massachusetts as, between 1862 and 1864, I acquired of Virginia from the Potomac to the James. And now, on a cantering horse, I enjoyed greatly scampering over the country, noting "its miserable population, its half-tilled farms and hardly passable roads; its deserted houses, the benighted inhabitants of the houses not deserted, and the wretched cultivation. I could not but deplore the fact that so fine a portion of our heritage was cursed with slavery."

The evening of the 28th I passed with Andrew Johnson, whose acquaintance I had made in the Senate waiting-room a few days before. Johnson was then at the highest point of his reputation. A Southern Unionist, a "poor white" of Eastern Tennessee, who, by native energy, had elevated himself to the Senate, he was holding his own there against Davis and all the representatives of Sumner's "Slaveocracy," who were trying in vain to dragoon him. It was not given us to look into the future, and see Andrew Johnson as he later on exhibited himself from the unfortunate altitude to which Booth's pistol elevated him. In February, 1861, he bore himself very gallantly in a most trying position. And so I wisely called on him, with a view to better acquaintance. "I found him at home in his hotel, stived up in one miserable room, littered with folded speeches and copies of public documents, and otherwise containing a bed and some scanty chamber furniture. He received me cordially, and introduced me to his son, a by no means distinguished-looking specimen of the young Tennesseean. As we talked, he paced slowly up and down the room, or sat facing me, speaking slowly and very carefully, with force though not with much feeling. We first discussed a convention election which had just been held in North Carolina, with the result of which he was greatly elated, though to evince feeling one way or the other is evidently no part of his philosophy. The great thing about the man is evidently his nerve — his apparent force and coolness in a position of danger. I spoke to him of his colleague, Nicholson. 'I can't,' he said, 'speak with freedom of my colleague because of our position; but when I became convinced that this conspiracy existed, it seemed to me very desirable that we should act together, and I consulted him. But I soon found that he had been swept away in the general current. When I spoke to him, Sir, there was dismay depicted on that man's countenance.' 'But,' he went on to add, 'though I can't speak of him personally, I will make a general remark, with no particular application: there are, you know, some men of a nature so selfish and conceited that they can't take a broad, generous view of any subject; and so mean and cowardly that they dare not pursue it if they could.' Of Sumner, he said that he knew him slightly — enough to exchange ordinary civilities; but he seemed to him on the present issues to be morbid and diseased, in fact, actually crazy. The feeling towards him on the Democratic side of the Senate he described as one of rather 'contempt' than anything else. He talked freely of political questions, agreeing with me that no remark had ever been more ingeniously misconstrued and misrepresented than Seward's 'irrepressible conflict'; and he admitted that slavery was, as an institution, opposed to the spirit of Christianity. The constitutional amendment framed by my father [and which Lincoln expressly approved in his inaugural of the following week] he said was enough for him to go home on, and sustain himself in Tennessee. He then went off on the secession conspiracy. He declared that nearly all the Senators from the South were parties to it, and he was afraid that Breckenridge and 'Joe' Lane were both of them in it. He was most amusingly severe over the secession of Florida. 'There's that Yulee,' he said, 'miserable little cuss! I remember him in the House — the contemptible little Jew — standing there and begging us — yes! begging us to let Florida in as a State. Well! we let her in, and took care of her, and fought her Indians; and now that despicable little beggar stands up in the Senate and talks about *her* rights.' Towards Jews, he evidently felt a strong aversion; for, after finishing with Yulee he began on Benjamin, exclaiming: 'There's another Jew — that miserable Benjamin! He looks on a country and a government as he would on a suit of old clothes. He sold out the old one; and he would sell out the new if he could in so doing make two or three millions.' The seceded States, he said, must come back; the remote and northern portions of the States would, he declared, pass other ordinances, and bring them back. He denounced Wigfall, of Texas, as 'a damned blackguard,' who had n't a cent; and 'that's his way! the strongest secessionists never owned the hair of a nigger.' His conclusion was that somebody would be, and ought to be, hanged for all this. I was with him about an hour and a half, and left, considerably edified by Andrew Johnson."

On Sunday, March 3d, the day preceding Lincoln's inauguration, I called on the Sewards in the afternoon. "I found them at dinner; but Governor Seward's son chanced to be in the hall, and he urged me so strongly that I went in and joined them at the dinner-table. There I found, much to my gratification, General King, of Milwaukee [one of my travelling companions during the trip of the previous summer], and also General James Watson Webb, of the New York *Courier and Enquirer*, besides some Auburn friends of Governor Seward's. He was comparatively quiet, and seemed less exuberant in spirit than usual; but almost the only thing he did say caused with me a long breath of relief. Referring to the coming inaugural, he remarked that he had been reading it, and that while it would satisfy the whole country, it more than covered all his [Seward's] heresies."

Seward at the same time made another remark which, though I failed to note it down at the time, made an impression on me, and I have since often repeated it, and noticeably in some remarks I made at the meeting of the Historical Society in 1909, on the observance of Lincoln's Centennial.[1]

[1] *Proceedings,* XLII. 145–54.

I there put on file my recollections of that mid-day Washington Sunday dinner of 1861. Seward then said, referring to Lincoln and his intercourse with him: "The President has a curious vein of sentiment running through his thought, which is his most valuable mental attribute." Long subsequent events gave a noticeable significance to those words, and caused me to bear them freshly in recollection. They showed, in my opinion, not only considerable insight, but a most creditable spirit of appreciation on Seward's part. Few men in public life, then or now, would have noticed the attribute at all; and the few who did would, most of them, have taken it as an element of weakness. It was one of not a few casual remarks of Seward in those days which have caused me to realize that, with all his "outs," he was after all a man of finer fibre than the rest.

Lincoln's inauguration (Monday) came with a sudden change of weather. The sun shone brightly, but a strong wind carried on it clouds of that Washington dust, which, then much more than now — for the streets were not yet asphalted — was wont to render walking detestable on days of early March. I wrote two accounts of what took place; one in my diary, which, however, was rather short, as I also wrote for publication a long descriptive letter, printed a few days later in the Boston *Transcript*.[1] It was dated March 4th. From the Senate gallery I saw Lincoln walk in, arm in arm with Buchanan, and the two seated themselves in front of the desk of the Vice-President. And, "in spite of the wry neck and dubious eye, the outgoing President was," to my mind, "undeniably the more presentable man of the two; his tall, large figure, and white head, looked well beside Mr.

[1] March 7, over the signature of "Conciliator."

Lincoln's lank, angular form and hirsute face; and the dress of the President-elect did not indicate that knowledge of the proprieties of the place which was desirable." Then followed the inaugural, delivered from "the miserable scaffold" on the east front before "a vast sea, not exactly of upturned human faces, but of hats and shirt-bosoms of all descriptions." Of the inaugural, I did not hear one word; for I was standing on a projection of the unfinished Senate wing of the Capitol, watching the scene, and was thus too far removed. But "Mr. Lincoln's delivery struck me as good; for it was quiet, with but little gesture and small pretence of oratory; the audience did not strike me as very enthusiastic — not such as they tell us hailed Jackson when he stood on the same steps on the occasion of the first invasion of Washington by the hordes of the youthful West — but it was silent, attentive, appreciative, and wonderfully respectable and orderly. At length a louder and more prolonged cheer announced that the inaugural was delivered. The Chief Justice administered the oath of office, and the long, eager, anxious struggle was over. A Republican President was safely inaugurated.

"Not until the ceremony was over did the curious cease to speculate as to the probabilities of 'a bead being drawn on Mr. Lincoln,' and the chances of assassination; and the question was curiously discussed whether the whole South would not yet furnish one Ravaillac." Now the procession was re-formed, and the new President was escorted to the White House. I started for home. As I walked up by way of F Street and the Patent Office, parallel with Pennsylvania Avenue, the procession's route, I chanced to meet Mr. Sumner, and joined him. "He seemed satisfied with the inaugural, and remarked of it: 'I do not suppose Lincoln had it in his mind, if indeed he ever heard of it; but the inaugural seems to me best described by Napoleon's simile of "a hand of iron and a velvet glove."" At home, on the other hand, I found my father in high glee over the endorsement that same inaugural gave him, and he was declaring the party saved. I also met Winter Davis, who pronounced himself as ready to stand on the President's position." Thus, that day, every one was, as Seward predicted they would be, "satisfied."

Returning to my walk home with Mr. Sumner; "all day I had looked in vain for the tall, commanding figure of General Scott; he was not in the procession; he was not in the Senate. As I left the Capitol" and was walking home-ward in company with Mr. Sumner, I came, at one of the intersecting avenues where a view was obtained in several directions, "upon a small carriage, drawn by a single horse and surrounded by mounted staff officers and orderlies, the whole the centre of a crowd of idlers. It was Scott's carriage, and in it sat the old General himself, in full uniform, anxiously observing the procession as it passed in the street beyond, and holding himself ready for any emergency. What was now dreaded was, of course, assassination followed by riot and panic, and an immediate necessity for a display of force; the fear of a *coup de main* was passed." Mr. Sumner stopped, and exchanged greetings with Scott through the open win-dow of his carriage. The old General shook hands with us, and seemed in high spirits and greatly relieved, as he watched intently the perfectly quiet progress of events below, on Pennsylvania Avenue. In his staff were several officers destined soon to have high rank and participate in great movements; they also were now in high spirits — satisfied with themselves, and feeling that the situation was well in hand. We walked in a street converging with the movement of the procession, which, at length, "enveloped in its cloud of dust, reached the White House, and I drew a long breath when I saw Mr. Lincoln leave his carriage; and turned away confident that the last danger was passed."

We all, the hope being father of the thought, had then nursed ourselves into a feverish faith, and anxious rather than real belief that, with a peaceful inauguration, the crisis would be really in safety "passed," and I closed this letter of mine in that spirit. "From this time," I wrote, "the secession experiment, I believe, will die away, and the Union feeling rise almost visibly, day by day, unless again the secession feeling is revived by some sort of strange folly on the part of the Administration. Within the last few days I have conversed with many men from the South, including even South Carolina, and all announce a better, kinder state of feeling, needing only gentleness and conciliation to ripen into Union." The one fact to which we then pinned our faith in an ultimate peaceful solution was in the avoidance as yet of any act of overt violence resulting in the shedding of blood. Until this should actually occur we nourished a hope, amounting almost to a faith, that, somehow or other, it was fated not to occur. Yet all the time we were conscious that we were drifting with neither guidance nor control. It was a period of anxious suspense; a fading reliance on "something."

A few days later, I attended the new President's first evening levee. "A pretty business it was. Such a crush was, I imagine, never seen in the White House before, on a similar, or any other, occasion. After two vain attempts to get into the reception room, Dexter and I resolutely set ourselves in the main current, and were pushed and squeezed along. It was a motley crowd. There they were — the sovereigns; some in evening dress, others in morning suits; with gloves and without gloves; clean and dirty; all pressing in the same direction, and all behaving with perfect propriety. There was no ill temper; no vulgarity or noise; no rudeness; in spite of the crowd and discomfort, everything was respectful and decorous. The sight was one not pleasant to see, and even less pleasant to participate in; but still good of its kind. Here, as everywhere, the people governed themselves. At last, after the breath was nearly out of our bodies, Dexter and I came in sight of the President — the tall, rapidly bobbing head of the good 'Abe,' as he shook hands with his guests, and quickly passed them along. The vastly greater number he hurried by him; but, when any one he knew came along, he bent himself down to the necessary level, and seemed to whisper a few words in the ear, in pleasant, homely fashion; though not exactly in one becoming our President. I hurried by as quickly as I could, and retreated into the rear of the room, there to observe. I stayed about an hour and a half, meeting Mr. Sumner, Mr. and Mrs. S. A. Douglas and others, and subsequently, leaving by the south front, reached home with 'tir'd eye-lids upon tir'd eyes.' "

The following Sunday it accidentally fell in my way to do an excellent turn to Dr. John G. Palfrey, than whom I may now say I have never in my life known a more truly estimable character. I do not think it is possible for a man to live more consistently up to conscientious ideals than Dr. Palfrey did through his whole life. He was almost morbidly victim to the terrible New England conscience. No man had sacrificed more than he in his advocacy of the anti-slavery cause; but wholly unimaginative, he was not sympathetic in

the human way and altogether the reverse of magnetic.
Kindly, he was of conscience all compact. Very sensitive, he
was in no way self-assertive; and the popular movement had
passed him by. In the day of triumph, he seemed likely to go
unrewarded; buried there at Cambridge, immersed in his
history of New England, but needy and craving recognition.
I had talked with both Sumner and my father about him,
and had written home to ascertain what sort of an appointment would be agreeable to him. As yet, we had been unable
to fix on anything. Sunday, the 10th, I called to see Mr.
Sumner at his lodgings — a sitting- and bed-room on F Street,
I think. Presently, after some office-seekers had betaken
themselves away, we began to discuss Dr. Palfrey's case. He
alluded to a letter he had received from him [Palfrey] on the
subject, in which he had spoken of what he would like, but
nothing definite seemed to come out of it all; and then "he
[Sumner] suddenly turned to me, saying: 'By the way, I have
drawn an elephant, and don't know what to do with it.
Yesterday I was at the Post-Office Department, and Mr.
Blair [the Postmaster-General] informed me that the Boston
Post-Office belonged to me, as a Senator living in that city;
and I'm sure I don't know what to do with it.' It seemed
that the postmastership in the place of his residence was a
bit of patronage conceded as a perquisite to a Senator,
though Mr. Sumner was not even aware of the fact, having
always been in opposition. I at once hesitatingly suggested
Dr. Palfrey for the appointment; and, finding it not unfavor-
ably received, pressed the idea hard upon him. Feeling that
I had made an impression, I got him to promise to dine with
us." This was a happy stroke on my part; for it had been
Sumner's habit to take his Sunday dinner in a perfectly

informal way at my father's. He came uninvited, but with absolute regularity, and was always very welcome. When, however, my father had, during the winter, shown indications of a conciliatory bearing towards the South, Sumner had discontinued his Sunday dinner practice. So doing was intensely characteristic. A difference of opinion even on a question of policy in a man's manners and bearing in the conduct of the issue on slavery, he then classed with moral delinquencies. His friendship and family intimacy my father and mother then valued highly, their personal regard was almost traditional; and seeing him in a kindly mood, I now struck in as a conciliator. I knew, also, that my advocacy of Dr. Palfrey would be potently seconded by my father. So I hurried home, and apprised my father of the state of the case. Presently Sumner came, and that was the last time he ever sat at my father's table — he who, for over a dozen years, had been the guest most constant at it. It was, and to my mind, still is a great pity; and there was no sufficient reason for a break. However, intent on Palfrey's case, that day I got Mr. Sumner there once more, and, as it proved, for the last time. "He was in great feather. Such a wonderful change I never saw in mortal man. The excitement and other peculiarities, which had so disgusted me in our previous interviews during this visit to Washington, had disappeared. They had vanished wholly under the soothing influence of success, and beneath the calm dignity of the chairmanship of the Senate Committee on Foreign Affairs. He now aired his new importance; and, in place of his former fierceness, he roared as gently as a sucking dove. The pleasant way in which he looked upon propositions, which, only the week before, were 'compromises' with Hell, was, indeed, beautiful

to behold. To-day he was great! He talked of Seward and
the diplomatic corps; and told us all the secrets of the Cabinet, so far as he knew them; how Mrs. Lincoln wanted to
make a Collector of the Port of Boston, on account of her son
'Bobby,' and *had* made a naval officer; how disgusted the
diplomatic corps was at the possible nomination of Schurz
to Turin; how Lincoln and Seward had a conversation about
Schurz, in which Seward convinced Lincoln that Schurz
ought not to be sent, and Lincoln sent him to Seward, for
them to fight the matter out together; how the Western
barbarians had invaded the White House, and Mr. Lincoln
was meddling with every office in the gift of the Executive.
Finally, he began on Palfrey, so I took myself off, leaving
him in my father's hands."

That evening I went to the reception at Mrs. Eames's.
"If the President caught it at dinner, his wife caught it at
the reception. All manner of stories about her were flying
around; she wanted to do the right thing, but, not knowing
how, was too weak and proud to ask; she was going to put the
White House on an economical basis, and, to that end, was
about to dismiss 'the help,' as she called the servants; some
of whom, it was asserted, had already left because 'they must
live with gentlefolks'; she had got hold of newspaper report-
ers and railroad conductors, as the best persons to go to for
advice and direction. Numberless stories of this sort were
current; and, while Mrs. Lincoln was in a stew, it was obvious that her friends, the Illinoisans, were in a rumpus. Much
fun is brewing in Washington." It was now the dead season
in Washington, or rather, that year, the season of lull before
the fierce bursting of the storm. Congress had dispersed;
and expectancy was in the air, with greedy office-seekers

thronging streets and corridors. And such streets and such corridors! The unheroic was much in evidence.

We all left Washington on the 13th. Two evenings before Seward dined with us. He was now Secretary of State, and just two weeks later Russell, of the *Times*, reached Washington and had those conversations with him of which he has in his *My Diary* given such a vivid, picturesque *résumé*. By the 10th of the month the Cabinet complications, which reached a climax three weeks later, had begun to develop. The question of mastery was yet to be settled. The President was an absolutely unknown quantity; so much so that a little later, as subsequently appeared, Seward invited him practically to abdicate, delegating full authority to himself. We, of my father's house, were all ardent Sewardites. We thought that in him, and the pursuance of the policy he either had devised, or at the proper time would devise, lay the single chance of peace and the preservation of the Union. As I now see it, his usefulness was, however, in fact then over. He had been of great service, during the interim period, holding things together and tiding over dangerous shoals. This he had done; but he had done it under an entire misapprehension of the real facts of the situation and with an absolutely impossible result in view. As I have said, he believed in the existence of a strong underlying Union sentiment in the South; he looked forward with confidence to a sharp reaction of sentiment there, as soon as the people of those States realized that no harm was intended them; and he nourished the delusive belief that a recourse to force could be avoided; that, if it was avoided or postponed, the secession movement would languish, and gradually die out. Thus he was now exerting all his influence, greater by far than that of any other one man, in a wrong direction. The possession of the Government having been secured, the true policy to be pursued, it is now obvious, was to let events take their course, inducing or compelling the seceded States to put themselves in the wrong by assuming the initiative, striking the first blow. A statesman equal to the occasion and grasping the situation in its full scope, would undoubtedly have pursued this course. Gathering his resources, he would have bided his time, perhaps covertly provoking the blow. But Seward was no Bismarck, and this was just the course Seward did not wish to have pursued.

That evening, the 11th, he talked freely, and the next day I incorporated the substance of all he said in a letter printed shortly after in the Boston *Transcript*.[1] It is before me now, pasted in my Scrap-book, and is supplemented by passages in my diary. Talking in his off-hand way, Seward then expressed to us, as four weeks later he did to Mr. Russell,[2] "the fullest confidence that things were coming out right; but he at the same time admitted that, three months before, it was in no way impossible that Jefferson Davis might, at the time he was speaking to us, have been in possession of Washington. 'Ever since Congress met,' he said, 'we have been on a lee shore. The sails have been flapping, and more than once we have thugged on the bottom; but we have been making offing all the time, and are now getting safely off shore and into deep water.'" As Russell the moment he got into the Confederacy afterwards became satisfied, Seward knew nothing of the real state of feeling in the South.[3] He derived what little knowledge he had from local and unreliable, or misinformed, sources. So, this evening, he did not hesitate

[1] March 15. [2] *My Diary*, i. 88, 103. [3] *Ib.*, i. 168.

to assert that "the fever of secession" was "fast disappearing, before the strong reaction for Union. The political traitors of that region," he said — "the Hunters, Masons, Wises, Clingmans and Garnetts — are trembling for their lives, and their only chance, and they know it, of retaining their power, lies in the revival of the excitement." The abandonment of Fort Sumter, he argued, would therefore not be taken by the South as a sign of weakness, but, on the contrary, would give "a new and tremendous emphasis to the now rapidly reviving Union spirit. The true men of Virginia will, at the close of the coming April, sweep every representative, even suspected of treason, from the National Congress, and forewarn the chuckle-headed Mason and sophistical Hunter of their impending fate; and Virginia would but set an example to other States. To hold Fort Sumter longer" was, therefore, "to stop the mouth and palsy the arm of every Union man, and there are many of them, throughout the seceded States, for no important end." The abandonment of Sumter he considered, therefore, "a mere question of time. It might be done then, and made the basis of a claim of gratitude by the Administration; or it might be done thirty days hence as a matter of necessity, and no credit gained. If we set out to reinforce it, we must join battle at our weakest point, and the enemy's strongest; our loss might be heavy, while our gain could not be great." Hence, I argued in the *Transcript*, the abandonment was decided upon, and might be looked for any day. Thus at this stage of the development of affairs—with a crisis immediately impending — Seward was pursuing an impossible result in pursuance of a policy devised under an entire misapprehension of facts. Meanwhile, to abandon the Tortugas or Fort

Pickens was no part of Mr. Seward's plan. Those could be held and defended; what he had in mind was to avoid a collision at a point where we could not hope to escape defeat.

Accompanied by his family, my father left Washington, and returned home, all of us nourishing this delusive hope of peace and a restored Union. Once in Boston, we heard nothing. On the 19th came the telegraphic announcement of my father's nomination to the English Mission. "It fell on our breakfast-table like a veritable bomb-shell, scattering confusion and dismay. It had been much discussed in Washington, but Seward had encountered so much difficulty, and the President had seemed so intent on the nomination of Dayton, that the news finally came on us like a thunderbolt. My mother at once fell into tears and deep agitation; foreseeing all sorts of evil consequences, and absolutely refusing to be comforted; while my father looked dismayed. The younger members of the household were astonished and confounded." Such was my diary record. It is droll to look back on; very characteristic and Bostonese. My father and mother had lived there steadily for nearly thirty years. They had grown into a rut, and begun to entertain a species of religious cult on that head. My mother, in some respects remarkably calculated for social life, took a constitutional and sincere pleasure in the forecast of evil. She delighted in the dark side of anticipation; she did not really think so; but liked to think, and say, she thought so. She indulged in the luxury of woe! So now, I remember well how she nursed herself into a passing belief that somehow she was very much to be compassioned, and something not far removed from disgrace had fallen upon us and upon her; and when she went out people would look at her, and say, "Poor woman," etc., etc. It seemed to give her quite a new view of the matter, when presently every one she met, instead of avoiding a painful subject or commiserating her, offered her congratulations or expressions of envy. So she cheered up amazingly. As to my father, he had then lived so long in the atmosphere of Boston, that I really think the great opportunity of his life when suddenly thrust upon him caused a sincere feeling of consternation. He really felt that he was being called on to make a great personal and political sacrifice.

As for me, I now went back to my office. Presently my father was summoned on to Washington to confer with the Secretary. He was there during the closing days of March, getting home on the 1st of April. I well remember his return. It then lacked only four days of a full month since the inauguration of Lincoln, and there were no visible signs of that reaction in the sentiment of the South which Seward had looked for with such confidence. On the contrary, though the new Administration did not threaten to resort to coercion, the Confederacy seemed to be fast consolidating. Nor in the border States did the aspect of affairs improve; on the contrary, it day by day grew unmistakably menacing. My diary read as follows: "My father, summoned by Seward to Washington a week ago, got home last night. For several days, now, I have been conscious of a vague presentiment that things were not going well. Instead of righting itself and coming up into the wind as soon as it was free of the incubus of a Democratic Administration — as I all along had so confidently hoped and predicted — the ship seemed, on the contrary, to be steadily and helplessly drifting upon the rocks, Secession and Reconstruction. So strongly had this feeling got a hold on me, that, when my father came into the breakfast-room, I feared to ask him any question on the subject. I did at last; and, at first, he seemed to deny that any change for the worse was apparent. Yet a few more inquiries were enough. It was at once apparent that my apprehensions were not only well founded, but that the real truth was worse than I supposed. We are drifting; and drifting fearfully. Our last card has proved a low one; the card on which we relied for everything. It is not the ace of trumps, but only the deuce; if, indeed, it be a trump card at all."

Whether my father then still clung to the hope of a peaceable solution of the troubles, I cannot say. On that point I never satisfied myself. In immediate presence of the inevitable, I think we were all, and he especially, in a state approaching mental bewilderment; we would not acknowledge that of which we could not help being inwardly conscious. We were, in fact, exactly in the position of people, passengers and landsmen, on some battered hulk drifting slowly but surely on the reefs that outlined a menacing lee shore. The ship had not yet struck, but we waited breathlessly to hear and feel her strike. Seward had in Washington evidently still talked to my father in the old, optimistic, hopeful vein; just as, a week later, he still talked in it to Russell. That, however, would not longer pass current; and for myself, I can only say that, from the moment I saw my father after he got back, I ceased to hope. War, I felt, confronted us. As I wrote, it was a bitter day — "without, a furious snow-storm raging; within, for me at least, doubt, hesitation and gloom." The only consolation I had was in the nomination of Dr. Palfrey as Postmaster of Boston; a result I had been instrumental in bringing about, "a long deferred act of political justice," for which Dr. Palfrey, by a note written immediately after receiving the news of his appointment, signified his sense of obligation to me individually. Three days later I wrote: "Fast day! and never did this country stand in greater need of aid from above than now. Still drifting — drifting — drifting! Our case resembles nothing so much as that of a ship, which, close on a lee shore, has only just weathered a violent storm. Morning has broken, not fresh and bright, but murky and sullen. The wind has died away, but a strong under-tow is bearing us imperceptibly nearer and nearer those rocks over which tremendous seas are dashing. Unless God helps us, we shall in a few moments be in the breakers." Then follow the usual weak observations and objurgations over the absence of a guiding hand at the helm, useless to repeat now, though natural enough then. Ten days afterwards, on the 14th, I wrote: "The war has begun! Fort Sumter is taken! Two bad announcements together. Yet strangely enough no drop of blood has yet been shed; or rather no life has been lost. Still, the first gun in civil war is fired, and its echoes will reverberate through years."

I continued to keep a sort of intermittent diary — making entries sometimes every day, but more usually once a week or so — for the next year and a half, the last record being written on the transport steamer which brought my regiment up from Hilton Head to Fortress Monroe, at the time of Pope's ignominious Virginia campaign, in August, 1862. This portion of my diary had, however, little, if any, value. I find I rarely recorded what I saw, or noted conversations; and, living in a provincial city, I had no special sources of information, nor did I often meet persons of any particular note. It was the dreary, commonplace existence of a young man, wasting his time in a professional life for which he, correctly enough, believed himself most illy adapted, in an out-of-the-way region but during a curiously exciting but most critical crisis in public affairs. Thus my diary naturally became almost wholly introspective; my worse than useless introspections being diversified by lengthy lucubrations over the varying aspects of the situation.

I did find in my diary before destroying it a few passages worth transcribing, having reference to incidents which occurred during those memorable eight months, April to December, 1861. It was on the 13th of April that the Confederate whip came down across the Northern face; and my father sailed for Europe on the 1st of May. Nominated on the 18th of March and at once confirmed, he did not reach his London post until the 13th of May — exactly eight weeks, or fifty-six days, later. Such a delay, at such a crisis, seems inexplicable, as it was, in fact, inexcusable. Considering the extremely critical state of affairs and the possible consequences delay might entail, the newly appointed minister should have left on the steamer first following his appointment, his instructions, if necessary, following him. He should have been in London at least a month earlier than my father got there. As it was, the Southern Commissioners were on the ground first, and scored the apparently great success of a recognition of belligerency before he arrived. For reasons I have set forth in my *Life of Charles Francis Adams*, this turned out in the sequel of events a most fortunate occurrence;[1] that it did so turn out was, however, a bit of good luck saving the country from the consequence of a piece of unpardonable laches. There is a secret history

[1] *Life*, 173.

attached to the incident, and I, then and later, came into possession of it.

One day, I think it was during the third year of the Civil War, when I chanced to be in Washington, Seward, then Secretary of State, remarked to me in his off-hand but consequential way: "The greatest misfortune that ever happened to the United States was that the marriage of your brother occurred on the 29th of April, 1861." We had been talking of the rebel rams, and the attitude of Great Britain towards this country, then very uncertain and menacing. I knew what he meant. At the time my father was appointed to the English Mission — a month before Sumter — my brother John was about to be married. The date was fixed for April 29th. My father wanted to be present; and, when, immediately after his confirmation, he went on to Washington, he intimated that he would defer his sailing until the 1st of May, if no exigency was thought to exist requiring an earlier departure. Seward assented, whether reluctantly or against his better judgment, I do not know; but at that time he was still dwelling in his "Southern Unionist" dream-land, and apparently had no realizing sense of the extremely critical state of affairs, in Europe as well as at home. He quite a time afterwards prepared in a leisurely way the memorable instructions which he characteristically read to Russell, of the *Times*, on the evening of April 8th.[1] The crisis of Sumter came on five days after that reading, and then followed the brief isolation of Washington. Those instructions, thus communicated in advance to the correspondent of a London newspaper, did not accordingly reach my father until April 27th, and he sailed four days afterwards. Every stage of our

[1] *My Diary*, i. 102.

action was thus marked by extreme deliberation; and the Confederate Commissioners took full advantage of the fact. There can, I think, be no question that my brother John's marriage on the 29th of April, 1861, led to grave international complications. It is creditable to neither Seward nor my father that the latter was allowed to dawdle away weeks of precious time because of such a trifle. It was much as if a general had permitted some social engagement to keep him away from his headquarters on the eve of a great battle; and, in his absence, the enemy secured possession of some coigne of great vantage. The course of subsequent events, as I have elsewhere pointed out,[1] transformed this apparent mishap into a fortunate occurrence.

[1] *Life of Charles Francis Adams*, 173; see also the paper on "The British Proclamation of May, 1861," in *Mass. Hist. Soc. Proceedings*, XLVIII. 190.

IV

WAR AND ARMY LIFE

At that time I had already entered into a sort of military life. A member of the Fourth Battalion of Massachusetts Volunteer Militia I was in garrison at Fort Independence, in Boston Harbor, and a most useful and instructive elementary military school that experience proved. Elementary in the extreme, it was all the preliminary training I ever had. But on that head I shall have more to say presently — confessions, I might call them, to record. Sumter was fired on upon a Friday; but the lines of communication were broken, and "all day Sunday it was curious to notice the agitation of the people; there was but one subject of thought or of conversation. Vague and distressing rumors were flying freely about. Next morning the head-lines of the daily papers told us that it was war." The call for troops — the first of many such — went forth that day; and, my diary fairly admitted, was the occasion to me of a very uneasy night. Seven months later, I received my long wished-for commission, and started off with my regiment, with positive elation. I had in the interim been educated up to the full fighting figure; but, in April, it was like an alarm-bell at midnight. It was with a shock I realized the situation. "War," I wrote that day, "is no plaything, and, God knows, I have no wish to trifle with it. I, therefore, shall not now volunteer, or expose myself to unnecessary service. But I can, and will, obey orders at any sacrifice, and, if called upon, shall go into active service. Not to do so, would be to incur lasting disgrace, in comparison with which the hardship and boredom and danger of a campaign would be a festive pastime. If I must do it — and I hope I must n't — I may as well put a good face on it. The back is ever strengthened to the burden. To-day, I shrink from the idea of a skirmish. Three weeks hence, I doubt not, my mind will be trained up to fierce battle, if need be." I at least then understood myself to that extent!

The same day the regiments began to come in from the country, turning out full ranks. I should think much better of myself now, if that day I had turned the key in my office-door and gone off in the ranks of the Quincy company. But so doing never even occurred to me. I simply was n't equal to the occasion — my ordinary experience in life — before, then and since. As it was, I wrote of the regiments that day pouring into Boston: "They say there were strange scenes at the country railroad stations — more weeping than is usual. In Boston here there would have been a tremendous demonstration, but for the weather; it was sufficiently striking even as it was. It has been a dreary, dismal day, storming heavily from the eastward; a day with rain enough to extinguish any degree of enthusiasm; and, as the poor devils plashed through the streets, less than half drilled and most insufficiently clad — for few country companies are supplied with overcoats — they were greeted with well-deserved applause. But I could n't help feeling badly for them." A few days later I wrote: "These be indeed stirring times, and the age has in it, after all, the elements of the heroic. It is now three days that our streets have been crowded with soldiers and draped in flags; while our populace, usually so staid and quiet, is crazy with patriotism. The contagion is, in fact, hard to resist; and often, within these three days as

I have seen these men go by, half armed and a quarter uni-
formed, many of them mere recruits, unarmed and with no
pretence of a uniform, following, carpet-bag in hand, the
rear of the column, I have felt a rising in the throat and been
conscious of a moisture in the eye, which caused me to feel
little of the soldier." Some days later there came along one
of those storms of alarmist rumors that then from time to
time developed, and one evening it was reported at one of
our leisure haunts that every available man was called for,
to be off next morning. "If this was true, it meant fight; and
we received it accordingly. Half of our battalion were new
recruits who had never handled a musket, all our officers
were inexperienced, nor was there a single uniform amongst
us; and yet we were to be ordered into immediate active
service. The men showed their pluck. Among them, there
was an outer gaiety and flow of humor; but it only covered
gravity and dismay. There was n't anywhere the faintest
sign of funk. For myself, though I kept up my spirits as well
as the best, I certainly realized how unprepared I was to go,
and what a doubtful experiment I thought it. As John and I
a little later walked up Beacon Street on our way home, the
sensation was certainly new. How many times we had trod
the same pavements before — grave and gay, drunk and
sober, from weddings and to funerals — but never until now
on the eve of battle."

At last, on the 24th of April, our battalion was ordered to
do garrison duty at Fort Independence, and so, closing my
office, I with the rest reported at the armory. We went down,
and took possession of the fort that afternoon, remaining
there five weeks. A pleasanter or more useful five weeks in
the educational way, I do not think I ever passed than those

during which I played soldier at Fort Independence in April and May, 1861. I enjoyed the experience thoroughly, and what I there learned — the details of drill and of guard duty — proved afterwards of the greatest value to me. But it was only a military kindergarten. The first night down I was in the guard detail. The guard-room — long unused and very damp — was awful; but my description of my beat was not bad, and covered many later experiences. My subsequent brother officer and life-long friend, Harry Russell, and I that night lay waking side-by-side. "The sky was at first overcast; but the clouds scattered after the rising of the moon, and, as the wind had fallen, I found my first tour of duty on the ramparts far from unpleasant. The surroundings were picturesque: on one side, beyond the parapet, the bay was gently rippling in the moonlight, which flooded the islands and shipping at anchor in the roadstead; while on the other were the walls around the parade-ground of the fort, white in the beams. In front of the guard-room a little knot of the relief were smoking and chatting, and, now and again, a cold gleam of light was reflected from the bayonet of the sentry patrolling the opposite rampart. As I walked my beat, stopping occasionally to admire the scene, I pondered the question of active service and reached my own conclusions concerning it in my particular case; and, finally, it struck me that I had never known two hours pass more rapidly than did those my two first on guard. Later, I saw the sun rise, and at six I was relieved."

John was married on the evening of the 29th of April, at Mrs. Crowninshield's house in Longwood, and my father, with the remainder of the family, sailed on the 1st of May. That afternoon I went back to Fort Independence, for which

I already felt homesick; and there, without once even desiring to go to the City, I remained for the next three weeks. The hint was a most forcible one, and I now wonder that I did not take it. I then actually loathed my office, and felt no call to my profession. My new life charmed me. I was young, strong, loved existence in the open air, was not afraid of hardship, alone of the whole garrison did I take my daily plunges from the wharf, and I had in me the elements of a thoroughly good soldier in the ranks. And yet I lacked the spirit of adventure, and the daring to throw myself into the new life. No young fellow there would have enjoyed it more.

We were relieved, and came up to town on the last day of May. After we had been dismissed at the armory, I went home to the house in Mt. Vernon Street to don my citizens' clothes, and, before going out to Quincy where the newly married John then was, I dropped in at the Parker House, on School Street, to join some friends. At their request, "I looked at myself in the mirror, and was amazed. I had in every respect the aspect of a prize-fighter. My face was brown and tanned, my hair was cut close to my head, my loose coat and blue shirt gave me a brawny reckless bearing, and I thought I had never looked so rollicking and strong, or felt so well, in all my life."

Going back to my office and its inanimate routine, the five ensuing months, though I did not then realize it, were educational. I was a conscientious young fellow in a way, with a sufficing sense of my obligation to others, especially my father. In reality everything then combined to carry me into the army. I was young, unmarried, vigorous, and, in a sense, in the way in my father's house, which my brother then occupied with his newly married wife; moreover, I was doing nothing in a profession profoundly distasteful to me. But I fostered a delusion that my presence in Boston was very essential to the proper conduct of my father's affairs, and I felt no call to arms from any love of adventure. So, ashamed to stay at home, conscious that one at least of the family ought to be with the colors, I argued the matter continually with myself. But it was only slowly, and by increasing attacks, that the ever-spreading epidemic got possession of me.

In June, I was suffering from an earlier and intermittent attack, and wrote to my father. Presently I got a letter from my brother Henry, who was with him in London. This letter has disappeared, together with all my correspondence and papers of the years before the war. I am sorry to have lost that particular letter, for it now would have an almost historical value. Few points in connection with my work on my father's life have more deeply interested me than the study of Seward's foreign-war panacea for the cure of civil dissension, in April-June, 1861; and my diary, under date of June 25, 1861, contained a reference to this letter, written by Henry the day after the receipt by my father of that despatch No. 10, of May 21st, from Seward, which Lincoln emasculated: "To-day I received a letter from Henry which fell on me like a thunderbolt from a clear sky; for, after six pages of general matter, he closed in a grand panic, telling me that the day before a despatch had been received from Seward which meant European war — that it would come within two months. His own faith in Seward was, he said, shaken, for he seemed resolved to lash the country into a foreign war. As for me, he advised me to keep cool, not gratifying my military ardor at present, but holding in reserve for a great

Canadian campaign. This letter almost terrified me, chiefly
because of Seward. Would it not be foolish under present
circumstances, and wicked under any, to force a third party,
against its will and without provocation into a bloody war,
merely because domestic contentions were getting too hot?"

But, all the same, the letter served to cool my immediate
ardor. The struggle in which we found ourselves engaged was
at that time just beginning to assume its correct proportions
in our eyes; and I chafed bitterly over the empty escort duty
I was doing as one of the rank and file of the Fourth Battalion
— tramping the streets continually, seeing the three-year
regiments from Maine and New Hampshire off on their way
to Washington; and I wrote in reply to Henry that I was
"still eager for release. And why should I not be? Have I
not failed in my profession? Am I not continually hungry
for some outside stimulus? Is it not now offered me? And in
what respect has my past been so successful, or in what way
is my future so brilliant in promise, that I should so long
hesitate to risk my life in this quarrel?"

A few weeks later my diary recorded a portent I still well
remember; though I have never seen it alluded to in any book
on that period. One evening early in July we had been drilling in the armory of the Battalion, then in the old Boylston
Market Building, corner of Washington and Boylston Streets.
As we left it, turning towards the Common, the exclamation
burst from several at once, "Why, there's a comet!" It was
the great comet of 1861 — the comet which took the whole
scientific world by surprise; for its advent had not been fore-
told, and of it nothing was known. As striking as it was unforeseen, it fairly burst on a startled world. The next day
the astronomers confessed themselves as much at a loss con-

cerning it as the most superstitious layman, and I wrote of it: "Close to the Dipper and, as it were, in the centre of our Heavens, with its head not far from the North-star, its trail streamed away to the southward like a milky way. But the question which perplexed all — astronomers and laymen — was: Where did it come from, and how did it get here? But here it is, brilliant beyond description as it streams across the sky. Already it is vanishing, and in a few nights will be invisible. What a curious coincidence! In Europe, it can hardly have been seen at all, for it shone high in our Heavens. It has come on our National Anniversary, bursting upon us unheralded and in the midst of our civil commotions. Its stay seems likely to be as short as it is brilliant. Who can read us the riddle?"

On the 4th of July, Gordon's regiment, afterwards the memorable Second Massachusetts Infantry, went off, we, the Fourth Battalion, doing escort service. It was largely officered by my old friends, who crowded the platforms of the cars and waved salutes as the train got in motion. It was a day of great heat; and "then, as usual after thus seeing others on their way to the real strife, we quietly marched back to our armory — and were not ashamed!" A few days later "Stephen Perkins, one of the very few close friends of my own I ever had, went off, too; and I did not even see him before he went. At the last moment he accepted a second lieutenant's commission in the Gordon regiment, and followed it two days after. I had advised his going; but, when he departed so suddenly, his going fell heavily on me. Whether I ever see him again depends on the fate of war." I never did see him again. Thirteen months later he was killed at Cedar Mountain, in Virginia. I realized that a place was made vacant in my circle not again to be filled. I have the sense of that loss still.

The Bull Run experience came a few days after the departure of the Second. My diary contained a long entry relating to it, simply setting forth the sensations of one individual American far removed from the scene of action. That incident of the war and the ensuing stampede occurred on a Sunday. I passed the day at Quincy, and the battle, well known to be impending, was the one topic of thought or talk. Monday morning the papers were full of encouraging reports; but very general. Getting to my office I had just finished a letter, when "my heart sank within me as I suddenly heard the newsboys shout in the street, 'Retreat of the Federal Army!' Just then Dana (R. H.) came in on some business; often have I seen Dana under trying circumstances, but never before *distrait*, or outwardly flustered. But now the tidings of a reverse weighed heavily on him, and he could n't even pretend to think or talk of anything else. At that time we supposed it was simply an orderly retreat to Centreville, which seemed bad enough; and, though I could n't work, in this pleasant faith I remained until, leaving the office, I met Caspar Crowninshield looking absolutely pale, and he then poured out to me the frightful tale of running men, captured artillery, abandoned arms and blasted honor. I too turned pale as I listened. We started for the news-room, and, passing through State Street, we could not help observing those strange and significant little knots of men with troubled faces, so suggestive of times of deep excitement." Dining at Quincy, we were unable to resist the desire to know what further tidings might have come, and Caspar and I drove back to town to see Boston in the hour of bitterest defeat. "The news we found, in some respects, a little less discouraging; but, as for the city, its quiet was remarkable. A few crowds lingered about the telegraph offices and the newspaper buildings, long closed, and those composing them stood in small knots, talking in subdued tones, and circulating the most awful rumors as to the dead and missing. Nervous excitement was the feature of the night; but the city was wholly quiet, and no news could be obtained."

Bull Run was followed by a regular panic — one of many, preceding and following, in which Washington either was, or was believed to be, in danger of capture. During it, my mind was always balancing arguments, should I go, or stay? I then began to realize the mistake I had made in not going earlier, and I wrote: "Would to God now that I had been ordered away, or had of my own accord joined some organization sent forward to Washington in April last, that I too might have been found ready, when to be ready was the duty of every man. But not," etc., etc., through the whole gamut of honest self-deception. There was then, as subsequent events showed, no earthly reason why I should not have gone, and the best of reasons why I should go, and go at once; but, I argued, if I now go, "I do so because I am carried away by the enthusiasm of those around me, or in the desire of a new and exciting life, with a chance of military distinction. I feel that war is not my vocation; and that, in deserting the law for it, I should give up a profession for which I am little adapted for one to which I am adapted even less. This disposes also of my chance of military distinction, and leaves only the question of yielding to the contagion about me. That a soldier's life would give a new impetus to my energies, I know; that in it I should be happy and grow, I am well enough aware; incidentally, also, it might, and, I fancy, would lead to many advantageous things; but these possible advantages, though they weigh heavily enough with me, will not justify my leaving the manifest duties which ought to keep me here. My father has entrusted me with the care of the bulk of his property, and never was property so difficult to manage as it now is," etc., etc., "and these considerations of real duty must outweigh the possible advantages to result from novelty, excitement and activity. Yes! this chance is gone by, and I feel that I shall not take part in the war." All of which shows that at twenty-five I was a good deal of a prig, as well as addicted to a mild form of sophistry. The fact was that my father, with the coldness of temperament natural to him, took a wholly wrong view of the subject and situation, did not believe in any one taking a hand in actual fight, and wholly failed to realize that it would have been an actual disgrace had his family, of all possible families American, been wholly unrepresented in the field. And I was the one to go! At the same time, I did understand myself, and recognize my own limitations. I had no natural call to a military life.

Early in September the Twentieth broke camp at Readville, and went to the Potomac. The Twentieth was largely officered by my friends. Frank Palfrey, wounded and disabled at Antietam, was its lieutenant-colonel; Paul Revere, killed at Gettysburg, was major. I saw them off. With them went Caspar Crowninshield, my household companion during the summer, destined to be my camp companion later on, and friend for long years. He died early in 1897, while I was living in Florence. It was a thoughtful day for me — that pleasant, soft September noon when I shook hands all around in the bustling camp, and then rode home to Quincy; and I wrote in my diary that "I tried to feel satisfied with Quincy and myself. I might have commanded the right of the line of that regiment; and, instead, I am scolding tenants, auditing bills, discussing repairs, rendering accounts, and so — doing my duty ! — Psh!"

This was in September, and the struggle went on all through that month and the following. At last things were ripe, and what may be termed the psychological crisis came about. On the 30th of October, I thus recorded a very memorable event in my life: "I have astonished myself within forty-eight hours. I have applied for the commission in the cavalry regiment, which, on Saturday last, I declined! Monday afternoon I went out to ride. It was a clear, windy afternoon, and the autumn leaves gleamed through the crisp October air in the afternoon sunshine. As I was walking my horse through the Braintree woods and meditating on my enforced staying at home, it suddenly flashed across me, Why do I stay at home? And sure enough the reasons that, two months ago, seemed so strong, all had vanished. The business questions were all disposed of; nothing more requiring my presence here seemed likely to arise; and so, Why should I not go? The first sensation was not pleasant; and I found myself instinctively clinging to my old, old reasons, now only excuses; but, in another moment, I was all aglow. During that ride, I thought of nothing else; and, when I got home from it, my mind was made up. I said nothing to any one; but, yesterday, I sent a note to Sargent, asking for a captaincy." The regiment in question was the

First Massachusetts Cavalry; Sargent was its lieutenant-colonel — Horace Binney Sargent, of the class of 1843; in 1861 a man of a little less than forty, whom I had known rather well for some years back; and, for some reason, had of him conceived a good opinion, which subsequent events in no way confirmed. Meanwhile, my delay had been productive, in one respect at least, of fortunate results. In the earliest stages of the war the powers that were had been slow in reaching any adequate conception either of its magnitude or of the time it would occupy. It had been assumed that no volunteer mounted regiments would be called into the service, as the preparation and training of cavalry required more time than could be given in view of the early ending of the conflict then anticipated as of course. No cavalry regiment from Massachusetts was called for until August; and though, like so many other of my friends, I might not improbably have then been transferred to it from an earlier infantry organization, I was in October just in time. Meeting Sargent in one of my afternoon rides, it had occurred to him to offer me a commission; which I, at the time, declined, in accordance with my earlier theory of duty at home. A few days later the cogitations of that afternoon ride through the Braintree woods in the October atmosphere settled the question. From that moment I did not again hesitate. The relief of a resolution taken was great. Even now, though more than fifty years have since passed on, I look back on that ride as at the moment of an inspiration — the time when I resolved to burst the bonds, and strike out into the light from the depth of the darkness. No wiser determination did I ever reach.

In November the news one day reached Boston of the

stopping of the *Trent* by Captain Wilkes, and the seizure of
Mason and Slidell, the Confederate "envoys." In view of
my subsequent investigations of this affair, and conclusions
thereon as set forth in the elaborate paper contained in the
published *Proceedings* of the Massachusetts Historical Society for November, 1911,[1] my contemporary record was
rather curious, reflecting the tempestuous character of the
time: "I have never known news spread so quickly, or seen
people so astonished, so delighted and so perplexed. First
came a cackle of joy; and then, immediately on its heels, the
question, What will England do? Immediately on hearing the
news I went round to Dana's (R. H.) office, and asked about
the law. The common fear as to England's attitude was
I found, not shared in that quarter; for Dana crowed with
delight as I told him, declaring that 'the Ambassador' could
on that issue 'blow Earl Russell out of the water'; and pro-
nouncing himself ready to stake his 'professional reputation
on the proposition.'" During the ensuing days, the seizure,
and the law relating to it, were the sole subjects of conversation, and the newspapers were prolific of arguments and
precedents; "but," I wrote, "no argument or citation of
authorities could shake off the sense of alarm, and, in the
face of the law, stocks would fall; which last fact clearly
showed that our talk of going to war with England had in it
a considerable infusion of brag. Still, our friends 'the Am-
bassadors' were in durance vile, which was a solid comfort;
and, in sleet and snow, in chilling winds and under cheerless
skies, my spirits rose as I walked to and from the railroad
station (for we were still at Quincy, and my walk to the
train was over the hill and commanded a full view of Boston

[1] XLV. 35.

Bay), and looked at the low, distant walls of Fort Warren, surrounded by the steel-blue sea, and reflected that those amiable gentlemen were there; and there they would remain! I remembered the last exhibition I saw Mason make of himself in the Senate-chamber; and I smacked my lips with joy."

It was on the 19th of December that I at last learned definitely that my name had been sent in for the commission of first lieutenant. That evening, in the exuberance of my joy, I wrote: "Well, at last my commission! Within the next four days I shall leave this room, and my native city. My office will know me no more, and to my profession I shall bid a long farewell. A new existence opens before me; and, when I return to the old haunts, I hope it will at least be in more prosperous times and with more sanguine feelings." My surprise would have been considerable, had I then been informed that five full and eventful years — eventful to me no less than to the community — were to pass away, before I, then married and in my thirty-first year, was again to find myself a resident in Boston. But, none the less, it was, for me, a great, a blessed break in life!

Meanwhile, at the moment, I bothered myself not much over the future. The cavalry regiment had that day come into town to show itself and be reviewed. I saw it pass through the streets; and, finally, by chance merely, went to the Common. "There I found an immense crowd; but I could not help being struck by the change. The enthusiasm and glow of the spring and summer were gone. It was the same place, and there were the outgoing soldiers and there were the people; but the spirit was gone. It was December; and very different from those pleasant days in June. I got within the lines, and went to headquarters. There I fell in with Colonel Harrison Ritchie, who astonished me by the information that my name had, the day previous, been sent in to the Governor, for a commission. Rarely have I ever felt more elated. I almost gasped with delight. I was then really off! Law and office seemed at once to vanish into a dim distance, as a new life opened. Its exposures, hardships and dangers I gave no thought to in my burst of genuine satisfaction."

Looking back now, fifty years after, were I asked whether I would give up as an experience of subsequent value, both educationally and in the way of reminiscence, my three years at Harvard or my three and a half years in the army, I would have great difficulty in reaching a decision. On the whole, I am inclined to think that my three and a half years of military service and open-air life were educationally of incomparably the greater value of the two. And especially was this so for me, constituted as I was and yet am. It gave me just that robust, virile stimulus to be derived only from a close contact with Nature and a roughing it among men and in the open air, which I especially needed. The experiment was, it is true, a somewhat risky one, and involved not a few hair-breadth escapes; but I succeeded in getting through without sustaining any lasting personal or physical injury, or any moral injury at all. I never was wounded; and though, when mustered out of the service in the summer of 1865 I was a physical wreck, eighteen months of change and a subsequent temperate and healthy life repaired all waste and injury. Thus, so far as physique is concerned, I from my army experience got nothing but good. I was, and at seventy-seven am, in every way the better for it. Otherwise, that experience was not only picturesque, but of the greatest possible educational value. For two years enjoying it keenly, it, so to speak, made a man of me.

And yet, somewhat paradoxically, I have never looked back on that army experience with any degree of unalloyed satisfaction. During my service — and it was a very active service — I did my duty as well as I knew how, and to the best of my ability. I never shirked, and never got into any trouble from which I did not extricate myself with a reasonable degree of credit, if not in every instance altogether to my own subsequent satisfaction. In many cases what I ought to have done or said was much clearer to me afterwards than at the time. And yet, in connection with that whole experience I am conscious of being more and more impressed with a sense of my own limitations, deficiencies and shortcomings. Not soldierly by nature, or of a daring and aggressive temper, I have come more and more to recognize that not only had my previous training in no way fitted me for the severe experiences I then challenged, but also I have grown painfully and ever increasingly conscious of the fact that I was not aware of my own lack of preparation and any preliminary training. So to me now it is simply shocking to think of the responsibilities we then lightly assumed, and the absence in us of any adequate realizing sense of the nature of those responsibilities. When I went into active service and the command of men, my sole acquaintance with military life and its duties was derived from my four weeks' tour of duty at Fort Independence, where, a member of the Fourth Battalion, M.V.M., I acquired a little knowledge of the manual and a smattering of the details of guard duty and of company and battalion drill. It amounted in fact to nothing at all —

not even the alphabet of a calling; and yet in my estimate it seemed all that was needful. If in 1861, instead of passing the summer at Quincy and in my office, I had served an apprenticeship for three months in any military school, no matter what, it would afterwards have been to me of infinite service and incalculable value. As it was, I, like all the rest, was a mere tyro, without even an adequate sense of my own utter insufficiency, and the consequent desire to be better informed.

This lack of preliminary training affected also my whole subsequent military life. I never was properly qualified as an officer; and yet, before I got through, I performed, and in doing so acquitted myself quite as well as the average, the duties and obligations of a colonel of a regiment of twelve hundred men. But as I think of the risks I in so doing ran, not only for myself, but for my command, I am dismayed. Still, what I most needed I never had — a competent and kindly instructor, a military preceptor and model. At the very outset ill fortune placed me in this respect in one of the most unfortunate and altogether trying positions any young fellow could have been projected into. I was put under the immediate command of two men even less qualified to instruct than I myself; and who together probably were as unfitted for the work to be performed as was possible. And these were my military preceptors! The constitutionally unqualified were to instruct the uninformed. Into that painful portion of my experience I do not care to enter. Let it pass into oblivion. I staggered and blundered through it. Nevertheless, educationally, my ill luck was indeed phenomenal; and so impresses me even more now than at the time. But that episode constitutes a page in my experiences to

which I refer in extenuation, as it were, of my own shortcomings. As an officer, all I ever learned I learned from
rough experience and as an outcome of my own blunders.
Nevertheless, though my case was in all these respects
exceptional, I was as an officer indisputably one of the better
class; for, though I did not appreciate my own deficiencies, I
at least had a sense of obligation, and a high standard of
duty. Nor did I ever try to advertise myself or to exploit
my services. Considering everything, I think I may say I got
out of it uncommonly well.

Recurring now to the course of events, it was on a Sunday, the 28th of December, 1861 — a very dull, gloomy and
generally forbidding day — that the First Massachusetts
Cavalry was loaded on to railroad cars, and started for New
York as its first stopping place, and subsequent point of
embarkation for Port Royal, then recently fallen into our
hands. I had reported for duty a day or two previous only,
and as first lieutenant been assigned to a company. Going
from a city house in Boston into a canvas camp at Christmas,
in Massachusetts, is, as I see it now, rather a severe experience. Then I was young and full of ardor, and disposed to
take everything in an uncomplaining spirit. But, certainly,
as compared with what I remembered of the same sort of
thing during the summer months, our home parting was to
the last degree dreary. So far as my own position was concerned, it was by no means so bad as it might have been.
I was not the utter greenhorn in uniform I would have been
but for my experience at Fort Independence; and I took hold
as one somewhat familiar with camp routine. None the less,
it was the very close of the year — cold, drear and pitiless;
and it required youth and health and buoyancy to stand it.

My description at the time of that Sunday of camp-breaking was not bad. My brother John came out from Boston to bring Caspar Crowninshield, his wife's brother, and me, some articles and bid us good-bye. He found us busy with preparation; but, at last, all was ready. "What a dreary three hours followed! A cold, grey sky overhead, with ice and frozen mud underfoot. In the distance, the familiar Blue Hills looked black and cheerless, their sides patched with snow. The air was rough and biting, and we, tired, hungry and impatient, waited for the ending of inexplicable delays. John alone was there to see me off; and, for this, I was thankful. I felt in a mood neither regretful nor sentimental; and, so far from lingering over farewells to home, I asked only to get away. It was dreary enough. Little knots of friends were collected everywhere; but no one seemed to care for anything. Grief and joy alike were frozen out. Finally, John gave out, and declared he could stand the dreary discomfort no longer; and I must say it was not without a sensation of envy I in thought followed him back to his comfortable dinner. At last we found ourselves on board the cars. I can pretend no sentiment at leaving home behind me; I felt none. The only strong sensation I had was one of relief at getting in motion and, at last, having something to eat."

I have dwelt in detail over this period of my life simply because, passing it in an eventful time, I then kept a contemporaneous record. That record extended through the larger part of the following year, until my regiment reached Virginia in early September, 1862, and I went into active field service. I then almost perforce discontinued it, nor was it renewed for twenty-six years; though I believe I always kept a brief daily memorandum of where I was, and what I was doing.

During my years of active service in the war, my correspondence with my family supplied, however, the place of a daily record, and much better than a diary; my letters have also been preserved. I have never looked them over except casually, one or two; but those I have looked over I found natural, vivid and extremely interesting. It has always been my intention to go over my family correspondence of that period, and prepare portions of it for publication as a contemporaneous war record, carried on, half in London and half from the camp. I have no doubt it would make a most interesting narrative, by no means without historical value; but now (1912) whether I ever get to it is more than doubtful. So much to do; so little done!

That, however, is no part of my present plan; but those letters, unlike my diary, I do not propose to destroy. For present purposes, from this point on what I have to say is mere reminiscence, and that at long range. Consequently, of small value. My army experience comes first, extending over three years and a half.

For a really considerable time I was now suddenly brought into close touch with Nature and man; and, in so far, I have not passed my entire life under conventional conditions. Yet, as I have already said, I had no particular military aptitude. Far from being a born soldier, I was in many respects unfitted for such a career. Not quick, daring or ready-witted, robust but not muscularly agile, I could not take advantage of sudden or unforeseen circumstances. With no personal magnetism, I was rather deficient in presence of mind in time of peril. The most that could be said of me was that, as a camp officer, I was distinctly above the average. I was conscientious, understood my duties fairly well, and cared anxiously for my men and horses. But I did not understand myself, nor did I take in the situation. Unseeing of my opportunities, I quite failed to realize in any broad way the nature of the occasion. I went into the service with a strong sense of duty, and a desire to see hard work, in no way seeking to save myself. I had no conception of army functions, or of the relative fields of usefulness of the staff and line. In common with most of my friends, I had rather a contempt for the staff positions; we wanted to be where the work and hardship were, and where the knocks were to be looked for. It was in some respects a praiseworthy feeling, and I lived up to it; but living up to it involved much hardship and danger, besides leaving out of sight, in my own individual case, that, while I had no particular aptitude for line work, I would have made a really valuable staff officer, had I only diligently qualified myself for the position. But on this subject, and my own insufficiency so far as my correct understanding of myself and the situation, and myself in connection with the possibilities of the situation, were concerned, I a few years ago set forth my more enduring conclusions in the *Memoir* I prepared of my friend Theodore Lyman, for the Historical Society.[1] He was more mature; I was like all the rest. As it was, I had to learn by hard experience that, in warfare on a large scale, a regimental officer, no matter how high his grade, sees nothing and knows nothing of what is going on. He is a mere minor wheel, when not simply a cog, in a vast and to him in greatest part unintelligible machine, moving on given lines to a possible result; wholly regardless of his comfort or even life. Obedience, self-sacrifice and patient endurance are the qualities most in

---

[1] 2 *Proceedings*, xx. 158–61.

demand for him; but as for any intelligent comprehension of the game in progress, that for the regimental officer is quite beyond his ken. Even a colonel of cavalry — in many respects a most delightful grade — knows only his own command, and is acquainted with nothing beyond his brigade front. He and his are but one small factor in an immense whole. A well-organized staff, on the contrary, constitutes the army's brain, and everything centres at Headquarters. There, and there alone, you know and see. So, the ideal position at which I should have aimed, had I only known enough, would have been the inspector-generalship of an army corps under a well-qualified corps commander. For this part, had I only realized it, I was well qualified; I needed only a well-defined plan in my own mind, and a patient study of functions. My lack of an early training was to be supplied by close observation and constant tact. At the close of the war, in February, 1865, that very position was offered to me, and by A. A. Humphreys, the best corps commander in the whole army; and I declined it! I stand aghast now at my own folly; I threw such a chance away! But I will do myself the justice to say that I did so most regretfully; and only from a strong sense of obligation to the regiment of which I had then just been made colonel. Duty or no duty, I have regretted it ever since. Though now I realize how little qualified I was for the position, had I accepted it.

As I have already intimated, my initiation into military life was most unlucky — that is the only word to apply to it. It was a case of hard luck! I set out wrong; and my mistakes and misfortunes followed me. It is all plain enough now; but then I blunderingly groped my way, and the course of events was dead against me. It is a long, disagreeable story; and, while I do not propose unduly to dilate upon it, it has its interest. Then, as ever since, my great misfortune lay in my utter lack of a nice, ingratiating tact in my dealings with other men and difficult situations. I was born deficient in true objectiveness. It is an inherited deficiency, a family trait; but it has been my great handicap and hindrance in life, and never so much so as in the army. Interfering with my success, it destroyed my comfort; and help it I could not. Well-meaning, conscientious, kind-hearted as I felt myself to be, it was not in me — it never has been in me — instinctively to do or say the right thing at the proper time.

This fact undoubtedly aggravated my difficulties, and prevented me from extricating myself from them, as any more adroit man would readily have done. On the other hand, I was extremely unlucky; and, wholly by accident, found myself during the first six months of my army life — my initiation period — in the most trying and spirit-breaking position I have known. Looking back on it now, I do not see how I stood it; nor, on the other hand, do I now quite see what I could have done other than I did do. It came about in this wise.

The First Regiment of Massachusetts Volunteer Cavalry was essentially a body of picked men. I have seen many military organizations, and soldiers of all kinds and climes; and I do not believe there ever were twelve hundred better men got together than those composing that regiment. It was the first complete cavalry regiment ever organized in New England. It was made up largely of Americans, young, athletic, ingenious, surprisingly alert and very adaptive. I always got along well with my men. We were kith and kin.

Not that I was popular or adored by them, as was Caspar Crowninshield, for instance; but they respected me, and I did well by them. I had a thoroughly good company — considered the best in the regiment. That was "D" Company; but originally I was assigned to "H." The colonel of the regiment was a Virginian — Robert Williams, a West Point graduate and officer of the regular army, strongly recommended by General Scott, and carefully selected by Governor Andrew first to organize and then command the initial cavalry regiment. Perfectly trained, and a gentleman of the Virginia school, very striking in appearance, Robert Williams may then have been some thirty-two years old, and he was a good organizer as well as a severe disciplinarian. I propose to deal kindly with him; but, in point of fact, he was all-outside! There was no real stuff in him, and — he could n't help drinking! Brought up in the regular service, he did not understand our Massachusetts men, and his discipline was severe to brutality. He had a set of us young Harvard fellows for officers, who served him like dogs, who bowed before him in blind, unquestioning obedience. Better material out of which to make officers never existed; but we needed kindly, sympathetic instruction. We did n't get it! Still, Williams did know his business, and was a good officer in camp; but in the field he got speedily demoralized, and, in moments of emergency, invariably drunk. Later, I was his personal aid, and the adjutant of the regiment; and, first and last, I went through incredible experiences with him. As an officer in presence of the enemy or under the stress of campaign, Williams was an utter failure; and so recognized. Prone to quarrel, he never got any promotion; and, shortly after Antietam, left the regiment, and returned to his adjutantgeneralcy, in Washington. Still, from Williams I did learn something.

Williams, as I have said, was a Virginian and a West Pointer; typically, both. I got along fairly well enough with him; but in no single respect was he a man I took to, or who took to me. He was far, very far, from my ideal of the head of a military family. He lacked innate courtesy as well as stability; and, above all, he was wholly deficient in character and in the sterling qualities. Still, I got on with him. My trouble, curiously enough, came from Massachusetts men — men I ought to have known all my life and been as of one family.

Leaving Massachusetts at the close of December, and after a short stay in New York, we were shipped to South Carolina, where we arrived about the middle of January. Two battalions went into camp at Hilton Head. Company H was in the Beaufort battalion; and there I remained four months. It was my apprenticeship. I was starting in on a new life; I had everything to learn. I look back on it now with a shudder of disgust. Fortunately, I liked the life; and the climate, after Boston, was delightful. I had, too, among the officers many friends; but, in spite of all that, it was the worst experience I ever had. Colonel Sargent was in local command of the Battalion; Captain Sargent commanded H Company. I was the only lieutenant of that company on duty; Davis, the second, shrewdly getting himself detailed as battalion adjutant. Lucius Manlius Sargent, their father, was well known in Boston, a great antiquarian and news-paper writer ("Sigma" and "A Sexton of the Old School" in the columns of the *Evening Transcript*) — a man of stand-ing and wealth. Horace and Manlius were children by different mothers. Both brothers were men of large figure and great muscular strength; very proud of their physique and, unquestionably, men of courage. Manlius, a graduate of Harvard in the class of '48, had studied medicine, and, in 1862, must have been about thirty-five.

In May, Williams was made commander of the post at Hilton Head; Sargent was transferred to the command of the two battalions there stationed, and my old and life-long friend — before, then, and now — Henry L. Higginson, recently made major, came up and assumed command at Beaufort. I now in my diary described my life as "a very pleasant and comfortable one." In early June, operations began on James Island, and, by a fortunate combination of circumstances which I at the time regarded as most unlucky, I was sick in the hospital when H Company was ordered off, and I never again rejoined it. For, when I was well enough to report for duty, I was assigned as an aid to Williams, then acting as brigade commander, and I continued to serve in that capacity until, in early September, the regiment was ordered to Virginia. In that capacity, and under Williams, I had what they are pleased to call "my baptism of fire," or, in other words, took part in my first engagement.

A day or two later came the James Island fight. We of the staff knew that something was impending, and we were called at 1 a.m. My record reminds me that, as we moved forward in the grey of the early dawn, I felt in no way heroic. Presently, Williams, whom we were following, "rode through a hedge, along a road, and then over a wall into an open field; and there we were directly in front of the enemy's works. Here I saw my first shell fall. It did not explode. It fell a few yards to our right, bouncing, and then rolling along in a very vicious way. It impressed me unpleasantly. Here we stayed a long time." We of the staff were kept very busy carrying orders, etc. "Though a heavy and incessant fire of infantry was going on, the roar of the artillery and the exploding of shells after they had hurtled and shrieked over our heads, so completely drowned the musketry that I do not think I heard the report of a small arm during the entire engagement. Yet, when I was sent with an order to our extreme left, I distinctly saw the puffs of dust raised by the musket-balls dropping about me. But I now found I had lost all sense of danger, and was thoroughly up to my work. My little mare did beautifully. Nothing scared her; not even the explosion of shells close by; and she carried me handsomely through morasses and over ditches without end; and she alone of all the staff horses followed the colonel wherever he went. After the action was well on, I began to enjoy it." The affair was badly managed, and the single attack was soon repulsed, our loss being heavy. We had some queer experiences that day, and it was a wonder we were not all killed. "Still, it was a pleasant feeling, that of riding out of my first fight, having done well in it. I don't think I ever experienced so genial a glow. As we rode out of the woods we passed our regiment — the cavalry — drawn up behind them, where they had been waiting the last four hours. We had been engaged; they had not. We felt, or at least I did, like a veteran of an hundred fights; and I got off my horse with a new and exalted sense of my own importance. It was very pleasant. In fact, it was not until I had dismounted that I realized how much I had enjoyed myself that day. But, honestly and unaffectedly, I do not think I ever passed a more pleasurable morning in my life. The excitement of a battle-field is grand."

Such was my contemporaneous record of my first engagement. Afterwards I was in many; and those I do not propose to particularize, or to give any descriptions of my part therein. I copy this, a part of the long record of my first experience in that way, merely because it was written at the time; also, as showing the extremely adverse and disheartening conditions under which I entered on army life. That I never for a moment even was sickened of that life, or looked back regretfully to my office and civilized existence speaks well, it seems to me, for my robustness; as, also, it is highly suggestive of my extreme distaste for the law and for office routine. But, assuredly, I never at that juncture did look back regretfully. My only fear was that I might be forced to give the new life up.

Meanwhile, as usual in face of steady persistence, luck slowly turned. In August, as a consequence of McClellan's reverses in Virginia, the regiment was ordered up from South Carolina; and, so far as I was concerned, it was high time. There was in my destroyed record a rather curious entry bearing on this subject. It was under the date of April 19, 1862; just a year from the fall of Sumter. When that occurred, and the President's call for troops immediately followed, the object of the muster was declared to be the re-taking of the captured fort [Sumter]; and I well remember the dread I felt of, possibly, being sent down to languish in what I assumed to be those fever-smitten swamps. And now, exactly one year from that time, I wrote thus: "A year ago my great apprehension was lest I might be sent to rot on the islands before Sumter; but now, here I am, just there, and the 'rotting' process has not yet begun. Again on picket duty at the Milne plantation; and it is beyond description beautiful. On my table are three bouquets of magnolias, roses, and sweet-smelling flowers, a fresh, fragrant atmosphere creeps in through the wide-open window, while beyond is the soft green foliage, such as we at home see only in early June. Altogether the spring here, though somewhat warm, is a pleasant season, and one good to live in."

In June, we lay before Sumter. After the failure of the expedition and our return to Hilton Head, I continued acting as aid to Colonel Williams. My duties were nominal only; but, in camp, my commander forswore sack and lived cleanly, and I certainly had nothing to complain of. But Hilton Head in July and August I found a wholly different place from Port Royal Island in April. The heat was great; also, continuous. I was young, and had never known what it was to take care of myself physically; so I neglected all precautions of diet and exposure; of course, with the usual result. The beach was directly in front of my quarters, and the bathing was superb; but the heat was as great by night as by day; and, gradually, I broke down under it. By the middle of August, though fit for duty, I was in a bad way. The news from home was, also, depressing; a succession of reverses; and, on the 18th of August, I thus wrote, hearing of our reverse at Cedar Mountain — when Banks came up against "Stonewall" Jackson — "the Massachusetts Second has been badly cut to pieces, and I have lost several old friends, and, among them, one, the first of our old Fort Independence mess, Harry Russell. More, and most of all, Stephen Perkins is reported killed; and if that be true, the ablest man I ever knew, the finest mind I ever met, is lost forever in the briefly reported death of a second lieutenant of volunteer Infantry. It is indeed bitter."

The news proved true of Perkins, but not of Russell. He was captured, and did not die till 1905 — over forty years afterwards; and I heard of his death at Assuan, in our second visit to Egypt. But in August, 1862, we did not have much time to count losses or lament the dead; our turn had come! For, only six days later I made the last diary record I was to make for twenty-six years, while lying on the transport *McClellan*, off Fort Monroe, on our way to Alexandria. There was one portion of that final record which tends to show that at the time I was at least in a recipient mood. It was rather creditable. On the voyage up, time hanging heavily on my hands, I chanced upon Tom Hughes's story of *Hodson*, in his *Twelve Years of a Soldier's Life in India*. It made a deep impression on me. We, too, were on our way to the awful fighting ground, and Hodson's experience and letters seemed strangely applicable. I remember writing to my people in London about it; and now I find this other record: "One lesson I wish I could learn from Hodson — that of patience and subordination. He makes me ashamed of myself. He, a captain at thirty-five and when he had long been the first soldier in the Indian army; and here am I, impatient and reckless, with that same rank in my grasp at the close of seven months of service. I am a very ordinary man; he was a most uncommon one: it would be well for me and my happiness could I take many pages from his book. Is it not possible for me also to do my duty unrepiningly in the place where I find myself, and, by doing it well, fit myself for higher? Cannot I too take fortune's buffets and rewards with equal grace? It does not seem so. Yet it is strange that one small feature in Hodson's army career in India should produce such an effect on me here!"

This is the last quotation I have to make from my contemporaneous records; and it is not my purpose to write a book of war reminiscences. From this point, therefore, I go on rapidly. The regiment was forced at once into the most active of campaign work — the Antietam episode. We were wholly unprepared, and Williams at once became completely demoralized — went all to pieces! I was now made the regimental adjutant; and a lovely time I had of it! Something had happened at Washington, I never quite knew what. But Williams disappeared altogether for two days, during which he was very much wanted. The regiment meanwhile was kicked about in a state of orphanage; and, when Williams turned up, looking very shame-faced, his chance of a higher command was gone. Consequently, he took the field in a totally demoralized frame of mind. Then came that awful campaign. Williams did not appear well, or do well. I was wholly inexperienced. He then gave us the benefit of his regular army jealousies; for he had a great contempt as well as dislike for his commanding officer — Pleasanton, in fact a decidedly poor stick — and an angry flare-up took place, with a fine display of West Point insubordination.

Williams, very wisely, decided to resign his Massachusetts commission, and return to his desk in the Adjutant-General's office at Washington. He did so, and his career as a cavalry officer, or in the field, then came to a close. It was well for him it did. He was utterly unfitted for the stress and excitement of active service; while, in his office, he acquitted himself well. He rose to be Adjutant-General of the Army, and died somewhere about 1902 or 1903, on the retired list, utterly broken in health.[1]

Sargent succeeded Williams, I remaining adjutant. This, however, lasted only a few weeks, when I got my company. It was a happy day for me. Meanwhile, forced into active campaign immediately on landing from South Carolina, the regiment, naturally, went all to pieces. Of our original excellent mount, there was hardly a horse left. The officers were disheartened; the men demoralized. So we went into camp to await a new mount and reorganize. Greeley Curtis had now become second in command, with Henry Higginson next to him. Both good officers, though with no more experience than I, strong personal friends, fearless and with some sense; much trouble was soon lifted off my shoulders, and assumed by them. As adjutant, I knew my duties fairly well; and did them.

In his *Memoir of Colonel Henry Lee*, published in 1905, John T. Morse, Jr., says that Harry Lee "said what others knew and liked to have said by some one, though themselves shirking responsibility"; and as illustrative of this he repeats a terse characterization of Colonel Lee's, made to his kinsman, T. Wentworth Higginson, when editing the *Harvard Memorial Biographies*. Harry Lee then said to Colonel Higginson: "Put it down that it will always remain an uncertainty whether it was the insane vanity of the elder brother, or the drunken insanity of the younger, which utterly ruined the finest regiment that ever left Massachusetts."

The two Sargents were the only superiors I had during my entire army experience with whom I was wholly unable to

[1] He died August 24, 1901.

get on, or to whom I failed to give satisfaction. Subsequently, I was urged for promotion, out of course, over the head of Captain Sargent, by Curtis and Higginson; but I refused to allow myself to be considered. I afterwards always had a good reputation as an officer; and, at the end of six months of excellent opportunity for observation, General Humphreys tendered me the highest position on his corps staff.

The winter following the Antietam campaign was passed by the regiment in camp at Acquia Creek. Sargent, now become colonel, was in command, and we learned nothing; unless it were to carry insubordination to a fine art. I now got my captaincy; and I must do myself the justice to say that, while my company was an excellent one, I took great pride in it and devoted myself to my duties and its improvement. Between me and it the most friendly relations existed. The trouble, however, was that we were all so inexperienced; we knew nothing of the laws of health and self-preservation, and we thought those laws not worth knowing. Why any of us survived, I cannot now see; but we were young and robust as a rule; we lived in the open air; and we were at least temperate. On the other hand, we had no schools of instruction; the regimental quarrels were incessant; the spirit of insubordination was rife and in the air. None the less, the material was all there, and it would assert itself. When the Spring came, it was a superb regiment.

Then followed the long Gettysburg campaign in which we were veterans — always, as I now see, self-taught. In the very height of it Colonel Sargent somehow got a leave-of-absence, and went to Europe. Curtis broke down, poisoned by malaria; Higginson and Chamberlain, the two majors, were both incapacitated by wounds; so also was Captain Sargent. So a few of us, boy-captains, ran what remained of the regiment. Curtis and Higginson — my old friends, with whom my campaign life was happiness — never came back. So, on the whole, this was my best period in the service. Somehow, the life agreed with me; I actually enjoyed its hardships, its adventure, its nearness to Nature and men. I alone of the officers asked for no leave of absence; I desired none. Perfectly well physically, I was in every way developing. That dreary Court Street office seemed a disagreeable dream; I was separated from it by a whole existence; I was never going back to it; it was the only period of my life in which I lived for the present, and took no thought of the future. It was a truly glorious existence.

It was now autumn (November, 1863), and I had been nearly two years in the service without a break. That autumn campaign was continuous and very severe; and, when we went into winter quarters at Warrenton — somewhere in early December — the regiment was reduced to a skeleton. Well do I now recall my tour of picket duty the night the brigade arrived there. The days were the shortest of the year, and a heavy freezing rain was falling. My line of outposts covered a broken, unsheltered country, and my reserve was stationed among the stumps of a recently felled grove. It was dark as Egypt, and all was desolation; and so the dreary hours wore themselves away. Late the next morning I was relieved; but for what? The newly formed camp was, I well remember, as comfortless and dreary as the outpost. How we stood it, I do not now see; but, as I have repeatedly said, we were young and strong, buoyant and full of resource.

That winter I got a leave of absence; my company re-enlisting and going home — the first in the regiment to do so — while I, seeing them to Boston, went to Europe. This closed my severe military experience; and it was enough. Two full years of company life had completely exhausted it; more would have been mere repetition. My letters, doubt-less, give a vivid enough picture of what that experience was — and it was far and away the greatest of my life — nor have I any disposition to indulge in reminiscence. Three episodes I have since at different times set down, and they are the most striking I recall.

The first describes the march of the Sixth Corps to Gettys-burg on the 2d of July, '63. That was the finest thing in a military way I ever saw. There was in it more of the spirit and splendor of war. I included it in the Fourth of July Address I delivered at Quincy, in 1869, and it has since been reprinted in the papers frequently, even in the West. In-deed, I came across it somewhere, not long ago. The passage is as follows, and I recall the scene now, after an interval of close on fifty years, as if of yesterday: "It was late on the evening of the first of July, that there came to us rumors of heavy fighting at Gettysburg, near forty miles away. The regiment happened then to be detached, and its orders for the second were to move in the rear of Sedgwick's corps and see that no man left the column. All that day we marched to the sound of the cannon; Sedgwick, very grim and stern, was pressing forward his tired men, and we soon saw that for once there would be no stragglers from the ranks. As the day grew old and as we passed rapidly up from the rear to the head of the hurrying column, the roar of battle grew more distinct, until at last we crowned a hill and the contest broke upon us. Across the deep valley, some two miles away, we could see the white smoke of the bursting shells, while below the sharp incessant rattle of the musketry told of the fierce struggle that was going on. Before us ran the straight, white, dusty road, choked with artillery, ambulances, caissons, ammunition trains, all pressing forward to the field of battle, while mixed among them, their bayonets gleaming through the dust like wavelets on a river of steel, tired, foot-sore, hungry, thirsty, begrimed with sweat and dust, the gallant infantry of Sedgwick's corps hurried to the sound of the cannon as men might have flocked to a feast. Moving rapidly forward, we crossed the brook which runs so prominently across the map of the field of battle and halted on its further side to await our orders. Hardly had I dismounted from my horse when, looking back, I saw that the head of the column had reached the brook, and deployed and halted on its other bank, and already the stream was filled with naked men shouting with pleasure as they washed off the sweat of their long day's march. Even as I looked, the noise of the battle grew louder, and soon the symptoms of movement were evident. The *rappel* was heard, the bathers hurriedly clad themselves, the ranks were formed, and the sharp, quick snap of the percussion caps told us the men were preparing their weapons for action. Almost immediately a general officer rode rapidly to the front of the line, addressed to it a few brief energetic words, the short, sharp order to move by the flank was given, followed immediately by the 'double quick,' the officer placed himself at the head of the column, and that brave infantry which had marched almost forty miles since the setting of yesterday's sun; which during that day had hardly known either sleep, or food, or rest, or shelter from the July heat, now, as the shadows grew long, hurried forward on the run to take its place in the front of battle and to bear up the reeling fortunes of the day. . . .

"Twenty-four hours later we stood on that same ground. Many dear friends had yielded up their young lives during the hours which had elapsed; but, though twenty thousand fellow creatures were wounded or dead around us, though the flood-gates of heaven seemed open and the torrents fell upon the quick and the dead, yet the elements seemed electrified with a certain magnetic influence of victory, and, as the great army sank down over-wearied in its tracks, it felt that the crisis and danger was passed — that Gettysburg was immortal."

The two other passages of war reminiscence are contained in my "Fenway" Address of April 13, 1899, before the Massachusetts Historical Society, and those, also, holding the journalistic stage in the usual limited and transitory fashion, were extensively printed at the time of delivery. They are as follows:

"As I have already mentioned, it was my fortune at one period to participate in a considerable number of battles — among them none more famous, nor more fiercely contested, than Antietam and Gettysburg. The mere utterance of those names stirs the imagination — visions arise at once of attack, repulse, hairbreadth escape, carnage and breathless suspense. There was, indeed, on those occasions enough and to spare of all these; but not, as it chanced, in my particular case. Some here will doubtless remember that English fox-hunting squire, who has gained for himself a sort of immortality by following his hounds over Naseby's field, I think it was, while the epoch-marking battle was going on. More yet will recall that ploughman, twice referred to so dramatically by Zola, intent upon his uninterrupted day's work near Sedan, when a dynasty was reeling to its fall. So my abiding recollection, as a participant in both Antietam and Gettysburg, is, not of the fierce agony of battle at its height, but the enjoyment of two exceedingly refreshing naps. As a statement, this, I am aware, is calculated to startle rather than to excite admiration; but, to the historian, truth is sacred; and the truth is — as I have said! Neither does the statement imply any exceptional nerve or indifference to danger on my part: I make no claim to anything of the sort. It happened in this wise. In the campaigns of both Antietam and Gettysburg I was an officer in a regiment of cavalry, a mere subordinate, responsible only for obedience to orders. At Antietam, in the height of the engagement, the division to which my regiment belonged was hurried across the narrow stone bridge at the point where the little river intersects the Sharpsburg road, and deployed on its further side. We were then directly in front of Fitz-John Porter's corps, and between it and the Confederate line, covering Sharpsburg. A furious artillery duel was going on, to and fro, above our heads, between the batteries of Porter's command and those of the enemy, we being down in the valley of the river, they on the higher ground. The Confederate batteries we could not see; nor could they see us. When we first deployed on the further side of Antietam Creek, it seemed as if we were doomed — so deafening was the discharge of artillery on either side, and so incessant the hurtling of projectiles as they passed both ways over us. Every instant, too, we expected to be ordered to advance on the Confederate batteries. The situation was unmistakably trying. But no orders came; and no one was hurt. By degrees it grew monotonous. Presently, to relieve our tired horses, we were ordered to dismount, and, without breaking the ranks, we officers sat down on the sloping hill-side. No one was being struck; I was very tired; the noise was deadening; gradually it had on me a lulling effect; and so I dropped quietly asleep — asleep in the height of the battle and between the contending armies! They woke me up presently to look after my horse, who was grazing somewhat wide; and, after a time, we were withdrawn, and sent elsewhere. I believe that day our regiment did not lose a man, scarcely a horse. Such is my recollection of that veritable charnel-house, Antietam; — and I was a participant — indeed in the fore-front of the battle.

"Gettysburg was different; and yet, as respects somnolence, in my case much the same. During the days preceding that momentous struggle, my command had been frequently engaged, and suffered heavy loss. We who remained were but a remnant. On the 3d of July the division to which we belonged occupied the high, partially wooded ground on the right of the line, covering the army's flank and rear. It was a bright July day; hot, and with white clouds slowly rolling across the sky, premonitory of a thunder-storm during the later afternoon. From our position the eye ranged over a wide expanse of uneven country, fields broken by woods, showing nowhere any signs of an army movement, much less of conflict. A quiet, midsummer, champaign country. Neither our lines nor those of the enemy were visible to us; and the sounds of battle were hushed. Waiting for orders and for action, we dismounted, out of regard for our horses as well as ourselves, and sat or lay upon the turf. Inured to danger by contact long and close, and thoroughly tired in body as overwrought in mind, we listened for the battle to begin; and, shortly after noon, the artillery opened. We did not know it — we could see nothing in that direction — but it covered the famous advance of Pickett's Virginia division upon Meade's centre — that wonderful, that unsurpassed feat of arms; and, just then, lulled by the incessant roar of the cannon, while the fate of the army and the nation trembled in the balance, at the very crisis of the great conflict, I dropped quietly asleep. It was not heroic; but it was, I hold, essentially war, though by no means war as imagined in the work-room of the theoretic historian."

Of my first trip to Europe — that delightful burst of sunlight from the midst of the awful storm-clouds of those years — I have elsewhere made record; so here I pass on. The change from home and office life was to me at that period so thoroughly enjoyable that I never at all realized what line and company life in war was until released from it. Once released, and knowing another existence, a return to it seemed unendurable. While on my English leave I shrank from the thought. It so chanced that my college as well as life-long friend, Theodore Lyman, was then attached to Meade's Headquarters. He had no army rank, but, knowing Meade personally, the matter had been arranged. He had got Governor Andrew to appoint him on his military staff, and then to detail him for service at the Headquarters of the Army of the Potomac. It was an ingenious and to me as well as to him a most useful arrangement; and Theodore at least availed himself of it to the utmost. More than any of us he rose to the magnitude of the occasion and derived advantage from the opportunities of a great experience. I have elsewhere expressed my sense of this.[1] He now by an act of extreme friendliness got me out of the most disagreeable and trying position in which, on the whole, I ever found myself involved, rendering me a service I never adequately repaid; though subsequently I did write his *Memoir* — forty years later, in 1906, for the *Proceedings* of the Historical Society.[2] It was a somewhat elaborate *Memoir* also, and gave much satisfaction to his widow, an old friend of mine, and a grand-daughter of that Jonathan Russell, whom J. Q. Adams so victimized somewhere about 1822. The fact was, Theodore Lyman realized my position. In my great perplexity I wrote to him, and he explained the situation to Meade. So my squadron was by special order detached from the regiment and directed to report to the Headquarters of the Army of the Potomac for escort duty. Taken altogether, the most opportune act of friendship ever done me, it saved my army life from utter failure; but I did not know how to avail myself of my opportunities, and that life was not what it should have been.

Thus, when I returned from England in April, 1864, just in time for Grant's awful Wilderness campaign — full of doubt and anxiety, determined somehow to get away from the regiment — this order had preceded me, and I found my squadron already transferred. Only once do I remember going back to the regiment. Chamberlain was then in command. A large, rough, self-made man, he had been wild and adventurous in his youth, serving as a trooper in the Mexican war. Wholly lacking in refinement and education, he was a dashing fellow in his way; and on the whole, I fancy, the best officer that regiment ever had. Knowing his business

[1] *2 Mass. Hist. Soc. Proceedings*, XII. 62.   [2] *Ib.*, XX. 147.

fairly well, he was more in sympathy with the men. At Kelly's Ford he had the year before been severely wounded — two carbine bullets in his face. He was now lieutenant-colonel in command; for the regiment was not full enough to permit the mustering in of a full colonel. On my reporting back for duty, I saw Chamberlain, and he urged me strongly to get myself and the squadron returned to the regiment. We sat on the grass there in that dreary Virginia camp, discussing the matter, and he then offered me the place next himself in command. I, however, was obdurate. I declined even to consider the proposition — it involved a daily contact with the things I loathed. Chamberlain and I then parted good friends, and afterwards remained such. He a year later succeeded me in command of the Fifth Cavalry, at last getting his colonelcy.

My experience at the Headquarters of the Army of the Potomac continued about six months — from April to October. The change was great, and a pleasant one. There, and there only, did I see some of the large operations of warfare, and find myself in contact with men high in command. I went to the Headquarters a perfectly well man; but the seeds of malarial disease were, I imagine, implanted, and during the summer of 1864 I began slowly to break down. I now know well enough what the trouble was. I was poisoned by incessant feeding on hard-tack and meat freshly killed and fried in pork-fat, and the inordinate drinking of black coffee — quarts of it, each day. We all did so; we and the medical men evincing an equal lack of either knowledge of or regard for the most elementary rules of hygiene. My present realizing sense of our ignorance and recklessness fills me with a sort of disgusted surprise. We seem all round, at home as in the army, to have been little more than ignorant and unobservant children. This disregard of ordinary precautions I stood longer than most, living meanwhile during the summer of 1864 on the river-banks of the Appomattox, surrounded by decaying animal matter; but, with even the most iron of constitutions, it was only a question of time. I began to break down in August, 1864; and, in May, 1865, was a mere physical wreck.

At Headquarters I came in contact with, or had a chance in a way to observe, all the men whose names were then famous in Army of Potomac circles, from Grant down. Here, as everywhere, my lack of *savoir-faire* — of natural objectiveness — my utter deficiency in quick discernment and tact, my inability to avail myself of opportunity, and to do or say the right thing at the proper moment — all this, as I now see, stood sadly in my way. I did not ingratiate myself to the degree that would have been easily possible with one differently constituted. At the same time I must confess that even now, looking back, the men I saw handling large affairs in those military operations do not seem to me to have been as a rule imposing. The truth of old Oxenstiern's remark forced itself continually on me. General Meade was a gentleman and man of high character; but he was irritable, petulant and dyspeptic. He did not give the idea of calm, reserved force. Grant did; but Grant was a man of coarse fibre, and did not impress with a sense of character. Hancock was a dashing field-marshal; a handsome, superb commander of a corps. Warren left on me a sense of lightness. Humphreys and Sedgwick were the only two generals I ever met who inspired me with an adequate sense of force and reliability. Officers, they were also quiet, unassuming gentlemen.

About them there was no pretence, no posing for effect, no stage tricks. I felt for them a profound respect; and, could I have been a staff officer on the corps commanded by either, I should have found my proper army position. Sheridan I never saw until long after the war was over, and then only casually. He was essentially an Irish adventurer — a species of brilliant Charles O'Malley; with a well-developed natural aptitude for military life, he was not conspicuous for character. Thomas, I never laid eyes on; but I imagine he was a man of the Sedgwick type — solid and full of character. Sherman, I only saw after the war was over; but he then impressed me much, more than any of those I have named, not even excepting Humphreys. He bore the stamp of true genius. Curiously natural, very fond of talking, there was about him nothing of the *poseur*. He was a delightful dinner-table companion, humorous, easy, striking, full of reminiscence. He and Humphreys, very different, but each great, were my two army ideals; under either, it would have been a delight and glory to serve. This satisfaction did not fall to me, partly from that natural obtuseness which has ever stood between me and my opportunities, partly from a mistaken adhesion to that narrow sense of obligation and duty to which I have made reference, both here and in my *Memoir* of Theodore Lyman.[1]

I had joined the Headquarters a few days only before the opening of Grant's terrible Wilderness campaign. I was then in perfect health. I remember well the fine April morning when my bugler blew "To Horse" just as Meade mounted, and, followed by his staff, headed towards Richmond. He did not go far that day; nor for many following days. I was

[1] 2 *Mass. Hist. Soc. Proceedings*, xx. 160.

with the Headquarters from that time on, until we halted before Petersburg, and the long siege of Richmond was well advanced. At first, while the army was on its way to the James, continually fighting and flanking, I was, owing to the entire absence of cavalry, frequently called upon for difficult and dangerous service. I had to skirmish, scout and cover the army's flank under the orders and eye of the commanding general. I did my work fairly well, and when I was leaving for another command Meade in a personal letter mentioned all the occasions specifically, and kindly commended my conduct. While the army was in movement, therefore, I could not have desired a better position. My only trouble was that I did not know how to magnify it.

Of this very memorable campaign and the impressions it left on me at the time, I have little question my letters home and to my friends would to-day tell the story so far as I was concerned. That would be contemporaneous evidence; but speaking of it as reminiscence, I can only say that the general impression left upon me is one of monotonous discouragement. The heroic is not greatly in evidence. Looking back, the thing which stands prominently forth, writ very large, is my sense of the utter incompetence of Major-General Benjamin F. Butler of Massachusetts, and the terrible disasters and loss of life that incompetence directly involved. The figure cut by Grouchy in the Waterloo campaign is heroic and almost innocuous compared with it. On this point I have since expressed myself with such force and emphasis as I can command. Grant's plan of campaign went absolutely to pieces at the very outset because of Butler's utter military incapacity, and his inability either to see an opportunity, much more to seize it. At the beginning, as I have shown in my recently published papers, the winning card was in his hand, and the fact was pointed out to him clearly by his subordinates. He did not know enough to recognize it as the winning card, or to play it when pointed out to him as such. The military element did not enter in any degree into Butler's composition, and the Army of the Potomac, including myself, paid the penalty. I think it not too much to say that the loss of life and casualties thus entailed were to be numbered by the tens of thousands. As I remember that awful campaign and those months passed in front of Petersburg, I entertain a very bitter feeling towards Major-General Benjamin F. Butler. Though I never saw him while he was in command, yet I was very sensible at the time of the disappointment and loss his being in command entailed upon us. But I have borne my evidence on all these points in print, and on more than one occasion. It can be found, if any one is curious enough to look it up, in my original paper on Mr. Rhodes's fifth volume, in the *Proceedings* of the Massachusetts Historical Society,[1] in my *Memoir* of Theodore Lyman in the next volume of those *Proceedings*,[2] and finally, in my published *Studies: Military and Diplomatic*.[3] It is needless here to repeat what I have there said.

But here I would like to refer to a matter which has for years been to me a constant annoyance. Never since it was there placed have I passed by the front of the State House without feeling a sense of wrong and insult at the presence, opposite the head of Park Street, of the equestrian statue of Hooker. That statue I look upon as an opprobrium cast on every genuine Massachusetts man who served in the Civil

[1] 2 *Proceedings*, XIX. 348.   [2] *Ib.*, XX. 162.   [3] Pages 267–81.

War. Hooker in no way and in no degree represents the typical soldiership of the Commonwealth. His record, either as an officer or as a man, was not creditable. Chancing to be born in Massachusetts, he was in 1861 and from that time forward little better than a drunken, West Point military adventurer. A showy officer, and one capable of fairly good work in a limited command — that of a brigade or division — he was altogether devoid of character; insubordinate and intriguing when at the head of a corps, as a commander he was in nearly every respect lacking. It is true that after superseding Burnside he did some effective work towards organizing the Army of the Potomac. Nevertheless, that was a period in its history when, so far as character was concerned, the Army of the Potomac sank to its lowest point. It was commanded by a trio, of each of whom the least said the better. It consisted of "Joe" Hooker, "Dan" Sickles, and "Dan" Butterfield. All three were men of blemished character. During the winter (1862–63), when Hooker was in command, I can say from personal knowledge and experience, that the Headquarters of the Army of the Potomac was a place to which no self-respecting man liked to go, and no decent woman could go. It was a combination of bar-room and brothel. Then, as if it was not sufficiently annoying to any Massachusetts man who had borne a respectable part in the Civil War, it was proposed to erect in front of the State House a statue of Butler in addition to that of Hooker. This may yet be done. If it is done, I can only hope it will not be until after my death. That will be altogether too much! Hooker on one side, and Butler on the other! — two men in connection with neither of whom during the Civil War a good word can be said. An equestrian statue of

Charles Lowell would have represented something typical of Massachusetts, greatly to the credit of the Commonwealth. But Hooker and Butler! — as one who wore the uniform my feeling would be much that of a Frenchman if, in the most conspicuous place of Paris, he every day was forced to contemplate statues of Grouchy and Bazaine, supposed to be representative of the best soldier type France had to offer.

Returning to my individual experience at that time, after the army crossed the James in June, 1864, and settled down before Petersburg, the whole situation, so far as I was concerned, became changed. I was no longer called on for special duties; I did not move with the staff; I became in fact a mere commander of orderlies. Of this I soon wearied. We were, too, encamped in low lands, for convenience of access to water on account of the horses, and my health for the first time manifestly began to fail. I had stood it two years and eight months, and my turn had now come. It was a marvel it had not come before, and my exemption up to this late day spoke volumes for my constitutional strength. But, as I look back, I wonder at my own obtuseness. I seem never to have taken the trouble to observe or to draw inferences which should have been obvious. With a suggestively growing sicklist it never occurred to me to change my camp to higher ground or dryer soil, to put my men in motion on some pretext, or to alter my own diet. I stupidly blundered along, myself sickening day by day.

In September, the monotony became terrible, and my enteric troubles so pronounced that I went into hospital, under care of my college friend, E. B. Dalton, then in command of the Reserve Hospital of the Army. I shared his tent.

Of him I cannot speak too highly. He was one of the few absolutely first-class characters I ever knew. Gentle, manly, refined, high-toned, courageous and self-respecting—to be his friend was indeed an honor. He must now (1912) have been dead hard upon forty years. His picture still hangs in my dressing-room, and I remember him as a man of the loftiest order of character. His later history was awfully and dramatically tragic — afflictions rained upon him and broke him down. He was one of perhaps a dozen I have known, the deaths of whom have left distinct vacancies in my life; because of them the world has for me since been appreciably poorer.

Dalton soon saw the gravity of my case, and he advised me to go home, and get well. Curiously enough, he did not advise me to stop drinking coffee, to eat no fried food, and to change my camp. These simple precautions never seemed to suggest themselves to our army medical men. The fact was my intestines were actually corroded with concentrated nourishment. I needed to live on bread, vegetables and tea; I did live on pork, coffee, spirits and tainted water. Undoubtedly, also, I was suffering from malarial poison. I needed active campaign work; but I was tired of the war and of army life.

At just this time the unsought offer came to me of the lieutenant-colonelcy of the Fifth Cavalry, a regiment at the head of which was my old Fort Independence friend, Harry Russell. I hesitated long; but, at last, determined to accept. I did not care for the increased rank, still less for the pay; but I was tired of orderly duty; sick, I needed a change, and I felt, and felt rightly, that a colored regiment would prove an interesting study. I left my old command at Petersburg, and never saw it again; in early October, I think it was, I joined my new regiment, then not mounted and doing guard duty at Point Lookout, Maryland, where was a camp of Confederate prisoners of war. Here my disease grew rapidly on me. I was now a thoroughly sick man; and, in November, I got myself ordered home. I had then been three years away. Getting somewhat better, I shortly returned to duty; but only to break down again. Before the close of the year I was back in Boston.

This was for me a memorable leave of absence, for, in it, I became engaged. I had met the young lady a year before, while staying at Newport with my sister, Mrs. Charles Kuhn, just before sailing for Europe. Fresh from two whole years of army life, I suppose I was then in a susceptible state. In any event, I thought I had never met so charming and attractive a person as she who, twenty-one months later, became my wife. The second daughter of Edward Ogden, originally of New York, then living at Newport, I had thought much of her during the year which elapsed after my flying visit to Newport in January, 1864, and now, invalided in Boston, I found myself attracted to Newport. My sister had gone to Europe; the Ogdens were in deepest affliction over the death of the only son, killed in action in Virginia six months before; and I had no excuse for going to Newport. I went all the same; and, in less than a week, we were engaged. That last sick-leave was thus made a very pleasant as well as memorable episode for me.

Things now came in rapid sequence. The war was manifestly drawing to a close: for the capture of Fort Fisher followed hard on the battle of Nashville; and that seemed a mere sequence to Sherman's march to the sea, and the fall of

Savannah. During those winter weeks of 1864–65 the flags were incessantly displayed in honor of some new victory. I was engaged, and in a Newport dreamland. A letter from Harry Russell next advised me that he had resigned, and that I must take charge of the regiment; and, almost at the same time, a message reached me from General Humphreys, telling me that he was about to succeed Hancock in command of the Second Corps, and inviting me to take the place of inspector-general of his command. That was a very intoxicating period. Patience, and minding my own business had carried me through my troubles, and I was rising surfaceward, corklike.

Large and small, I have made many mistakes in my life; not more perhaps than the average man, but still a sufficiency — mistakes of judgment, mistakes of temper and utterance, social mistakes, and, above all, mistakes due to lack of discernment. One or two of these, mistakes of judgment, have been vital, affecting my whole subsequent course of life; mistakes like taking the wrong fork of the road to a destination, when it was a mere turn of the hand which road was taken. Other of my mistakes, though not vital, were important; matters for life-time regret. Among my half-dozen mistakes of this sort, I now distinctly scored one. Acting, I will do myself the justice to say, largely under a sense of obligation and duty, I did not hesitate an instant; I elected to remain with my regiment. From every point of view I decided wrong; for I did the regiment no good and myself much harm. The whole experience afforded an excellent instance of good intentions misdirected. In the first place, by an ingenious move through my influential friends at the Headquarters of the Army of the Potomac, I got the regiment mounted. Mistake number one. The regiment was doing very good service, dismounted, as a garrison and on guard over the prisoners' camp at Point Lookout. To mount it, meant only the waste of twelve hundred much-needed horses. Then, having got it mounted, through the same channels I worked it into active service. Mistake number two; as the only result of so doing was to afford myself convincing proof that the negro was wholly unfit for cavalry service, lacking absolutely the essential qualities of alertness, individuality, reliability and self-reliance. He could not scout; he could not take care of himself in unfamiliar positions. That regiment was in exactly its proper place at Point Lookout. I merely took the negro out of it, and put him where he was of no possible use. I did the service harm, the regiment no good. As for myself, I sacrificed the whole ripe reward and happy culmination of my three years of service. True, I had the satisfaction of leading my regiment into burning Richmond, the day after Lee abandoned it. I did have that satisfaction; and it was a great one. But it was purchased at a great cost. And that was all I got. Then came a few weeks of wretched breaking down, until I became a confirmed invalid, and had to crawl ignominiously home, leaving my regiment ordered to Texas and almost in a state of mutiny. It was a bitter and humiliating termination of nearly four years of faithful effort. And all from a sense of duty! And I might have been in at the death with Humphreys and the Second Corps! It was all very bitter and so wholly unnecessary!

Forced to be content with the march into Richmond, a few weeks later, about the 20th of May, I dragged myself on to my horse, and left my command. I was then a mere wreck

— pitiably reduced and weak. Eaten up with malarial poison, I weighed scarcely one hundred and thirty pounds, while my knees would at night so ache from mere weakness that sleep was out of the question. Intestinally corroded, I was never free from the influence of opium, which acting on my nerves drove me almost to insanity. Weeks later, a short sea voyage brought me relief; the physicians were of no use. Had they in May prescribed an ocean voyage to Europe and back, I would have been convalescent in a month. As it was, in June, I think, I was quietly mustered out of the service, and became once more a civilian. A great experience was over, and its close was for me a Dead Sea apple. But I intended it well!

V

PUBLIC SERVICE AND HISTORY

PASSING the summer in Newport, I was married in November, and went immediately to Europe. The next eleven months I passed — or rather we passed — in London, at Rome and Paris, and finally in England, getting back to America in the following October (1866). My going to Europe was a wise move, for it enabled me to recover my health. The process was a slow one, for my system was permeated by disease. I had slowly to work the poison out. I much fear I was far from an amiable or considerate husband during those twelve months; more especially as I was weighed down by the ever-present consciousness that I was now to go back to civil life, and, somehow, while earning a living, work out my destiny. The outlook was indeed dreary.

Still, I did enjoy Europe — after a fashion! That I failed, and failed woefully, to avail myself of my opportunities, goes without saying; for it was I! My father was then American Minister to Great Britain, and, had I possessed the happy, ingratiating, social faculty only in a moderate degree, I could have seen much I never saw of things, and met many men I now have only heard of. It was not so, and I have little to record; for at that period I kept no diary. On the Continent, it was the same; I failed to avail myself of my opportunities. But those were at least the days of the temporal dominion of the Pope, and Rome was mediæval and unique. It had not yet been at once modernized and vulgarized. It was old Rome, under the Papacy. When we left it, we left it by carriage, driving to Perugia. We also drove from Genoa to Nice along the famous Cornice Road. France and Paris were very different in 1866 from what they now (1912) are. It was in the days of the Empire; the battle of Sadowa, ominous of the fate of Napoleon III, was fought while we were at Paris. I am free to confess that, for a foreigner, France of the Second Empire was an infinitely more attractive country than France of the Republic. It may have been all sham and tinsel; but Paris was then undeniably brilliant, gay and clean. It is now a cheap caravansary — cheap in everything but its prices. It has since grown common. Even the boulevards, the theatres, the "garçons," and the police have deteriorated. But on this head I expressed myself in full in my *Memoir* of Robert C. Winthrop.[1] *Mutato nomine*, etc.

We got back to America late in September, 1866, and I confronted the world, so to speak, face to face. It bore a far from inviting aspect. I had been away nearly five entire years, and both I and the conditions were greatly changed. Married, and thirty years of age, I was to begin anew; and at the foot of the ladder. The change was something terrific; nor did those around appreciate, I think, how great it was. I had been a full colonel, in command of a regiment. Within the beat of his sentries there is no one on earth more of a despot than a colonel commanding a regiment. He is supreme; he breathes a constant atmosphere of deference and subordination. This I had been thoroughly accustomed to; and, now, I found myself an office-boy — a mere tender-out — a confessed applicant for — something! People, I knew well enough and felt keenly, looked at me, half curiously, half sympathetically, waiting to see what I would find

[1] 2 *Mass. Hist. Soc. Proceedings*, xx. 186–89.

to do. It was more, far more than merely discouraging — it was humiliating.

I must do myself the justice to say that under these circumstances I addressed myself to the ordeal before me, not only with a good deal of courage, but promptly and in a large way, evincing withal a somewhat surprising degree of good sense. Nominally, I found I had to go back to a law office. I had no choice. I had to do something; but I did it with a sinking heart. I felt I had no aptitude that way. In my case people have always been over-ready to talk of "family influence" and all that sort of thing in an owlish way, so accounting for about everything I ever accomplished. So far as I have ever been able to see, however, "family influence" never was of any assistance to me; and, in those ordeal days, never I am sure was put forth in the faintest in my behalf. Paraphrasing Pistol, the world was my oyster then, which I with pen did open; and I did it, unaided.

But, curiously enough, I had meanwhile worked out my problem in advance; and worked it out correctly. Surveying the whole field — instinctively recognizing my unfitness for the law — I fixed on the railroad system as the most developing force and largest field of the day, and determined to attach myself to it. I now stand amazed at my own inexperience and audacity; but, having made up my mind, within a fortnight of my dreary home-coming, and, in perfect good faith, evolving my facts from my inner consciousness, I proceeded to write an article on "Railroads" for the *North American Review!* James Russell Lowell and Charles E. Norton were then editing that periodical — trying to infuse new life into its aged system; for it was being slowly but surely crowded out of existence by the newer and more superficial, but also more readable swarm of monthlies then coming into vogue. Norton was kind enough to accept my suggestion of an article; and, even now, I retain a profoundly grateful feeling towards him for that helping hand in an hour of submerged distress. I wrote the article — *currente calamo* — at Newport, while wondering what I was going to do for a winter shelter; and I hardly consulted a book, while, certainly, I knew nothing of my subject. As I think of it, I must say I decidedly admire my own energy and directness; even if I have to confess to a considerable degree of simple-minded assurance. The article appeared — "judiciously edited," I am glad to say, by Norton — in the *North American* for April, 1867, and it helped me much. I have not read it for over forty years; and I should be somewhat afraid to read it now; but then it was a first step; undeniably ill-considered and rash, it showed life.

Meanwhile, trying somehow to catch on to the railroad interest, I did make an honest effort at the law. It simply would not go! There was something inherently unsympathetic — *antipatica* — between it and me. Not only did I feel it, but I was conscious, or thought I was conscious of the fact, that, somehow, every one else realized it also. I never had, to my recollection, a *bona-fide* client. The whole experience was to the last degree humiliating; it may have been healthy, but it certainly was not agreeable.

Again, time, patience and persistent pegging away worked a salvation. Fortunately, I had enough to live on in a small but sufficiently comfortable way, and the dreary clientless months crept on. But my pen was always busy; I wrote article on article, almost always on railroads, or railroad law, for the *North American* or the magazines, law and other, and in that way identified my name with railroads; but it was a discouraging process. I never seemed to get anywhere; the outlook did not brighten. Then, as is wont to be the case, day suddenly broke. Up to that time, Massachusetts had no department of government specially connected with its growing but still wholly unregulated railroad system. I fixed my mind on the great probability of such a department being soon created, and determined to try for a place in it. In this, I succeeded; nor, as things go in life, did I have long to wait.

It was in October, 1866, that I began operations; in July, 1869, my purpose was accomplished. An act creating a State Board of Railroad Commissioners was passed by the Legislature, in the spring of 1869, largely through my instrumentality; and, making a strike for the position, I was appointed the third member of it. I had worked my problem successfully out in two years and nine months; a very creditable consummation.

Again, as in February, 1865, everything, so to speak, flowered simultaneously, all my long efforts seemed to mature together, wholly changing my position at once and permanently. I at last had my foot firmly on the lower rung of the ladder, and was on the way up. My father had returned from London in the spring of 1868. Leaving his house in Boston, which until then I had occupied, we, in the autumn of 1868, established ourselves on the Neponset turnpike, in Quincy. It was a wise thing to do; though, at the time, I did not so consider it. I went there most reluctantly; but in Quincy I was known. There, during that Winter, I with infinite pains, sparing no labor, wrote my *Chapter of Erie*. That showed progress; it was really a careful piece of literary

work. In the spring also I was invited by the Grand Army
Post, at Quincy, to deliver a Fourth of July Address. I
agreed to do it; and on that, also, I spared no pains. I actually memorized it; a thing I could not possibly now do.
When July came, my nomination as Railroad Commissioner,
my Fourth of July Address, and the *Chapter of Erie* all came
at once, and together. Careful preparation told. The success of each effort was considerable; my chance was secure.
That Fourth of July, 1869, was, distinctly, one of my life's
red-letter days. It stands out in memory as such. The preliminary struggle at last was over; the way was open before
me. At last I had worked myself into my proper position
and an environment natural to me.

I served on the Massachusetts Board of Railroad Commissioners exactly ten years, from July, 1869, to July, 1879;
for seven of the ten, I was chairman, and for the whole ten
by common consent the controlling mind of the Board. In
1879, my fourth commission expired, and I declined a re-
nomination. I had done all I could do in the position; and,
so far as I personally was concerned, I had got out of it all
it had to give. It was time I left, and looked elsewhere. But
certainly, those ten were prosperous, active, useful years for
me — years good to live, good to look back on. My two
colleagues on the original commission were very ordinary
men; both much older than I. But, all the same, they let
me do nearly all the work of the Board, and write all the
reports, and the reports were thought well of. When,
through the chapter of accidents, those two associates were
retired, I came to the chairmanship, and then my two colleagues — Mr. Briggs, of Springfield, and Mr. Johnson, of
Newton — were, as associates, all I could ask for. It was a

really excellent board, as good as such a board well could be, able, honest, perfectly harmonious. It was a very pleasant official life; and, as the initial Railroad Commission, the success of the Board was pronounced and generally recognized.

As for myself, looking back, I think, all things considered, I did well. I made some mistakes of judgment, and bad mistakes. Frequently, I proved unequal to the occasion. More than once, I now see, I was lacking in firmness, and even in courage. I did not take the position I should have taken. On the other hand, on the one great occasion which offered I did prove fully equal to it, and my success then more than counterbalanced all my shortcomings elsewhere. I refer to our action and report on the strike of engineers on the Boston & Maine Railroad, in February, 1877. On that occasion our Board rendered a really considerable public service, putting a sharp stop to a rapidly increasing epidemic, and courageously laying down some very salutary doctrines which were productive of lasting effects. That was twenty-three years ago (1900); and there has not since been a strike of railroad train operatives in New England. I wrote the whole of the report, at Quincy, during the evening which followed the hearings. My associates adopted my draft the next day, without the change of a word; it was immediately published; and, as a leading member of the Legislature — General Cogswell, of Ipswich — afterwards remarked to me: "It cleared the air like a thunderclap." On the action then taken, I now (1912) pride myself. In my judgment great and unnecessary friction would have been since avoided and industrial results of the utmost importance secured had the precedent there established been since generally followed.

The appeal in industrial difficulties was to an enlightened public opinion, based on facts elicited by a fair-minded public investigation. As labor conflicts have since occurred, I have repeatedly called attention to that experience and precedent; but it was a voice crying in the wilderness. Our people as a community do not share in my faith in publicity; but, all the same, public opinion and patience are the best possible agents for successfully solving industrial, social and economical problems. Twenty-five years subsequently (1902) I told the story in a paper entitled *Investigation and Publicity as opposed to Compulsory Arbitration*, read before the American Civic Federation, and then printed by me in pamphlet form. The Roosevelt Commission on the Pittsburg Anthracite Coal Strike of that year formally adopted my views, and recommended accordingly; but nothing came of it. That action and report of 1877, however, I still hold to have been as creditable a piece of work as I ever did; it was also courageous. Perhaps I ought to have followed it up; made in fact the following of it up my work in life. Who knows? It is a supremely wise man who recognizes his mission when the call comes and occasion offers. I certainly have in life not been over-wise, much less supremely so.

On the other hand, not impossibly my turn of thought is too philosophical for practical, every-day purposes; and, being so, it fails to make proper allowance for the natural in human nature — the desire of the man in the street to get things done and, as he imagines, once-and-for-all disposed of. Hence, as I see it, the growing tendency to excessive legislation — to the everlasting issuing of new legislative edicts in which the supposed popular will is crystallized and penalized. For myself, I don't believe in it. I never have believed in it; and for this reason, perhaps, have failed to be in sympathy with the sturdy champions of the "Dear Peepul." But, after all, such are but the old-time courtier, the sycophant and the parasite of the Tudor and Stuart periods thinly disguised and in a slightly different rôle; and the lot of the man who talks of Reason, Publicity and Patience now differs not greatly from the lot of him who three centuries ago questioned Divine Right, or gave open expression to a doubt as to the infallibility of the British Solomon. And so it goes! The potter's wheel has turned; the clay and the potter remain the same.

So, as Chairman of the Massachusetts Board of Railroad Commissioners, I for ten years consistently and persistently preached my doctrine. It, too, proved in the outcome a mere phase in a process of development along the old lines. A stronger diet is called for; mine is pronounced a Milk-and-Water Dispensation. Unquestionably the late Thomas Carlyle would have so denominated and denounced it. Fortunately, however, the Strong-Arm Policy is restricted in its application to the domain of Politics and cannot reach out into those of Science, Art, Literature or Medicine. Hence, the world does get on; but, for all I see, industrial controversies still remain in the old chaotic stage, or a little more so; while, as to the so-called transportation abuses, if any real progress to more satisfactory conditions has been made, a knowledge of the fact has not reached me. Whatever improvement has been secured has been through the operation of natural influences and not as a result of legislative edict.

But my activity during those ten years (1869–1879) was by no means confined to railroads, or my official duties as a commissioner. In other fields I did a great deal of work; and in my work I took pleasure. I was in every way prosperous; successful in business, I was happy at home. They were good years — those with me between thirty-four and forty-four. I had, in 1870, found myself so well off in a worldly way that I projected, and built, on land my father gave me, the house on President's Hill in Quincy; where we lived from 1871 to 1893. Four of my five children were born in that house; and in it no death occurred during our occupancy. We moved into it, a new house, when my wife was twenty-nine and I was thirty-six; we moved out of it, when Quincy, ceasing in the way already described to be a town, had been metamorphosed into a most commonplace suburban municipality; and, as such, was to me no longer bearable. We then by a most fortunate cast in the dice of life, changed environments, moving into a far better abode in much more congenial surroundings.

Still, in Quincy, for more than a score of years I was very active as a worker, and was an influential citizen. My record too was creditable. I left a mark on the town government — on its schools, on its Public Library, on its Park system. I have told the whole story, always leaving out my own name and carefully suppressing reference to myself, in the third of my *Three Episodes of Massachusetts History*. So far as the producing of results was concerned, I was, also, between 1870 and 1890, most fortunately placed. I worked with and through my brother, J. Q. Adams. I never was sympathetic or popular; he, somehow, was. He was in close touch with the people of Quincy; me, they were disposed to look at a bit askance. But he and I, in town matters, always acted together. I was much the more active-minded; he was inclined to indolence. But, when set in motion, provided he did not encounter too much opposition, he had a really remarkable faculty of accomplishing results. He was, however, by nature prone to be too easily discouraged. We both delighted in town-meeting. Its atmosphere — in the olfactory way pretty bad at times — came naturally to us; we were bone of their bone, flesh of their flesh; and the mass of those there knew it and felt it; and, for twenty years, we together practically managed Quincy affairs. It was also Quincy's golden age. The town-meetings were reduced from a mob to a model; the finances were straightened out; the school system was reorganized and made famous; the Public Library building was erected and endowed; a system of Parks was devised and developed; and, finally, Quincy was actually freed from debt. The last fact stated is significant — eloquent even. That was under a town government, and in largest extent because of my steady urgency. The levy then was ten dollars in the thousand of valuation. Now (1912), twenty years later under a city government, Quincy has a debt of two million dollars and is considering an annual levy of twenty-five dollars on the thousand! Judging by the balance-sheets of the respective periods, my brother John and I certainly exercised a not unsalutary influence.

I have told the story in my *Three Episodes*, carefully, as I have said, suppressing all claim for personal credit. But the historic fact is that whatever was then accomplished our town owed wholly and exclusively to us; and, moreover, I do not hesitate here to add that, in so far as I was not, as in the cases of the Library and Parks, the immediately active force, I was the stimulating spirit. That record of local and municipal activity and usefulness is one pleasant to look back on. During those twenty years, I was a member of the School Committee, of the Trustees of the Public Library, a Park Commissioner, and a Commissioner of the Sinking Fund. There never was a time when I was not actively engaged in town work; nor was I ever defeated when a candidate for office. I never before reviewed that record; to do it now (1912), after a lapse of twenty years, affords me satisfaction. It was eminently creditable — far more so than I supposed. Out of pure public spirit I did a great deal of work, and I did it well; and, though it nowhere so appears, the Thomas Crane Library building and the Merrymount Park remain in Quincy permanent memorials of that fact.

In my life I seem to be able to put my finger on two accidental epoch-marking incidents. One was the coming across a certain book at a crucial period of mental development; the other was being invited to deliver an occasional address. When in England in November, 1865, shortly after my marriage, I one day chanced upon a copy of John Stuart Mill's essay on Auguste Comte, at that time just published. My intellectual faculties had then been lying fallow for nearly four years, and I was in a most recipient condition; and that essay of Mill's revolutionized in a single morning my whole mental attitude. I emerged from the theological stage, in which I had been nurtured, and passed into the scientific. I had up to that time never even heard of Darwin. *Inter arma*, etc. From reading that compact little volume of Mill's at Brighton in November, 1865, I date a changed intellectual and moral being.

The other individually epochal incident occurred eight years afterwards. It was curious, and, though commonplace enough at the moment, in remote consequences in its way dramatic. Wholly unconsciously on my part and with no sense of volition, I entered on a path which led far — for me very far! Indeed, I then found my vocation — a call had come! The incident occurred in 1874, and thirty years later I gave in another address [1] delivered at Weymouth a somewhat autobiographical account of it. It is only needful to premise that the James Humphrey referred to was typical of the old New England stock. A man then advanced in life, plain in dress and aspect, he was very lame — walking always with the aid of two canes, one in each hand; but his whole presence was somehow suggestive of honest shrewdness. The "Judge" was a man of a stamp common enough formerly, but now rarely found within a radius of twenty miles of Boston, if not indeed in that region extinct. For example, since I went to Lincoln to live in 1893, the type, then familiar enough there, has disappeared — it was the going of the Massachusetts village squire, the town-meeting stand-by, the traditional moderator and selectman.

Getting back to my story, the 1904 account of the incident was as follows: "Just thirty years ago last spring, on a day in April, if my memory serves me right, your old-time selectman, James Humphrey — remembered by you as 'Judge' Humphrey — called at my office, then in Pemberton Square, Boston. Taking a chair by my desk, he next occasioned wide-eyed surprise on my part by inviting me, on behalf of a committee of the town of Weymouth, to deliver an historical address at the coming two hundred and fiftieth anniversary of the permanent settlement of the place. Recently returned to civil life from four years of active military service, and nominally a lawyer, I was at that time, as chairman of

[1] *Weymouth Thirty Years Later*, Weymouth Historical Society, no. 3, 115-16.

the State Board of Railroad Commissioners, devoting my attention to questions connected with the growth and development of transportation. To independent historical investigation I had never given a thought. As to Weymouth, I very honestly confess I hardly knew where the town so called was, much less anything of its story; having a somewhat vague impression only that my great-grandmother, Parson William Smith's daughter, Abigail, had been born there, and there lived her girlhood. Such was my surprise, I remember, that I suggested to Mr. Humphrey he must be acting under a misapprehension, intending to invite some other member of my family, possibly my father. He, however, at once assured me such was not the case, satisfying me finally that, a man sober and in his right mind, he knew what he was about, and whom he was talking to. Subsequently, I learned that he did indeed act as the representative of a committee appointed at the last annual Weymouth town-meeting; for an explanation of the choice appeared — as 'a great-grandson of Abigail (Smith) Adams, a native of Weymouth,' I had been selected for the task. Overcoming my surprise, I told Mr. Humphrey I would take the matter under consideration. Doing so, I finally concluded to accept. Though I had not the faintest idea of it at the time, that acceptance marked for me an epoch; I had, in fact, come to a turning-point in life. That, instinctively, if somewhat unadvisedly and blindly, I followed the path thus unexpectedly opened has been to me ever since cause of gratitude to Weymouth. For thirty years it has led me through pastures green and pleasant places. But at the moment, so little did I know of the earlier history of Massachusetts, I was not aware that any settlement had been effected hereabouts immediately after that at Plymouth, or that the first name of the place was Wessagusset; nor, finally, that Thomas Morton had, at about the same time, erected the famous May-pole at Merrymount, on the hill opposite where I dwelt. Thus the field into which I was invited was one wholly new to me, and unwittingly I entered on it; but, for once, fortune builded for me better than I knew. I began on a study which has since lasted continuously."

I prepared that Address, and delivered it on King-Oak Hill on the Fourth of July, 1874. The morning of that day was propitious, and the meeting, an open-air one, passed off well enough. Taken by surprise, I had to convert what was meant for a discourse from manuscript into an oral *ex tempore* address, but I acquitted myself fairly; and, after the thing was over, went home without attending the other features of the occasion. I felt tired, and a storm was plainly gathering; that afternoon how it did rain! The flood-gates were opened. That, and the afternoon rain of the third day at Gettysburg, well do I recall them.

But returning once more to the 1874 performance, the historical investigation preliminary thereto interested me; and though a somewhat crude and 'prentice-like piece of historical work, the address itself brought me a certain degree of notice as well as credit, leading among other things to my election in the following year (1875) as a member of the Massachusetts Historical Society. Step by step, as leisure and occasion offered and called, I was led further and yet further in the investigation upon which I then entered, and it occupied me, on and off, twenty years. It was not until November, 1892, that, in my *Three Episodes* of *Massachusetts History*, I finished and published the story I first got acquainted with while preparing my Address of June, 1874.

Returning to my narrative, the year before this for me epochal episode — that is, in 1873 — I was concerned in the earliest of the many outside commissions to which I have first and last been appointed, and upon which I have done some of the work I shall ever do of most lasting value. My father-in-law, Edward Ogden, had died in Paris, in June, 1872, and his wife — one of the most lovable characters I ever knew, affectionate, unselfish and immensely capable — had followed her husband suddenly, dying of heart disease in the railroad station at Lyons, while on her way from Geneva to Paris, in November following. Her three daughters had remained in Europe. I thought of going out, to arrange certain business matters and bring them home, when Governor Washburn suddenly appointed me chairman of a commission provided for by the Massachusetts Legislature to attend the Vienna Exposition and report thereon. I went out in April, and returned in September. My experience was pleasant enough, and in a way instructive; though I was generally quite unqualified for the task. Of course, as I always have, I failed fully to avail myself of my opportunities, and the experience left on my own mind a distinct sense of self-insufficiency; but, passing all that, it was my supreme good fortune on this occasion to have associated with me Frank D. Millet, who was appointed Secretary of the Commission, and met me as such in Vienna. He and I, at any rate, were sympathetic. Coming together at once, we remained together ever after; and until his terrible death in the frightful *Titanic* disaster of April, 1912. I then gave public expression [1] to the value I put upon his friendship, and the more than esteem I felt for him. He was a very rare character, and his unaffected friendship I held more than the equivalent of a diploma — it was a decoration. Through nearly forty years correspondents, we were also in the earlier and the better period companions in numerous vacation trips. I have had more days on the water with him, in close touch with Nature — days of good companionship and keen yachting enjoyment, days a delight to look back upon — than with all other persons I have ever met put together; for Millet was incomparably the most perfect holiday companion it was ever my fortune to encounter. So I reckon his and my chance association that Vienna summer, one of the bits of supreme good fortune which in all my life have come my way. Millet was one of perhaps a half-dozen in all whose going left for me a void and permanent sense of loss not again to be made good — and the void and sense of loss thus in his case left were the largest and most sensible of all.

In 1877, I think it was, I was again appointed a member of a special commission created to report a plan for utilizing the Troy & Greenfield Railroad — that Hoosac Tunnel elephant then a problem on the hands of the Commonwealth; and I prepared its report. Nothing came of it immediately; but that report foreshadowed the course subsequently pursued.

Once more, in 1878, I was made the Chairman of the Board of Government Directors of the Union Pacific Railroad Company, and, for the first time, visited the Pacific Coast. This was through the influence of Carl Schurz, then Secretary of the Interior in the Hayes Cabinet. I prepared

[1] *Art and Progress*, vol. III, no. 9, July, 1912.

the report; but, though at the time it was merely put in the Department files, much to me a little later on resulted from that experience.

In 1892 I was appointed chairman of the preliminary and advisory commission provided for by the Legislature of Massachusetts to devise a system of Parks and Public Reservations in the vicinity of Boston; and, a year later, when, to my utter surprise, our recommendations had been approved and adopted, I became chairman of the permanent commission organized to carry the system we had outlined and recommended into effect. I served on this Board until June, 1895. I then resigned, feeling that my task was accomplished, and I had best quit betimes. Wholly opposed to the policy of rapid growth and what I could not but regard as premature development, I found myself powerless to check it. I was, in fact, frightened at our success in the work we had to do, and the expenditure step by step involved in it. A few years later, however, I again served (1903) as chairman of a special commission appointed to apportion the cost of maintenance of the system of reservations among the several cities and towns responsible therefor. Eleven years had elapsed since I first got concerned in the development. My connection with it then at last ceased. And yet I greatly doubt whether at any period of my life, or in any way, I have done work more useful or so permanent in character, as that I did in this connection; for I was largely instrumental in saving to the people of Massachusetts the Blue Hills and the Middlesex Fells. In one more year the former, at least, would have been gone beyond the possibility of redemption. The granite-quarry man had obtained a footing in it, and the work of exploitation was actually in

process. The Blue Hills were, so to speak, in my special baili-
wick — the region of my *Three Episodes*. To their inclusion
in the Reservation I especially devoted my efforts. Thus I
may also not unfairly claim the Blue Hill Park Reservation
as in part my monument.

In 1897 I was appointed chairman of a Massachusetts
commission provided to inquire into the relations between
street railways and municipalities. In this connection I
visited Europe, inquiring into systems in use there; and,
subsequently, prepared the report of that commission also,
which became the basis of comprehensive general legislation.

On all these commissions my relations with my colleagues
and associates were perfectly harmonious, and generally
more than merely friendly. Never in any case was there serious friction in any one of them, or any considerable difference in our conclusions and recommendations. Uniformly the
drawing-up of the reports was entrusted to me. It has, therefore, always been a rather curious subject of reflection in my
mind, how it chanced that in the early days of my army experience alone — the period and position in which harmonious
relations with my superiors were most important — I found
myself in an utterly impossible position. Still vaguely impressed with the idea that it must have been largely my fault,
in subsequent relations of life I have never proved a person
difficult to get on with. I am, therefore, forced to the conclusion that it was simply a case of infernal bad luck. The
fault was mine in no respect; and the only possible alterna-
tive to the course I took would have been an unseemly
regimental quarrel, followed by my resignation. I could not
but have come out of the affair irremediably discredited.
It was better as it was. And yet, looking at it in all coolness

through the vista of fifty years, I am not sure I would not now feel better satisfied had I shown myself a fighting man of the old duelling school.

Again, however, returning to my narrative, apart from these minor public functions, my trouble all my recent life — that is, since I got my foot firmly on the rungs of the ladder in July, 1869 — has been a too active mind. I have continually attempted too much — always had too many irons in the fire. Besides my official and my literary life, for over forty years I led a very active business life. I managed a variety of considerable interests; was concerned in many enterprises. There is an old saying that the unsuccessful man is he who is wrong three times out of five; the successful man, he who is right in the same proportion. As I now look back on experiences stretching through more than a generation, my respect for my own judgment is the reverse of inflated. I have throughout dealt with large affairs; several times, I have made decided successes; but, as a rule, the fallibility of my judgment has been noticeable. A few successes, however, more than made good, in my case, almost innumerable blunders, the very thought of which is now most unpleasant to dwell upon. One great business success I did achieve; and it is the only one on which I can fairly plume myself. Going into it at its inception, in 1869, I have for over forty years been at the head of the Kansas City Stock Yards Company, directing its policy and development. When I became President, it was a concern of $100,000 capital, earning, perhaps, $20,000 a year gross. From this I stage by stage have built it up, always its President, until to-day it is capitalized at above ten millions, and earns annually over $1,200,000 gross. The second largest institution of the kind in the world in all these years it has missed but a single quarterly dividend; and that owing to a cataclysm — the Kaw Valley flood of 1903, which in three days swept away at least $600,000 of the values of enterprises of which I was the originator, and in which I was personally most largely interested. Financially, it was for me as a brick falling on the head as I walked along a familiar street. The loss was never recouped. Managed in a broad, liberal spirit, the Kansas City yards have been a great public benefit as well as a considerable commercial success. The success of the company drew down on it, of course, a populistic political attack of the most dangerous character about 1907; and this too it survived. I take much pride in its record; and feel I have a right so to do. *That,* I did.

I also early foresaw the future commercial importance, and consequent rapid growth, of Kansas City, arguing the proposition out fairly and from first principles; and I acted on my convictions, making there large purchases of real estate. Here I reasoned soundly, and acted boldly and with judgment. One of the enterprises I there organized and had a large interest in made in one year twelve dividends of ten per cent each (1886), has divided over four hundred per cent on its capital, and is now (1912) being closed out. Another investment there, long since having reimbursed its entire outlay several times over, represents still several-fold what I put into it.

While, therefore, in view of the opportunities I have had — the chances that have fallen in my way, not less numerous than superb — I have little to pride myself on on the score of sagacity or business judgment; yet, considering that my real thought has all the time been occupied in other directions, I cannot accuse myself of any glaring lack of discernment. The result speaks in a way for itself. In 1878, when I had been engaged in my operations for eight years and carrying what was for me a heavy load incident to the financial collapse of 1873, my liabilities exceeded my assets, as I then figured their value, by about fifteen thousand dollars. In 1879, with the return of the country to a gold basis, the tide turned. That thereafter for a season I was simply floating with the stream — a piece of flotsam borne along by the flooding tide — I realized at the time; but that I had in a degree foreseen the tide, and the channel in which it would flow, should to a certain extent be put down to my credit. On the other hand, I in no degree foresaw the almost unprecedented readjustment of values involved in the demonetization of silver, and the subsequent increase in the output of gold; and I further plead guilty to the fact that I allowed my head to be turned by the rush of my own prosperity. The mistakes I then made affected markedly the whole tenor as well as ease of my subsequent life — that after fifty-five. They turned the current awry.

On the other hand, looking back, I wonder at my own lack of insight and foresight. It seems to have required a certain degree of skill on my part to escape the opportunities, the great opportunities, fortune flung in my way; as, also, a certain perverseness seems to have been necessary to cause me to wallow, as it were, into the misadventures in which I from time to time involved myself. For instance, a participation in the great success of the Calumet and Hecla — the bonanza mine on record — was in 1868 almost thrust upon me; but I preferred to "invest" in some wretched Michigan lumber railroads, which I long ago dropped as hopeless.

None the less, however, I did get through; and got through better than I had any right to expect — indeed, successfully, as success in such things goes. That, in place of my suffering financial shipwreck, it so fell out was the result partly of persistence, partly of judgment, largely of luck.

Indeed, as I approach the end, I am more than a little puzzled to account for the instances I have seen of business success — money-getting. It comes from a rather low instinct. Certainly, so far as my observation goes, it is rarely met with in combination with the finer or more interesting traits of character. I have known, and known tolerably well, a good many "successful" men — "big" financially — men famous during the last half-century; and a less interesting crowd I do not care to encounter. Not one that I have ever known would I care to meet again, either in this world or the next; nor is one of them associated in my mind with the idea of humor, thought or refinement. A set of mere money-getters and traders, they were essentially unattractive and uninteresting. The fact is that money-getting, like everything else, calls for a special aptitude and great concentration; and for it, I did not have the first in any marked degree, while to it I never gave the last. So, in now summing up, I may account myself fortunate in having got out of my ventures as well as I did. Running at times great risks, I emerged, not ruined.

Taken as a whole, my life has not been the success it ought to have been. Where did the fault come in? I think I can put my finger on it. I began with a scheme of life; nor was it a bad one. It was to establish myself at fifty; so that, after fifty, I would be free to exert myself in such way as I might then desire. Life, also, I regarded as a sequence

— one thing, accident apart, leading to another. I followed this scheme rather successfully, and for a long time. I got well under way in 1869, being then thirty-four. I had been through my early experiences, nor had they been lacking in variety. I had enjoyed college and society, and got a glimpse of early professional life; a glimpse of that sufficed! Then came the army, an exceptional break. After that, I was married at thirty, and, by the time I was thirty-four, I had caught the step. At forty-four, I resigned from the railroad commissionership, having achieved a success, to become, first, the Chairman of the Board of Arbitration of the Trunk Line Railroads, and then, immediately afterwards, the President of the Union Pacific. These were both natural sequences from what had preceded. The Trunk Line Arbitration was not a success. The time for it had clearly not come. Just the right man in the position held by me might possibly have worked out very considerable results; but I doubt; and, certainly, I was not the man to do it. The whole thing depended on Colonel Albert Fink. I was merely his instrument; and I gravely question whether conditions were at that time ripe for a successful development on the lines Colonel Fink contemplated. Nevertheless, that I was tendered, and for three years held the position I then did, was a sufficient proof of the standing I had attained. Unconsciously I had now come to the parting of the ways. I knew it, thoughtfully pondered it — and took the wrong road!

In 1882 I became a member of the Board of Direction of the Union Pacific Railroad Company, and, in the spring of 1884, that company found itself in financial trouble. I went out to Omaha, with F. L. Ames, to look into its affairs; and they certainly were then in a shocking bad way. The concern was threatened with summary proceedings on behalf of the United States Government, its service was demoralized, it had just backed down before its employees in face of a threatened strike, and it was on the verge of bankruptcy, with a heavy floating debt. Sidney Dillon, then its president, was old, and had lost his nerve. He was involved with the company, and alarmed lest he should be compelled to suspend. He insisted, therefore, on being relieved. Everything pointed to me as the person to succeed him. I was at once sent on to Washington to avert the threatened action of the Government, which would have sent the company into the hands of a receiver; and then and there I had my first experience in the most hopeless and repulsive work in which I ever was engaged — transacting business with the United States Government, and trying to accomplish something through Congressional action. My initial episode was with a prominent member of the United States Senate. This Senator is still (1912) alive, though long retired; he has a great reputation for ability, and a certain reputation, somewhat fly-blown, it is true, for rugged honesty. I can only say that I found him an ill-mannered bully, and by all odds the most covertly and dangerously corrupt man I ever had opportunity and occasion carefully to observe in public life. His grudge against the Union Pacific was that it had not retained him — he was not, as a counsel, in its pay. While he took excellent care of those competing concerns which had been wiser in this respect, he never lost an opportunity of posing as the fearless antagonist of corporations when the Union Pacific came to the front. For that man, on good and sufficient grounds, I entertained a deep dislike. He was distinctly dishonest — a senatorial bribe-taker.

However, when I went to Washington in May, 1884, to look after the Union Pacific interests, I succeeded, after a fashion, in effecting a settlement; and, when I got back to New York, I was duly made President of the company in place of Dillon, resigned. I remained its President six and a half years, until November, 1890, and of my experience in that position, and its outcome, I do not propose to say much. I took the position advisedly, and from purely selfish considerations. I was then only forty-nine, and ambitious. With a good deal of natural confidence in myself, I looked upon assuming the management of a great railway system, and correctly enough, as the legitimate outcome of what had, in my case, gone before. I was simply playing my game to a finish. I was not yet fifty, and I did not want to break off, and go into retirement, in mid-career. So I assumed charge of the Union Pacific, quite regardless of the fact that, in so doing, I took the chances heavily against myself; for the concern was in bad repute, heavily loaded with obligations, odious in the territory it served; and, moreover, though I had no realizing sense of the fact, a day of general financial reckoning was at hand.

And yet, with all these chances against me, my scheme, so far as my future was concerned, was, as I now see, well-conceived, entirely practicable, and even it justified itself in the result. Unfortunately for myself, I lacked the clean-cut firmness to adhere to it. Had I only done so, I should have achieved a great success, and been reputed among the ablest men of my time. The trouble was — and a very common trouble it is — I did not know when to lay down my hand, and leave the game. My original plan was perfectly defined. It was to retain the railroad presidency for five years, and then to retire, being at that time fifty-four. My first five years in control of the affairs of the company were most successful. I got its finances in order; greatly improved the service; reëstablished its credit; paid off the whole of its floating debt; improved its relations with the communities it served. I did not, however, succeed in effecting a settlement between it and the United States Government. Thus, when I ought, upon every possible consideration, to have resigned the presidency and retired from active management — for I was tired of it and had grown to long for other pursuits and more congenial associates — I went lumbering on, chasing the *ignis fatuus* of a government settlement; and, at last, absolutely a victim to the duty delusion, laboring under the foolish idea that I owed some sort of obligation to my company, and that my services could not well be spared. I paid the penalty!

During the last eighteen months of my connection with the Union Pacific I was — there is no use denying it, or attempting to explain it away — wholly demoralized. I hated my position and its duties, and yearned to be free of it and from them. My office had become a prison-house. Loathing it, I was anxious, involved, hopeless. I had accordingly become a plunger; rapidly getting beyond my depth. I have nothing to say in extenuation. I displayed indecision and weakness — almost as much as Napoleon showed in his Russian campaign. Comparing little things with big, and a small man with a great one, the one situation had become as impossible for me as was the other for him. I simply now rode for a fall; nor did I really care when or how I got it. Taken altogether, this was, I think, my least creditable experience; and certainly that upon which I look back with the most dissatisfaction. Though ultimately I purchased my freedom at a great price, it was worth to me all it cost; and though I have deeply regretted the folly and lack of will-power which got me into such a wretched position, I have never for a moment grudged the price exacted of me in leaving it. In the course of my railroad experiences I made no friends, apart from those in the Boston direction; nor among those I met was there any man whose acquaintance I valued. They were a coarse, realistic, bargaining crowd.

Railroads, and the railroad connection, thus occupied over twenty years of my life; and, when at last, in December, 1890, I got rid of them, it was with a consciousness of failure, but a deep breath of relief. I was emancipated; and, from that day to this, I have eschewed the subject. I had a surfeit; and the surfeit super-induced disgust. The equivalent to a professional life on my part ended, therefore, in December, 1890; it was then as if, being a lawyer, I had left my office, and closed my connection forever with legal affairs or problems. But, in my case, that meant merely an application to what had all along been those activities and pursuits which appealed to me — for which I felt a call, and in which I found my pleasure. Except when at the head of the Union Pacific I had never wholly given them up; and even then only at times. I must admit they were rather multifarious, those activities, and it does not speak highly for my judgment and controlling good sense that I allowed myself to be drawn off in so many directions. The fact is, as I have just said, not understanding well myself or my own limitations, I was cursed with a dangerous mental activity; and, physically, I was not less mobile. Accordingly for twenty years and more I was travelling incessantly; a large proportion of my nights were passed in sleeping-cars — and, curiously enough, I slept more soundly there than at home and in my own bed; while, on the intellectual side, an array of bound volumes — ten in number — and two volumes of occasional newspaper contributions, bear evidence to my intellectual restlessness. Creditable in a way, they constitute a record in which it is not possible for a man to take any considerable or real satisfaction; for it is a record of dissipation and of quantity rather than one of quality and concentration. But the fact is I worked in the way natural to me; and I did take pleasure in my activity. Undoubtedly I overdid it at times, and life was made temporarily somewhat of a burden; but the thing never ran into a dangerous excess.

The two forms of activity, the professional and the extra-professional, that which I carried on for the enjoyment and satisfaction, or interest, I got out of it or felt in it, ran along side by side. The professional life began in July, 1869, and ended, abruptly, in December, 1890. The extra-professional life — business, political, educational and literary — began earlier — about 1868 — and is not yet (1912) closed. It ran in many directions, naturally, under the circumstances, accomplishing large results in none. My *Chapter of Erie* was published in July, 1869. In the years that immediately followed I got interested in historical and educational work, as my Weymouth Address (1874) and my papers on the Quincy School System bore evidence. In 1875, I was elected a member of the Massachusetts Historical Society, a recognition which I at the time took somewhat lightly, but which afterwards implied much. All through those years I was, instinctively but unconsciously, gravitating to my vocation; for I was engaged at odd moments — as a recreation and because I liked it — in historical research. The local records and traditions of the region in which I lived had an attraction for me, I found a real and great fascination in re-creating the past — the Wessagusset settlement at Weymouth, "Tom" Morton and his May-pole, at Merrymount, John Wheelwright and his Chapel of Ease, in Braintree, the early settlement and church, the highways, the training-field, the town-meetings and the schools. Out of this I got enjoyment; and, now, I feel a sense of satisfaction in having put on permanent record the past of that region. *That*, I did; and the record is there, and will remain. It may not be great, and certainly has not, nor will it obtain a recognized place in general literature; but, locally, it is a classic; and, when you come to classics, "local" and "world" are relative terms. The great reading public never took note of my *Three Episodes;* but in the Quincy community, it will be more read as time goes on. Even two centuries hence it will there be referred to and quoted. In 1880 this work was practically completed. Between that year and 1884, I was very active. It was a period of intermission. I delivered the Phi Beta Kappa oration — *A College Fetich;* I edited the *New English Canaan;* I wrote the *Sir Christopher Gardiner.* I was on the verge of my vocation. It was a fruitful and satisfactory period. My privately printed volume, *Episodes in New England History*, bears the date 1883; and I recall the enjoyment with which, in the comparative leisure and quiet repose of Quincy, I then put those pages through the press. Nearly seven years of waste followed — the years devoted to the Union Pacific — and, during them, I had small leisure for historical investigation. Those years I passed in my office, largely in the society of stenographers. But in June, 1882, I was chosen one of the Board of Overseers of Harvard University, and on that Board, and a very active worker on it, continued through four terms of six years each; and my papers and reports on the English Department, representing a really large amount of work, were not without results of a more or less permanent character.

In 1890 I was at last thrown forcibly out of the utterly false position from which, I am obliged to confess, I did not have the will-power to extricate myself. Ejected by Jay Gould from the presidency of the Union Pacific, I at last, and instantly, fell back on my proper vocation. I was then fifty-five; but it was not too late. Though forced back into it by a kindly Providence, my scheme of life was being carried out with a greater degree of consistency than is usual with life-schemes. In spite of myself, I was working a way out. Disgust and discontent for and with my position had already produced results; and, for more than a year previous to my railroad downfall, I had been occupied with my biography of R. H. Dana. When the blessed crisis came, and the catastrophe occurred, the book was ready for publication. Somewhere in my *Memorabilia* I remember philosophizing over the fact — it was literally on two successive days that I ceased to be a railroad man and appeared as an author. A case of out of the darkness and into the light — it could not have been better arranged!

Finding my calling in December, 1890, I should then have been in good time to achieve such results in it as I was capable of, had it not been for the awful and inexcusable plunging of which I had been guilty during my final period of demoralization, towards the close of my business activity. I only just escaped utter shipwreck. It was in May, 1893, that the long-impending, plainly gathering financial storm broke — the most deep-seated and far-reaching in the history of the country. That I, placed as I then was, could have avoided it, would not have been possible. My whole scheme of life, and theory of the material situation and course of development of the country made it impossible. It was something of which I had no preconception — a readjustment necessitated by a change in the measures of value, a change such as had never occurred before. One of the precious metals was demonetized. For anything so world-wide and far-reaching, I was not prepared. I had always looked forward to a depreciation of values, especially in real estate; and for that I had made some degree of preparation; but I had not expected to see the bottom tumble out, and values become purely nominal. This, however, was what happened. As the spokesman of Tennyson's *Maud* expressed it, "a vast speculation had fail'd," and I had excellent cause to "mutter" and "madden" as the "flying gold" of a series of autumns "drove thro' the air." When in those June days of 1893 the collapse came, I was then carrying a large amount of sail — far more than was prudent; for, my head turned by long and considerable success, I had become reckless. But, after my sudden railroad dethronement, to reduce sail was impossible; and, at the same time, I had to assume heavy additional burdens on account of liabilities I had incautiously entered upon on account of the Union Pacific; but which now I had to shoulder myself. Thus, with much canvas spread, I was loaded down with a cargo I had never intended to take on.

The storm broke! There was the misadventure of my life. I was fifty-eight when the crash came. The fury of the gale was weathered; but its results were felt continuously through five long, precious years. They were for me years of simple Hell — years during which I had to throw everything aside, and devote myself to rehabilitating a wreck. It made no sort of difference that the wreck was the result of my own improvidence; there it was right under me, and the question of again reaching a port was the only one to consider. The dislocation this event caused — coming just when it did — shattered my whole scheme of life. Breaking in upon it, it broke it up. I was sixty-three years old, and a tired man, when at last the effects of the 1893 convulsion wore themselves out, and my mind was once more at ease so that I could return to my calling.

The mercury in the financial barometer touched its lowest point in the spring and summer of 1897 — the dead ebb of a tide steadily receding through four entire years. That winter we had passed at Florence, living, not unpleasantly, in a villa there — the Boutilene — I immersed in my father's diary and papers, and a very elaborate report I was drawing up as head of a committee of Overseers on written English at Harvard. I had an immense mass of material on this topic to work up; and I fear it was to a large extent a dissipation of force. At any rate, I cannot now — fifteen years later — see that any perceptible effect was produced — nothing appreciable; but I suppose it all went into the grand result, and is present somewhere. The University, however, I must say I found a hard and distinctly ungrateful subject on which to expend force. I was at it, on and off, and with a fair degree of steadiness, through twenty-five years, and

I might, I now think, have been more profitably employed. However, on that point I am on record; for, when my fourth term as Overseer came to a close in 1906, I said my say in the Columbia Phi Beta Kappa address *Some Modern College Tendencies*, and, so far as I am concerned, that tells the story. The world is very full of institutions calling loudly for a readjustment to bring about conformity with changed conditions — changed socially, morally, politically, financially, materially and, above all, educationally — and, of these institutions Harvard College — and, note — I say College and not University — is, to my mind, distinctly one. Indeed, I would say of it as Hamlet of Denmark, the world's a prison—"a goodly one, in which there are many confines, wards and dungeons; Harvard being one o' the worst." Like Gertrude's married life, it, in my judgment, needs to be reformed altogether. But this is a digression. My evidence as respects Harvard is on record in the little volume entitled *Three Phi Beta Kappa Addresses* (pp. 134–47); and I refer to the matter now only in connection with what was for me an episode occupying much time and thought on my part through twenty-five years.

Recurring to 1897, the tide, as I have said, then turned; the young flood began to make its influence felt. But it was still a very anxious period; the movement was slow, and I had reached the climacteric — I was in my 63d year. So, as my record shortly after (1900) made still tells, I took up the broken thread, conning to myself as I did so the lines from Tennyson's *Ulysses*, since college days a favorite among poems:

> Tho' much is taken, much abides; and tho'
> We are not now that strength which in old days

> Moved earth and heaven; that which we are, we are;
> One equal temper of heroic hearts,
> Made weak by time and fate, but strong in will
> To strive, to seek, to find, and not to yield.

That, and these other lines from Browning's *Paracelsus*, since 1853 a favorite:

> I will fight the battle out; a little spent
> Perhaps, but still an able combatant.

Meanwhile the great disturbance of that long and troubled period had been productive of two memorable changes in my way of life. I left Quincy and gave up my winter residence in Boston; in the closing days of 1893 I moved from Quincy to Lincoln, there thenceforth making my home, and a dozen years later (1905) I bought a house in Washington and fixed our winter abiding-place. In both cases, at the time of making it a wrench and a severe one, each proved a blessing in the end. The worst wrench, and by far the most painful one, was in the case of Quincy. That was awful! Quincy was bone of my bone — flesh of the Adams flesh. There I had lived vicariously or in person since 1640; there on my return from the war I had made my home, and later (1870) built my house; there I had fought my fight, not unsuccessfully, through the best years of life; there my children were born; in fact, I felt as if I owned the town, for every part of it was familiar to me, and it was I who had recounted its history. I felt about it exactly as Hawthorne felt about Salem. In his inimitable introductory chapter to the *Scarlet Letter*, he says: "This old town — my native place [I, by the way, was born not in Quincy but in Boston; but Quincy, none the less, ought to have been my birthplace, as it was my race-place] though I have dwelt much away

from it, both in boyhood and mature years — possesses, or
did possess, a hold on my affections, the force of which I
have never realized during my seasons of actual residence
there. . . . It is now nearly two centuries and a quarter since
the original Briton, the earliest emigrant of my name, made
his appearance in the wild and forest-bordered settlement,
which has since become a city. And here his descendants
have been born and died, and have mingled their earthy
substance with the soil; until no small portion of it must
necessarily be akin to the mortal frame wherewith, for a
little while, I walk the streets. In part, therefore, the attachment which I speak of is the mere sensuous sympathy
of dust for dust. . . . So has it been in my case. I felt it
almost as a destiny to make Salem my home. . . . Nevertheless, this very sentiment is evidence that the connection,
which has become an unhealthy one, should at least be sev-
ered. Human nature will not flourish, any more than a po-
tato, if it be planted and replanted, for too long a series of
generations, in the same worn-out soil."

It was in my case much as Hawthorne here describes in
his; and so it came about that the storm and stress of 1893
— and it was an awful storm, and a period for me as for
many others of severest stress — the storm and stress of
1893, I say, in the matter of my continuing at Quincy,
only precipitated the inevitable. It simply had to come;
nor had I failed to realize the fact.

During the spring of 1893 I had accordingly taken the
preliminary steps, and, when the financial troubles broke
out, what had been before merely contemplated became a
condition to be immediately dealt with. In May, just before
the 1893 crisis came, by great good luck I had committed

myself to the purchase of the place at Lincoln where I have since lived, intending to occupy it at some indefinite, if not remote, future time when Quincy should have become impossible. Then came the crash, necessitating immediate action; and this I took. Early one Monday morning in the latter part of November, 1893, I mounted my horse at the door of my house on the hill at Quincy — the sun being hardly above the horizon of the distant sea-line in the nipping atmosphere — and rode over to Lincoln. I have not passed a night at Quincy since.

As things resulted, the change was timely and most fortunate. I have never seen occasion to regret it; and, long since, the place on President's Hill, on which I dwelt, and the development of which between the years 1870 and 1893 was one of the leading interests of my life, passed into other hands. It has been cut up, and "improved," as the expression goes, by the building of well-nigh innumerable houses. I have never set foot on President's Hill since 1895, when I parted with the property. I never mean to again. The Quincy I knew has ceased to exist; and, with the present Quincy, I have neither ties nor sympathy. In fact, I never now go there without, as I come away, drawing a breath of deep relief. When I enter it, I seem going into a tomb; when I leave it, getting back to Lincoln, it is a return to the sunlight and living air.

As to Boston, as a place in which to live and have one's being, it is much the same. There, however, I passed my winters from '84 to '96, building and occupying the house at the corner of Gloucester Street and Commonwealth Avenue. As a place for social life, long before I parted with my house in 1896 the resources were exhausted. When I first went back to Boston as a winter residence in 1884, it was enjoyable enough, and made more so by my official connection with the Massachusetts Historical Society. As time passed, however, I was made to realize that my whole Boston social existence consisted of the annual exchange of dinners with a rather narrow circle, rapidly changing and perceptibly contracting. This is the trouble with Boston — it is provincial. Including Cambridge, one finds there what might be called a very good society stock company — an exceptional number, in fact, of agreeable people, intimate acquaintance with whom is rarely formed except in youth, unless subsequently by chance encounter in Europe. When thus casually met, they are apt to emerge from their social shells in curiously attractive shapes and phases. Socially, however, the trouble with Boston is that there is no current of fresh outside life everlastingly flowing in and passing out. It is, so to speak, stationary — a world, a Boston world, unto itself; and, like all things stationary, there is in it, as the years pass, a very perceptible lack of that variety and change which are the essence and spice of life; it tends to stagnate. I, accordingly, rate it as one of the fortunate accidents of my life that the long and disheartening financial depression which followed the crisis of 1893 finally decided me, if indeed it did not seem to compel me, to dispose of my Commonwealth Avenue house, and sever my residence connection with Boston. The winter climate of Boston is distinctly Arctic, and society life, from sympathy, perhaps, seems then to pass through a long period of cold storage.

Nevertheless, the change of life, whether from summers at Quincy or winters in Boston, has seriously affected continuous and successful application to the task I for years have had in hand. That is the working up of raw material of history — of the papers, etc., of my father. My plan of a *magnum opus* was to write what would have been a diplomatic history of the Civil War. A rough draft of this I completed some ten years ago (1890), and since then it has remained unfinished. During the intervening time I have been absorbed in other things, largely correspondence, and the preparation of numerous papers for the Historical Society, all of which appear in its *Proceedings*. Incidentally, the work thus done at times related to incidents and episodes connected with my chief subject. These, however, though preliminary "Studies," have never been worked up into a continuous narrative. In the mean time what in this way I have been able to do has undergone incessant interruption, through literary forays and excursions — demands on me to prepare "occasional" addresses, etc., etc. Of work of this sort I have done altogether too much; and, looking back on it, it seems to have been singularly resultless and barren. Indeed, of all these performances, involving an immense amount of labor, there is but one I recall with pure gratification. This was the address entitled *Lee's Centennial*, delivered before the Washington and Lee University at Lexington, Virginia, on the 19th of January, 1907. In every way satisfactory, that occasion and effort left no bitter after-taste lurking in the mouth. I had then been in Europe, and it was on my return that I received the invitation. My selection was, for obvious reasons which at once suggest themselves, a very pronounced compliment, due to the memory, on the part of those composing the faculty of Washington and Lee, of an address I had delivered five years previously, before the Phi Beta Kappa Society of the University of Chicago — an address entitled *Shall Cromwell have a Statue?* The earlier address can be found in the little volume published by me in 1907, entitled *Three Phi Beta Kappa Addresses* — the other two being *A College Fetich*, delivered before the Harvard chapter in 1883, and that to which I have just referred, entitled *Some Modern College Tendencies* before the Columbia chapter in 1906. The address I am now referring to — *Lee's Centennial* — may be found printed in its final form, in the volume of my *Studies: Military and Diplomatic*, published in 1911.

As I have just said, the *Lee's Centennial* is my one effort in that line which I now regard as having been somewhat better than a mere waste of time and force. Indeed, from the literary point of view, I should put it in the forefront of anything I may have done. When I first received the invitation, I gave it scant consideration. As respects General Lee, the risk incurred by an acceptance loomed in my case large. I at once, therefore, wrote, stating that it would not be in my power to accept. Shortly after, I received another and more urgent letter from President Denny, of Washington and Lee, begging me to reconsider my determination, and expressing in warm language the desire of all concerned that I should undertake the task, and the disappointment that would be felt should I decline so to do. I then, with great reluctance, came to the conclusion that for me, with my family connection with Massachusetts, and the relations Massachusetts and Virginia had from first to last borne with each other — for me, I say, to decline a second time an invitation thus emphasized, would be distinctly ungracious. I felt I had to accept, and do the best I could; and take my chances. I accordingly did so. And that I did so has ever since been for me one of the pleasant things in life to look back on. I went to Virginia, accompanied by my friend F. D. Millet, in the following January, and there, on Saturday, the 19th of the month, delivered my address, standing on the platform of the College Chapel with Lee's tomb, and recumbent image upon it, directly behind me. As I have said, the occasion was in every way a success, and constituted a very grateful incident in life — good and altogether pleasant to look back on. It was not marred, as I afterwards realized, by a single untoward incident. The weather was perfect; my audience was packed and sympathetic; and what I offered was received with a warmth of applause which I have never elsewhere or on any other occasion had equalled. Most of all, I gratified a large number of most excellent people. Altogether pleasant at the time, it was in retrospect an occasion yet more pleasant.

The story of my life is told — here and in the pages of my *Memorabilia*. I became a Vice-President of the Massachusetts Historical Society in April, 1890, with a view to succeeding old George E. Ellis in the Presidency. My consent was not asked; nor did I think it a matter of sufficient importance to decline the position. I just drifted. In 1895 I became its President, and am so still (1912).

Finally, I want to say that preparing this *résumé* has been for me a decidedly profitable use of time. It has caused me to review, to weigh and to measure. As a result of that process, I feel I have no cause of complaint with the world. I have been a remarkably, an exceptionally, fortunate man. I have had health, absence of death, of dissipation and worthlessness in my family, with no overwhelming calamity to face and subside under; and the world has taken me for all I was fairly worth. Looking back, and above all, in reading that destroyed diary of mine, I see with tolerable clearness my own limitations. I was by no means what I in youth supposed myself to be. As to opportunity, mine seems to have been infinite. No man could ask for better chances. In a literary way, financially, politically, I might have been anything, had being it only been in me. The capacity, not the occasion, has been wanting. It was so in the army; it was so in railroads, in politics and in business; it was so in literature and history. In one and all my limitations made themselves felt; most of all, in the Law. On the other hand my abilities, as ability goes in this world, have been considerable; never first-rate, but more than respectable. They have enabled me to accomplish what I have accomplished; and I have accomplished something.

Six years ago, on its fiftieth year from graduation, my class delegated me to speak for them at the Commencement dinner. I did so, and then gave expression to something autobiographic in a way, and from which now I am not disposed greatly to dissent. I had said that Dr. Jacob Bigelow, of the class of 1806, whom, I well remembered, had in his life accomplished the greatest feat given any man to accomplish, in that he left his chosen calling other and better than he found it—elevated through him. And I then went on: "So now, looking back over these fifty years—their victories and their defeats, their accomplishments and their failures to accomplish—I have of late often thought how I would have had it go could I have shaped events in my own case so as now to please me most. As the shadows grow long, the forms things assume are very different from those once imagined. The dreams of ambition are transformed. It so chances I have had to do with varied callings; but now, looking back, I find I would not have greatly cared for supreme professional success, to have been a great physician, or divine, or judge. I served in the army once; but military rank and fame now seem to me a little empty. As to politics, it is a game; art, science, literature — we know how fashions change! None of the prizes to be won in those fields now tempt me greatly; nor do I feel much regret at my failure to win them. What I now find I would really have liked is something quite different. I would like to have accumulated — and ample and frequent opportunity for so doing was offered me — one of those vast fortunes of the present day rising up into the tens and scores of millions — what is vulgarly known as 'money to burn.' But I do not want it for myself; for my personal needs I have all I crave, and for my children I know, without being reminded of the fact, that excessive wealth is a curse. What I would now like the surplus tens of millions for would be to give them to Harvard. Could I then at this moment — and I say it reflectively — select for myself the result of the life I have lived which I would most desire, it would be to find myself in position to use my remaining years in perfecting, and developing to an equality with all modern requirements the institution John Harvard founded. I would like to be the nineteenth-century John Harvard — the John Harvard-of-the-Money-Bags, if you will. I would rather be that than be Historian or General or President." To be this, and to do this, was not given to me. In other directions also I have, perhaps, accomplished nothing considerable, compared with what my three immediate ancestors accomplished; but, on the other hand,

I have done some things better than they ever did; and, what is more and most of all, I have had a much better time in life — got more enjoyment out of it. In this respect I would not change with any of them.

As long ago as my college days I came across the closet memorandum of the Calif Abdalrahman, in Gibbon's *Decline and Fall*, and it made an impression upon me — an impression so deep, that, since, I have not wearied of referring to it. It is in Gibbon's fifty-second chapter, and reads as follows: "I have now reigned above fifty years in victory or peace; beloved by my subjects, dreaded by my enemies, and respected by my allies. Riches and honours, power and pleasure, have waited on my call, nor does any earthly blessing appear to have been wanting to my felicity. ·In this situation I have diligently numbered the days of pure and genuine happiness which have fallen to my lot: they amount to Fourteen: — O man! place not thy confidence in this present world!" I cannot undertake to number my days of "pure and genuine happiness"; and such days vary greatly with mortals. Obviously, they are a matter largely of individual disposition and temperament, much affected in their greater or less frequency by the very commonplace factor of digestion, or the presence or absence in one's system of uric acid. Were I, however, to undertake, in my own case, to guess whether the number of those days had been more or less than "fourteen," I might hesitate in so doing; but, more or less, I am very confident they exceed in number those of any one of my forbears.

Finished, at Washington, Wednesday, March 27, 1912; 8.45 A.M.

The story of the last years is soon told. Much occupied by a desire to complete the *Life* of his father, which had been begun more than fifteen years before, and was practically in definite shape up to the time of his appointment as United States Minister to Great Britain, Mr. Adams seriously bent himself to preparing this, the most important, portion of the work. A series of preliminary studies on the more vital incidents of the father's service in England was prepared and printed in the *Proceedings* of the Massachusetts Historical Society. The *Trent Affair* appeared in November, 1912,[1] with a number of letters and papers drawn from the papers of Charles Francis Adams, Sr.; and the *Negotiation of 1861 relating to the Declaration of Paris of 1856*, in October, 1914.[2] Seward's foreign policy was described more at large, and in doing this Mr. Adams came, somewhat reluctantly, to the conclusion that his earlier estimate of Seward's measure for the situation in which he was placed required some modification not favorable to the Secretary of State. The reluctance arose from Seward's known admiration for and open imitation of the grandfather, John Quincy Adams, and from his long friendship for the father, Charles Francis Adams. The deeper he went in his investigation of this period the stronger became his conviction that no relation would be complete or even satisfactory without a knowledge of what the records, public and private, in England and France contained. Never having approached such an investigation of the foreign or European side of the questions involved in his father's diplomatic career, he came to realize that in spite of the abundance of material collected from American sources the story would be told in a one-sided

---

[1] *Mass. Hist. Soc. Proceedings*, XLV. 35–148.   [2] *Ib.*, XLVI. 23–81.

and partial manner. The broader aspects, and the full extent of the great victories won in England by his father, could only be developed by a study of the documents in the foreign office archives and in the carefully guarded private correspondence of ministers of foreign affairs and their agents in France and Great Britain. Without such a study he felt that the accomplishment of his task could result only in a conclusion unsatisfying to his own ideas of the possible and inherently defective from the standpoint of history. In printing the lives and correspondence of their public characters Englishmen passed over the American connection as of secondary interest, giving only a glimpse of what a collection contained on American questions. It was to develop this wealth that Mr. Adams desired to go abroad.

An opportunity came to accomplish in part this desire. Invited to deliver a course of lectures on American institutions at Oxford University, in succession to Mr. James Ford Rhodes, he accepted and sailed for England in March, 1913. He has given an account of his experience at Oxford, and the impressions left upon his mind by that experience. The conferences then being held in London on the situation in the Balkan States naturally overshadowed all other political interests. They emphasized the fact that historically Great Britain turned towards the East, and the history of America was not looked upon as a profitable field for study.[1] He framed his four lectures to meet this condition, selecting certain dramatic features in the War of Secession which might awaken interest and further investigation. He wished to "impress such as may study my Oxford course with a sense not only of the importance of our American history in

[1] *Mass. Hist. Soc. Proceedings*, XLVI. 435.

connection with that of Europe, but of the far-reaching world-wide influence it both has exerted and is hereafter destined to exert, from which Great Britain as a community has perhaps not least of all been exempt." This resulted in a volume containing the lectures in a somewhat expanded form, *Transatlantic Historical Solidarity* (Clarendon Press, 1913), and a renewal of his association with many of his English friends and correspondents.

In the second object of his journey he attained a great, yet, as it seemed to him, a partial success. To break through strict regulations, and to enjoy privileges refused to all others, offered no mean difficulties in a land where bureau methods prevail. But Mr. Adams had a special right as well as reason in his favor, and this was recognized by the state officials. With courtesy his application for access to special records was considered, and with generosity the rules were suspended. The Public Records, however, contained only a part of what was necessary; for it has long been the practice in the British diplomatic service to employ a private or personal correspondence between the ambassador and the Foreign Secretary in addition to the official dispatches. The greater freedom employed in this personal correspondence gives it a distinct historical value, for it includes many rumors, interpretations, conversations and incidents, trivial at the time, but later of value in illustrating characters and influences. These letters are looked upon as personal to the Foreign Secretary, and do not become part of the official records. To secure access to family papers of so recent a period offered even greater difficulties than to obtain privileges in the public records. The first approach, however, was fortunate. Hon. Rollo Russell, son of Earl Russell, the holder of the Russell Papers, met his request with singular generosity; not only showing great interest in his undertaking, but placing at his disposal whatever in the Russell Papers could serve his purpose. An examination of the American correspondence proved the richness of the material.

Returning to the United States in June, Mr. Adams, on receiving a part of the Russell transcripts, saw more clearly than ever that his English researches must be extended, so as to include other collections like that of Earl Russell. He determined upon a second visit to England, and in August was again in London. He had in mind also locating hitherto unknown Winthrop material, in view of the Society's proposed re-issue of the *History*. The search, no longer confined to London, took him far afield, and he visited many houses where papers were to be found, going twice over the Winthrop region in the neighborhood of Groton. He had the aid of friends, like Viscount Bryce, who were thoroughly in sympathy with his objects, and everywhere he was successful in overcoming the reticence natural to possessors of papers believed still to possess diplomatic possibilities. A welcome guest, rarely informed on public questions, and vital in his opinions, his tact, social qualities and intelligent inquiries were recognized, and his success should offer at least some moderation of the severe self-judgment he records in this "autobiography."

He visited Hardwick House, where his host, Mr. George Milner-Gibson Cullom, told him of traces of Winthrop material, and gave him the opportunity to meet the Suffolk Archæological Society, then assembled for one of its historical pilgrimages. There resulted the appeal sent out to that

Society for aid in the Winthrop problems.[1] Oxford University conferred upon him the degree of Litt.D. He renewed his friendly relations with Hon. Rollo Russell, who again gave him what he wanted from his father's papers.[2] One after another of the more important collections were thrown open to him, and he gained, under certain perfectly justifiable restrictions, more than he had deemed possible, and at last became himself somewhat impressed by the great mass of material to be digested for his volumes. The field seemed without limit, and he resolved to cut short the accumulation and, returning to Washington, to await another opportunity to complete his English research, and to plan a similar visit to French archives.

He now confidently expected to take up the *Life* of his father and complete it within two years, and in this expectation he called in the aid of others to reduce the new material to usable proportion, and to direct the study of printed sources. But other undertakings crowded upon him, which he did not feel inclined to set aside. At the urgent request of Johns Hopkins University he repeated in Baltimore his Oxford lectures, but rewritten in a much amplified form. He prepared an elaborate study of one incident in his father's career — the final defeat in the British Cabinet of foreign mediation between North and South in 1862 [3] — and intended to proceed in further studies as rapidly as his occasions would permit. The outbreak of the great European war aroused such interest in him and so engrossed his thoughts as to make concentration on the events of the past irksome

---

[1] *Mass. Hist. Soc. Proceedings*, XLVII. 56.
[2] Mr. Russell has since died.
[3] *A Crisis in Downing Street*, in *Mass. Hist. Soc. Proceedings*, XLVII. 372.

to him. In view of what was passing before him, the War of Secession became of secondary importance, and he confessed to a sense of weariness in dealing with a subject which had lost so much of its moment in the world's history. He did complete a paper on the *British Proclamation* [of Neutrality] *of May, 1861*, largely based upon his English material, and printed it in January, 1915,[1] but this formed his last contribution in the long series of historical studies he had made since 1876, a series as notable for its variety of topic as for its originality in presentation. Each constituted a study of a certain event or problem in the diplomatic history of the War of Secession; but it was "thinking aloud" and did not give that final conclusion which would have made a chapter in his book. To the last he was working over his material, recasting his sentences and moulding his opinion, and thus to the last his mind remained active, potent and creative. Exposure to cold overtaxed his body, and after a few days of illness the end came on March 20, 1915, in Washington.[2]

W. C. F.

[1] *A Crisis in Downing Street*, in *Mass. Hist. Soc. Proceedings*, XLVIII. 190.
[2] Tributes to his memory are given in *Mass. Hist. Soc. Proceedings*, XLVIII. 383–423.

THE END

Index

Index